THE
ARMED FORCES
OF THE
UNITED KINGDOM

Copyright © R & F Defence Publications 2006

ISBN 1 84415 489 0

Price £6.99

Pen & Sword Books Ltd
47 Church Street
Barnsley S70 2AS

Telephone: 01226-734222   Fax: 01226-734438
www.pen-and-sword.co.uk

The information in this publication has been gathered from
unclassified sources

Front Cover: The WAH64 Longbow Apache currently in service with British
Forces in Afghanistan (Copyright GKN/Westland)

Rear Cover: An RAF Eurofighter Typhoon during mid 2006
(Copyright Alister Taylor)

Contents List

Chapter 1 – The Management of Defence 11

CHAPTER 1 – THE MANAGEMENT OF DEFENCE

GENERAL INFORMATION

Populations – European Union – Top Five Nations

Germany	82.3 million
United Kingdom	58.7 million
France	59.1 million
Italy	57.9 million
Spain	40.2 million

Finance – European Union – Top Five Nations (2004 Figures)

	GDP	Per Capita Income
Germany	Euro 2,160 bn (US$2,570 bn)	US$31,227
United Kingdom	£1,150 bn (US$2,001 bn)	US$33,898
France	Euro 1,620 bn (US$1,927 bn)	US$32,619
Italy	Euro 1,340 bn (US$1,594 bn)	US$27,540
Spain	Euro 799 bn (US$950 bn)	US$23,651

US$/Euro conversion at early 2006 rates

UK Population – 58.7 million (2001 census)

England	–	49.1 million	Wales –	2.9 million
Scotland	–	5.06 million	Northern Ireland –	1.68 million

2006 Population estimate is approximately 60 million

UK Population Breakdown – Military Service Groups
(2006 estimate – figures rounded up)

Age Group	Total	Males	Females
15–19	3.6 million	1.8 million	1.8 million
20–24	3.6 million	1.8 million	1.8 million
25–29	3.6 million	1.8 million	1.8 million
30–64	28.2 million	14.4 million	13.8 million

UK Area (in square kilometres)

England	–	130,423
Wales	–	20,766
Scotland	–	78,133
Northern Ireland	–	14,160
Total		243,482

Government

The executive government of the United Kingdom is vested nominally in the Crown, but for practical purposes in a committee of Ministers that is known as the Cabinet. The head of the ministry and leader of the Cabinet is the Prime Minister and for the implementation of policy, the Cabinet is dependent upon the support of a majority of the Members of Parliament in the House of Commons. Within the Cabinet, defence matters are the responsibility of the Secretary of State for Defence. The Secretary of State for Defence has three principal deputies; the Minister of State for the Armed Forces; Parliamentary Under-Secretary of State for Defence Procurement and the Parliamentary Under-Secretary of State for Veterans.

THE MISSIONS OF THE ARMED FORCES

A recent MoD mission statement for the armed forces reads as follows "Defence policy requires the provision of forces with a high degree of military effectiveness, at sufficient readiness and with a clear sense of purpose, for conflict prevention, crisis management and combat operations. Their demonstrable capability, conventional and nuclear, is intended to act as an effective deterrent to a potential aggressor, both in peacetime and during a crisis. They must be able to undertake a range of Military Tasks to fulfil the missions set out below, matched to changing strategic circumstances." These missions are not listed in any order of priority:

Peacetime Security: To provide forces needed in peacetime to ensure the protection and security of the United Kingdom, to assist as required with the evacuation of British nationals overseas, to afford Military Aid to the Civil Authorities in the United Kingdom, including Military Aid to the Civil Power, Military Aid to Other Government Departments and Military Aid to the Civil Community.

Security of the Overseas Territories: To provide forces to meet any challenges to the external security of a British Overseas Territory (including overseas possession and the Sovereign Base Areas) or to assist the civil authorities in meeting a challenge to internal security. (An amendment to legislation in due course will formalise the change of title from "Department Territories" to "Overseas Territories).

Defence Diplomacy: To provide forces to meet the varied activities undertaken by the Ministry of Defence to dispel hostility, build and maintain trust, and assist in the development of democratically accountable armed forces (thereby making a significant contribution to conflict prevention and resolution).

Support to Wider British Interests: To provide forces to conduct activities to promote British interests, influence and standing abroad.

Peace Support and Humanitarian Operations: To contribute forces to operations other than war in support of British interests and international order and humanitarian principles, the latter most likely under UN auspices.

Regional Conflict Outside the NATO Area: To contribute forces for a regional conflict (but on an attack on NATO or one of its members) which, if unchecked, could adversely affect European security, or which could pose a serious threat to British interests elsewhere, or to international security. Operations are usually under UN or Organisation for Security Co-operation in Europe auspices.

Regional Conflict Inside the NATO Area: To provide forces needed to respond to a regional crisis or conflict involving a NATO ally who calls for assistance under Article 5 of the Washington Treaty.

Strategic Attack on NATO: To provide, within the expected warning and readiness preparation times, the forces required to counter a strategic attack against NATO.

This mission statement is further sub-divided into a number of Military Tasks (MT) which accurately define the way in which the missions are actually accomplished.

TOTAL BRITISH ARMED FORCES – OVERVIEW (AS AT 1 JANUARY 2006)
Regular: 195,960 (excludes approximately 3,350 Gurkhas, approximately 1,500 Full Time Reserve Service (FTRS) personnel, approximately 3,000 Royal Irish Regiment (Home Service) and 2,000 mobilised reserves).

Army: 107,400; Royal Navy 39,430; Royal Air Force 49,390; (figures include all trained and untrained personnel). Royal Naval figure includes some 7,200 Royal Marines.

Regular Reserves: 191,500; Volunteer Reserves 44,000; Cadet Forces 153,100 (Sea Cadets 16,350, Army Cadets 52,000, Air Training Corps 40,170, Combined Cadet Force 44,600); MoD Civilians 115,000 (includes 14,000 locally entered civilians).

Strategic Forces: 4 x Vanguard Class submarines capable of carrying 16 x Trident (D5) Submarine Launched Ballistic Missiles (SLBM) deploying with 48 x warheads per submarine. If necessary a D5 missile could deploy with 12 MIRV (multiple independently targetable re-entry vehicles). Future plans appear to be for a stockpile of 200 operationally available warheads and 58 missile bodies. Strategic Forces are provided by the Royal Navy.

Royal Navy: 39,430: 10 x Tactical Submarines; 3 x Aircraft Carriers; 1 x Helicopter Carrier; 2 x Assault Ships; 3 x Landing Ships; 26 x Destroyers and Frigates; 16 x Mine Warfare Vessels; 5 x Survey Ships; 24 x Patrol Craft; 1 x Antarctic Patrol Ship.

Royal Fleet Auxiliary: 2 x Fast fleet tankers; 3 x Small fleet tankers; 4 x Support tankers; 4 x Replenishment ships; 1 x Aviation training ship; 1 x Forward repair ship; 6 x Ro-Ro Ships (4 under civil management).

Naval Aircraft: 2 x Fixed wing (Harrier GR7/GR9) squadrons; ; 8 x Helicopter squadrons with 38 x Merlin Helicopters; 12 x Sea King MK6. 23 x Lynx Helicopters; 11 x AEW Sea King Helicopters; 41 x Sea King Commando Helicopters; 6 x Lynx Helicopters. Anti Tank role; 8 x Gazelle Helicopters.

Royal Marines: 1 x Commando Brigade Headquarters; 3 x Royal Marine Commando (Battalion Size); 3 x Commando Assault Helicopter Squadrons; 1 x Commando Light Helicopter Squadron ; 1 x Commando Regiment Royal Artillery; 1 x Commando Squadron Royal Engineers; 1 x Commando Logistic Regiment; 1 Commando Assault Group (Landing-Craft); 1 x Fleet Protection Group; 4 x Special Boat Service Squadrons.

Merchant Naval Vessels Registered in the UK, Crown Dependencies and Overseas Territories: 24 x Cruise ships (over 200 tons); 541 x Passenger and dry cargo merchant vessels; 5 x Roll-on roll-off passenger (over 200 berths); 47 x Roll-on roll-off freight (over 500 lane metres);

223 x General cargo (over 1,000 dead-weight tons); 60 x Refrigerated cargo (over 1,000 deadweight tons); 102 x Container (over 100 twenty foot containers); 195 x Product and chemical tankers (2,000 to 80,000 dead-weight tons); 31 x Large fishing vessels (over 2,000 horse power).

Royal Air Force: 49,390; 5 x Strike/Attack Squadrons (includes 1 x reserve squadron); 1 x Offensive Support Squadron; 4 x Air Defence Squadrons; 3 x Maritime Patrol Squadrons (includes 1 x Reserve Squadron); 5 x Reconnaissance Squadrons; 2 x Airborne Early Warning Squadrons; 9 x Transport and Tankers Squadrons; 10 x Helicopter Squadrons; 4 x Surface-to-Air Missile Squadrons; 6 x Ground (Field) Defence Squadrons.

Army: 107,400 (including some 3,350 Gurkhas); 1 x Corps Headquarters in Germany (ARRC); 1 x Armoured Divisional HQ in Germany; 1 x Mechanised Divisional HQ in UK ; 5 x Non-deployable divisional type HQ in UK; Germany: 3 x Armoured Brigade Headquarters and 1 x Logistics Brigade HQ; UK: 4 x Deployable Combat Brigade HQ and 1 x Logistics Brigade HQ; 10 x Regional Brigade HQ; 2 x Northern Ireland Brigade HQ.

Major Units: 10 x Armoured Regiments; 40 x Infantry Battalions; 14 x Artillery Regiments; 11 x Engineer Regiments; 11 x Signal Regiments; 7 x Equipment Support Battalions; 22 x Logistic Regiments; 8 x Medical Regiments.

JOINT FORCES

Joint Force Harrier: 2 x Royal Navy Squadron; 2 x Royal Air Force Squadrons.

Joint Helicopter Command: 4 x Royal Naval Helicopter Squadrons; 6 x Army Aviation Regiments (including 1 x Volunteer Reserve); 7 x Royal Air Force Helicopter Squadrons (including 1 x RAuxAF Helicopter Support Squadron).

Joint Special Forces Group: 1 x Regular Special Air Service (SAS) Regiment; 2 x Volunteer Reserve Special Air Service Regiments; 4 x Special Boat Service (SBS) Squadrons; 1 x Special Reconnaissance Regiment; 1 x Special Forces Support Group.

Joint Nuclear, Biological and Chemical Regiment

National Police Forces: England and Wales 125,000 Scotland 14,000, Northern Ireland 11,000.

MINISTRY OF DEFENCE (MoD)

In 1963, the three independent service ministries (Admiralty, War Office and Air Ministry) were merged to form the present MoD.

The UK MoD is the government department that is responsible for all defence related aspects of national policy. This large organisation, which directly affects the lives of about half a million servicemen, reservists and MoD employed civilians, is controlled by The Secretary of State for Defence and his deputies.

The Secretary of State for Defence has three principal deputies;

Minister of State for the Armed Forces

Parliamentary Under-Secretary of State for Defence Procurement

Parliamentary Under-Secretary of State for Veterans Affairs

The Secretary of State is assisted by two principal advisers:

Permanent Under-Secretary of State (PUS): The PUS is responsible for policy, finance and administration in the MoD. As the MoD's Principal Accounting Officer he is personally responsible to Parliament for the expenditure of all public money voted to the MoD for Defence purposes.

Chief of the Defence Staff (CDS): The CDS acts as the professional head of the Armed Forces and he is the principal military adviser to the Secretary of State and to the Government.

Both the PUS and the CDS have deputies; the Second Permanent Under Secretary of State (2nd PUS), and the Vice-Chief of the Defence Staff (VCDS).

In general terms defence is managed through a number of major committees that provide corporate leadership and strategic direction:

Defence Council
Defence Management Board
Chiefs of Staff Committee
Single Service Boards

DEFENCE COUNCIL

The Defence Council is the senior committee which provides the legal basis for the conduct and administration of defence and this council is chaired by the Secretary of State for Defence, The composition of the Defence Council is as follows:

The Secretary of State for Defence
Minister of State for the Armed Forces
Parliamentary Under-Secretary of State for Defence Procurement
Parliamentary Under-Secretary of State for Veterans Affairs
Permanent Under-Secretary of State for Defence
Chief of the Defence Staff
Vice-Chief of the Defence Staff
Chief of the Naval Staff and First Sea Lord
Chief of the Air Staff
Chief of the General Staff
Chief of Defence Procurement
Chief Scientific Adviser
Second Permanent Under-Secretary of State

Defence Management Board

This board is chaired by the PUS and is the MoD's senior non-ministerial committee. In essence the Defence Management Board is the MoD's main corporate board providing senior leadership and direction to the implementation of defence policy.

Chiefs of Staff Committee

This committee is chaired by the CDS and is the MoD's senior committee that provides advice on operational military matters and the preparation and conduct of military operations.

Single Service Boards

There are three single service boards: Admiralty Board, Army Board and the Air Force Board all of which are chaired by the Secretary of State for Defence. In general the purpose of the boards is the administration and monitoring of single service performance. Each of these three boards has an executive committee chaired by the single service chief of staff; Navy Board, Executive Committee of the Army Board and the Air Force Board Standing Committee.

CHIEF OF THE DEFENCE STAFF

The Chief of the Defence Staff (CDS) is the officer responsible to the Secretary of State for Defence for the coordinated effort of all three fighting services. He has his own Central Staff Organisation and a Vice-Chief of the Defence Staff who ranks as number four in the services hierarchy, following the three single service commanders. The current Chief of the Defence Staff is:

AIR CHIEF MARSHAL SIR JOCK STIRRUP KCB AFC ADC FRAES FCMI RAF

Air Chief Marshal Stirrup was educated at Merchant Taylors' School, Northwood and the Royal Air Force College Cranwell, and was commissioned in 1970.

After a tour as a Qualified Flying Instructor he served on loan with the Sultan of Oman's Air Force, operating Strikemasters in the Dhofar War. Returning to the United Kingdom in 1975 he was posted to No 41(F) Squadron, flying Jaguars in the Fighter Reconnaissance role, before taking up an exchange appointment on RF-4C Phantoms in the United States. He then spent two years at RAF Lossiemouth as a flight commander on the Jaguar Operational Conversion Unit, and subsequently attended the Joint Service Defence College in 1984. He commanded No II(AC) Squadron, flying Fighter Reconnaissance Jaguars from Royal Air Force Laarbruch, until 1987 when he took up the post of Personal Staff Officer to the Chief of the Air Staff.

He assumed command of Royal Air Force Marham in 1990, just in time for Operation GRANBY, and then attended the 1993 Course at the Royal College of Defence Studies. He completed No 7 Higher Command and Staff Course at Camberley prior to becoming the Director of Air Force Plans and Programmes in 1994. He became Air Officer Commanding No 1 Group in April 1997 and was appointed Assistant Chief of the Air Staff in August 1998. He took up the appointment of Deputy Commander-in-Chief Strike Command in 2000. At the same time he assumed the additional roles of Commander of NATO's Combined Air Operations Centre 9 and Director of the European Air Group. He spent the last few months of his tour, from September 2001 to January 2002, as UK National Contingent Commander and

Senior British Military Advisor to CINCUSCENTCOM for Operation VERITAS, the UK's contribution to the United States led Operation ENDURING FREEDOM in Afghanistan.

Air Chief Marshal Stirrup was appointed KCB in the New Year Honours List 2002 and became Deputy Chief of the Defence Staff (Equipment Capability) in March 2002. He was appointed Chief of the Air Staff, on promotion, on 1 August 2003 and became Chief of the Defence Staff in May 2006.

Air Chief Marshal Stirrup is married with one son and enjoys golf, music, theatre and history.

Air Chief Marshal Sir Jock Stirrup

CHAIN OF COMMAND

The Chief of the Defence Staff (CDS) commands and coordinates the activities of the three services through the following chain of command:

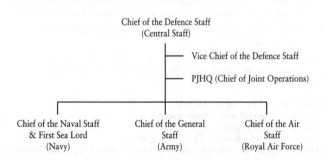

Chief of the Defence Staff
(Central Staff)

— Vice Chief of the Defence Staff

— PJHQ (Chief of Joint Operations)

Chief of the Naval Staff
& First Sea Lord
(Navy)

Chief of the General
Staff
(Army)

Chief of the Air
Staff
(Royal Air Force)

The three single service commanders exercise command of their services through their respective headquarters. However, the complex inter-service nature of the majority of modern military operations, where military, air and naval support must be coordinated, has led to the establishment of a permanent Tri-Service Joint Headquarters (PJHQ).

PERMANENT JOINT HEADQUARTERS (PJHQ)

The UK MoD established a Permanent Joint Headquarters (PJHQ) at Northwood in Middlesex for joint military operations on 1 April 1996. This headquarters brought together on a permanent basis, intelligence, planning, operational and logistics staffs. It contains elements of a rapidly deployable in-theatre Joint Force Headquarters that has the capability of commanding rapid deployment front line forces.

The UK MoD Defence Costs Study of January 1994 identified a number of shortcomings with the command and control of UK military operations overseas. The establishment of PJHQ was an attempt to provide a truly joint force headquarters that would remedy the problems of disruption, duplication and the somewhat 'ad hoc' way in which previous operations had been organised

MoD officials have described the primary role of PJHQ as 'Working proactively to anticipate crises and monitoring developments in areas of interest to the UK'. The establishment of PJHQ has set in place a proper, clear and unambiguous connection between policy and the strategic direction and conduct of operations. Because it exists on a permanent basis rather than being established for a particular operation, PJHQ is involved from the very start of planning for possible operations. Where necessary, PJHQ then takes responsibility for the subsequent execution of these plans.

PJHQ, commanded by the Chief of Joint Operations (CJO), (currently a three star officer) occupies existing accommodation above and below ground at Northwood in Middlesex. PJHQ is responsible for planning all UK-led joint, potentially joint, combined and multinational operations and works in close partnership with MoD Head Office in the planning of operations and policy formulation, thus ensuring PJHQ is well placed to implement policy. Having planned the operation, and contributed advice to Ministers, PJHQ will then conduct such operations. Amongst its many tasks PJHQ is currently (early 2006) engaged in planning and conducting UK military involvement in both Iraq and Afghanistan.

When another nation is in the lead, PJHQ exercises operational command of UK forces deployed on the operation.

Being a Permanent Joint Headquarters, PJHQ provides continuity of experience from the planning phase to the execution of the operation, and on to post-operation evaluation and learning of lessons.

Principal Additional Tasks of PJHQ Include:
♦ Monitoring designated areas of operational interest
♦ Preparing contingency plans
♦ Contributions to the UK MoD's decision making process
♦ Exercise of operational control of overseas commands (Falklands, Cyprus and Gibraltar)

- Managing its own budget
- Formulation of joint warfare doctrine at operational and tactical levels
- Conducting joint force exercises
- Focus for Joint Rapid Reaction Force planning and exercising

Overview Of International Operations.
From 1 Aug 1996 PJHQ assumed responsibility for military operations world-wide. Non-core functions, such as the day-to-day management of the Overseas Commands in Cyprus, Falkland Islands, and Gibraltar, are also delegated by MoD Head Office to the PJHQ. This allows MoD Head Office to concentrate in particular on policy formulation and strategic direction. As of early 2006 PJHQ has been involved with UK commitments in the following areas:

Afghanistan, Albania, Algeria, Angola, Bosnia, Burundi, East Timor, Eritrea, Honduras, Iraq (including operations during 2003), Kosovo, Montenegro, Montserrat, Mozambique, Sierra Leone, East Zaire, West Zaire (Democratic Republic of the Congo).

Operations for which PJHQ is not responsible include: UK Strategic Nuclear Deterrent; Defence of the UK Home Base; Defence of UK Territorial Waters and Airspace; Support to the Civil Power in Northern Ireland; Counter-terrorism in the UK and Operations in support of NATO (Article V General War).

Headquarters Structure.
PJHQ brings together at Northwood some 620 civilian, specialist and tri-service military staff from across the MoD. The headquarters structure resembles the normal Divisional organisation, but staff operate within multidisciplinary groups which draw from across the headquarters. The headquarters must have the capability of supporting a number of operations simultaneously on behalf of the UK MoD.

PJHQ in the MoD Chain of Command

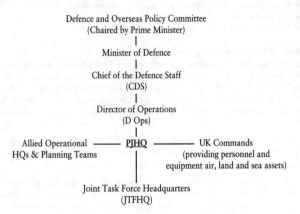

Defence and Overseas Policy Committee
(Chaired by Prime Minister)
|
Minister of Defence
|
Chief of the Defence Staff
(CDS)
|
Director of Operations
(D Ops)
|
Allied Operational ———— **PJHQ** ———— UK Commands
HQs & Planning Teams   (providing personnel and
equipment air, land and sea assets)
|
Joint Task Force Headquarters
(JTFHQ)

Note: The Defence and Overseas Policy Committee (DOPC) is responsible for the strategic direction of the UK Government's defence and overseas policy. The DOPC is chaired by the Prime Minister and members include the Secretary of State for Foreign and Commonwealth Affairs (Deputy Chair); Deputy Prime Minister and First Secretary of State; Chancellor of the Exchequer; Secretary of State for Defence; Secretary of State for the Home Department; Secretary of State for International Development; Secretary of State for Trade and Industry. If necessary, other ministers, the Heads of the Intelligence Agencies and the Chief of Defence Staff may be invited to attend.

PJHQ Headquarters Structure

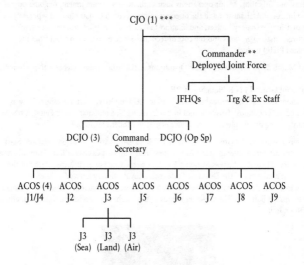

Notes:

(1) CJO – Chief of Joint Operations; (2) *** Denotes the rank of the incumbent (3) DCJO – Deputy Chief of Joint Operations; DCJO (Op Sp) Deputy Chief of Joint Operations (Operational Support); (4) ACOS – Assistant Chief of Staff.

CJO has a civilian Command Secretary who provides a wide range of policy, legal, presentational, financial and civilian human resources advice.

PJHQ Departments

J1	Personnel and Admin	J6	Communication and Information Systems
J2	Intelligence	J7	Doctrine and Joint Training
J3	Operations	J8	Finance
J4	Logistics	J9	Policy, legal and presentation
J5	Policy and Crisis Planning		

The annual PJHQ budget is in the region of UK£573 million (2005/06 – Capital + Resource DEL). The annual running costs of the Headquarters is estimated at approximately UK£50 million.

Included in the overall PJHQ budget are the costs of the UK forces in the Falkland Islands, Cyprus and Gibraltar. Major operations such as the Kosovo commitment, ongoing operational commitment in Afghanistan and the ongoing commitment in Iraq are funded separately by way of a supplementary budget, and in almost all cases this requires government-level approval. Small operations and the cost of reconnaissance parties are funded from the standard PJHQ budget.

As of March 2006 the Chief of Joint Operations (CJO) is Lieutenant General JNR Houghton.

Lieutenant General J N R Houghton CBE

Lieutenant General Nick Houghton was born in 1954 in Otley, West Yorkshire. He was educated at Woodhouse Grove School in Bradford, RMA Sandhurst and St Peter's College, Oxford, where he completed an in-service degree in Modern History.

Commissioned into the Green Howards in 1974, he had a variety of Regimental and Staff appointments before attending the Army Command and Staff Course at both Shrivenham and Camberley. Thereafter he was Military Assistant to the Chief of Staff British Army of the Rhine and a member of the Directing Staff at the Royal Military College of Science, Shrivenham. At Regimental Duty he was both a Company Commander in, and Commanding Officer of, 1st Battalion The Green Howards in the Mechanised and Airmobile roles, and in Northern Ireland.

Lieutenant General J N R Houghton

More recently Lieutenant General Houghton was Deputy Assistant Chief of Staff, G3 (Operations & Deployment) in HQ Land Command 1994 – 1997 and attended the Higher Command and Staff Course in 1997. He commanded 39 Infantry Brigade in Northern Ireland from 1997 to 1999 and was the Director of Military Operations in the Ministry of Defence from December 1999 to July 2002. He was Chief of Staff of the Allied Rapid Reaction Corps from July 2002 to April 2004 before becoming the Assistant Chief of the Defence Staff

(Operations) from May 2004 to October 2005. He was the Senior British Military Representative Iraq and Deputy Commanding General of the Multi-National Force-Iraq from October 2005 until assuming his current appointment as Chief of Joint Operations at PJHQ (UK) in March 2006.

JOINT RAPID REACTION FORCE (JRRF)

The JRRF is essentially the fighting force that PJHQ has immediately available. The JRRF provides a force for rapid deployment operations often using a core operational group of the Army's 16th Air Assault Brigade and the Royal Navy's 3rd Commando Brigade, supported by a wide range of air and maritime assets including the Joint Force Harrier and the Joint Helicopter Command.

The force uses what the MoD has described as a 'golfbag' approach with a wide range of units available for specific operations. For example, if the operational situation demands assets such as heavy armour, long-range artillery and attack helicopters, these assets can easily be assigned to the force. This approach means that the JRRF can be tailored for specific operations, ranging from support for a humanitarian crisis to missions including high intensity operations.

The 'reach' of the JRRF has been enhanced by the Royal Navy's new amphibious vessels HMS Albion and HMS Bulwark, currently entering service. Both of these ships will be able to carry 650 troops plus a range of armoured vehicles including main battle tanks. A flight deck will allow ship-to-shore helicopter operations.

Responsibility for providing units to the JRRF remains with the single service commands who ensure that units assigned are at an extremely high state of readiness. JRRF units remain committed to NATO.

Under normal circumstances, the Army would ensure that the the following land forces were available to the JRRF: a brigade sized grouping held at High Readiness and two Strategic Reserves – the Spearhead Land Element (SLE) held at Extremely High Readiness and the Airborne Task Force (ABTF) held at Very High Readiness. To command the JRRF a Joint Task Force HQ (JTFHQ) is maintained at 48 hours notice to move.

Since Operation Telic commenced the High Readiness Brigade has been routinely deployed to Iraq, and has therefore been unavailable to the JRRF. Nonetheless, the SLE and ABTF have been maintained throughout.

Joint Force Logistics Component

The Joint Force Logistics Component (JFLogC) provides a joint logistic headquarters with force logistics under the command of PJHQ. It delivers coordinated logistic support to the deployed Joint Force in accordance with the commander's priorities. The composition of the JFLogC will be determined by PJHQ during the mission planning stage. Two logistic brigades have been assigned to JFLogC.

STAFF BRANCHES

The Staff Branches that you would expect to find at every level in a headquarters from the Ministry of Defence down to garrison/station/port level are as follows:

Commander – The senior officer of the formation who in a large headquarters could be an Admiral, General or Air Marshal. The Army often refers to the commander as the GOC (General Officer Commanding), the Royal Air Force to the AOC (Air Officer Commanding) while the Royal Navy uses the term Flag Officer.

Chief of Staff – The officer who runs the headquarters on a day-to-day basis and who often acts as a second-in-command.

G1 Branch – Responsible for personnel matters including manning, discipline and personal services.

G2 Branch – Responsible for intelligence and security

G3 Branch – Responsible for operations including staff duties, exercise planning, training, requirements, combat development and tactical doctrine.

G4 Branch – Logistics and quartering.

G5 Branch – Civil and military co-operation.

An operational headquarters in the field will almost certainly be a tri-service organisation with branches from the Army, Navy and Air Force represented. The Staff Branches are the same for all three services.

NATO COMMAND STRUCTURE

The United Kingdom is a member of NATO (North Atlantic Treaty Organisation) and the majority of military operations are conducted in concert with the forces of NATO allies.

In 1993, NATO was reorganised from three into two major Commands with a further re-organisation of these two commands in 2003. The first is ACT (Allied Command Transformation) with headquarters at Norfolk, Virginia (USA) and the second is ACO (Allied Command Operations), with its headquarters at Mons in Belgium.

NATO operations in which the United Kingdom was a participant would almost certainly be as part of a NATO force under the command and control of Allied Command Operations (ACO). The current Supreme Allied Commander is General James L Jones.

SACEUR – GENERAL JAMES L JONES

General Jones is the Supreme Allied Commander, Europe (SACEUR) and the Commander of the United States European Command (COMUSEUCOM). From the Supreme Headquarters Allied Powers Europe, Mons, Belgium, General Jones leads Allied Command Europe (ACE), comprising NATO's military forces in Europe. The mission of ACE is to preserve the peace, security, and territorial integrity of the NATO member nations in Europe. As COMUSEUCOM, General Jones commands five US components: US Army, Europe; US Navy, Europe; US Air Forces in Europe, US Marine Forces, Europe and Special Operations Command, Europe. The European Command's mission is to support and achieve US interests and objectives throughout 93 countries in Central and Eastern Europe, Africa and portions of the Middle East. The command performs a variety of functions including planning for and conducting contingency operations such as noncombatant evacuations and humanitarian relief operations; providing combat-ready forces to both Allied Command Europe and other US unified commands; and conducting intelligence activities and security assistance.

General Jones spent his formative years in France, returning to the United States to attend the Georgetown University School of Foreign Service, from which he earned a Bachelor of Science degree in 1966. He was commissioned a Second Lieutenant in the Marine Corps in January 1967. Upon completion of The Basic School, Quantico, Virginia, in October 1967, he was ordered to the Republic of Vietnam, where he served as a Platoon and Company Commander with Company G, 2nd Battalion, 3rd Marines. While overseas, he was promoted to First Lieutenant in June 1968.

Returning to the United States in December 1968, General Jones was assigned to Camp Pendleton, California, where he served as a Company Commander until May 1970. He then received orders to Marine Barracks, Washington, DC, for duties as a Company Commander, serving in this assignment until July 1973. He was promoted to Captain in December 1970. From July 1973 until June 1974, he was a student at the Amphibious Warfare School, Quantico, Virginia.

In November 1974, he received orders to report to the 3d Marine Division on Okinawa, where he served as the Company Commander of Company H, 2nd Battalion, 9th Marines, until December 1975. From January 1976 to August 1979, General Jones served in the Officer Assignments Section at Headquarters Marine Corps, Washington, DC. During this assignment, he was promoted to Major in July 1977. Remaining in Washington, his next assignment was as the Marine Corps Liaison Officer to the United States Senate, where he served until July 1984. He was promoted to Lieutenant Colonel in September 1982. He was then selected to attend the National War College in Washington, DC. Following graduation in June 1985, he was assigned to command the 3rd Battalion, 9th Marines, 1st Marine Division, Camp Pendleton, California, from July 1985 to July 1987.

In August 1987, General Jones returned to Headquarters Marine Corps, where he served as Senior Aide to the Commandant of the Marine Corps. He was promoted to Colonel in April 1988, and became the Military Secretary to the Commandant of the Marine Corps in February 1989. During August 1990, General Jones was assigned as the Commanding Officer, 24th Marine Expeditionary Unit at Camp Lejeune, North Carolina. During his tour with the 24th MEU, he participated in Operation Provide Comfort in Northern Iraq and Turkey. He was advanced to Brigadier General on April 23, 1992. General Jones was assigned to duties as Deputy Director, J-3, US European Command, Stuttgart, Germany, on July 15, 1992. During this tour of duty, he was reassigned as Chief of Staff, Joint Task Force Provide Promise, for operations in Bosnia-Herzegovina and Macedonia.

Returning to the United States, he was advanced to the rank of Major General in July 1994, and was assigned as Commanding General, 2nd Marine Division, Marine Forces Atlantic, Camp Lejeune, North Carolina. General Jones next served as Director, Expeditionary Warfare Division (N85), Office of the Chief of Naval Operations, during 1996, then as the Deputy Chief of Staff for Plans, Policies and Operations, Headquarters Marine Corps, Washington, DC. He was advanced to Lieutenant General on July 18, 1996.

His next assignment was as the Military Assistant to the Secretary of Defence. He was promoted to General on June 30, 1999, and became the 32nd Commandant of the United States Marine Corps on July 1, 1999. General Jones assumed duties as the Commander of US European Command on 16 January 2003 and Supreme Allied Commander Europe on 17 January 2003.

General Jones' personal decorations include: the Defense Distinguished Service Medal with two oak leaf clusters, Silver Star Medal, Legion of Merit with four gold stars, Bronze Star Medal with Combat "V", and the Combat Action Ribbon.

General James L Jones

Allied Command Operations (ACO)
Allied Command Operations, with its headquarters, SHAPE, near Mons, Belgium, is responsible for all Alliance operations. The levels beneath SHAPE have been significantly streamlined, with a reduction in the number of headquarters. The operational level consists of two standing Joint Force Commands (JFCs) one in Brunssum, the Netherlands, and one in Naples, Italy – which can conduct operations from their static locations or provide a land-based Combined Joint Task Force (CJTF) headquarters, and a robust but more limited standing Joint Headquarters (JHQ), in Lisbon, Portugal, from which a deployable sea-based CJTF HQ capability can be drawn. The current organisation of Allied Command Operations is as follows:

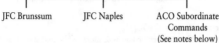

SHAPE
(Supreme Headquarters Allied Powers Europe)
Mons – Belgium
SACEUR
(Supreme Allied Commander Europe)

JFC Brunssum   JFC Naples   ACO Subordinate
Commands
(See notes below)

ACO Subordinate Commands

Immediate Reaction Forces (Maritime) – There are three Maritime Immediate Reaction Forces that provide NATO with a continuous naval presence and can be deployed NATO-wide, when required.

ACE Rapid Reaction Corps (ARRC) – The ARRC is prepared for deployment throughout Allied Command Europe in order to augment or reinforce local forces whenever necessary. The Headquarters of the ARRC are located in Rheindahlen, Germany.

NATO Airborne Early Warning Force (NAEWF) – The NATO Airborne Early Warning Force provides air surveillance and command and control for all NATO commands. It is based in Geilenkirchen, Germany, and Waddington, United Kingdom.

NATO Programming Centre (NPC) – The NATO Programming Centre maintains NATO Air Command and Control Software and provides system expertise to nations and NATO agencies and headquarters. It is located in Glons, Belgium.

Component Headquarters at the tactical level

The component or tactical level will consist of six Joint Force Component Commands (JFCCs), which will provide service-specific – land, maritime, or air – expertise to the operational level. Although these component commands will be available for use in any operation, they will be subordinated to one of the Joint Force Commanders.

Joint Forces Command – Brunssum

HQ JFC Brunssum

JFCC Air   JFCC Maritime   JFCC Land
Ramstein – Germany   Northwood – UK   Heidelberg – Germany

Joint Forces Command – Naples

HQ JFC Naples

| JFCC Air | JFCC Maritime | JFCC Land |
| Izmir – Turkey | Naples – Italy | Madrid – Spain |

Static Air Operations Centres (CAOC)
In addition to the above component commands there will be four static Combined Air Operations Centres with two more deployable as follows:

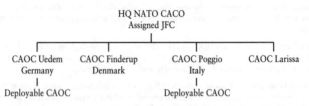

HQ NATO CACO
Assigned JFC

CAOC Uedem	CAOC Finderup	CAOC Poggio	CAOC Larissa
Germany	Denmark	Italy	
Deployable CAOC		Deployable CAOC	

As the deployable CAOCs will need to exercise their capability to mobilise and deploy, the current facilities at Torrejon Air Base in Spain will probably be the primary site for training and exercising in that region. A small NATO air facility support staff would be stationed at Torrejon to support this capability.

Allied Command Transformation (ACT)
In the future, Allied Command Transformation, with its headquarters in Norfolk, US, will oversee the transformation of NATO's military capabilities. In doing so, it will enhance training, improve capabilities, test and develop doctrines and conduct experiments to assess new concepts. It will also facilitate the dissemination and introduction of new concepts and promote interoperability. There will be an ACT Staff Element in Belgium primarily for resource and defence planning issues.

ACT will command the Joint Warfare Centre in Norway, a new Joint Force Training Centre in Poland and the Joint Analysis and Lessons Learned Centre in Portugal. ACT Headquarters will also supervise the Undersea Research Centre in La Spezia, Italy. There will be direct linkages between ACT, Alliance schools and NATO agencies, as well as the US Joint Forces Command. A NATO Maritime Interdiction Operational Training Centre in Greece, associated with ACT, is also envisaged. In addition, a number of nationally- or multinationally-sponsored Centres of Excellence focused on transformation in specific military fields will support the command.

The (2003) NATO concept

Under the 2003 concept, NATO forces should be able to rapidly deploy to crisis areas and remain sustainable, be it within or outside NATO's territory, in support of both Article 5 and Non-Article 5 operations. The successful deployments of the Allied Command Europe Rapid Reaction Corps (ARRC) to two NATO-led Balkan operations (the Implementation Force (IFOR) to Bosnia Herzegovina in 1995 and Kosovo Force (KFOR) to Kosovo in 1999) are early examples of non-Article 5 crisis response operations outside NATO territory.

The new concept will have its largest impact on land forces. Maritime and air forces are by nature already highly mobile and deployable and often have a high state of readiness. Most of NATO's land based assets, however, have been rather static and have had limited (strategic) mobility. In the new structure, land forces should also become highly deployable and should have tactical and strategic mobility. The mobility requirements will have great impact on the Alliance's transport and logistic resources (sea, land and air based). The need for quick reaction requires a certain amount of highly trained forces that are readily available. Further, interoperability (the possibility of forces to co-operate together with other units) and sustainability (the possibility to continue an operation for an extended period of time) are essential in the new force structure.

High Readiness Forces and Forces of Lower Readiness

There will be forces of two different kinds of readiness posture. First, forces with a higher state of readiness and availability, the so-called High Readiness Forces (HRF) to react on short notice. Second, forces with a lower state of readiness (FLR) to reinforce and sustain. Graduated Readiness Headquarters will be developed to provide these forces with command and control facilities.

Land forces: Their deployable headquarters will be able to command and control assigned forces up to the corps-size level. Also a wide range of options will be available to command and control land forces at the brigade and division size to operate as stand-alone formation or subordinated to a higher HQ.

Maritime forces: Their deployable headquarters will be able to command and control assigned forces up to the NATO Task Force Level. Also a wide range of options will be available to command and control maritime forces at NATO Task Unit level to operate as stand-alone formation or subordinated to a higher HQ.

Air forces: The air forces will use the air command and control facilities of the present NATO Command Structure.

High Readiness Forces (Land) Headquarters candidates available:

The Allied Command Europe Rapid Reaction Corps (ARRC) HQ in Rheindalen (Germany) with the United Kingdom as framework nation;

The Rapid Deployable German-Netherlands Corps HQ, based on the 1st German-Netherlands Corps HQ in Munster (Germany);

The Rapid Deployable Italian Corps HQ based on the Italian Rapid Reaction Corps HQ in Solbiate Olona close to Milan (Italy);

The Rapid Deployable Spanish Corps HQ based on the Spanish Corps HQ in Valencia (Spain);

The Rapid Deployable Turkish Corps HQ based on the 3rd Turkish Corps HQ near Istanbul (Turkey);

The Eurocorps HQ in Strasbourg (France) sponsored by Belgium, France, Germany, Luxembourg and Spain.

Note: The Eurocorps Headquarters which has a different international military status based on the Strasbourg Treaty, has signed a technical arrangement with SACEUR and can also be committed to NATO missions.

Forces of Lower Readiness (Land) Headquarters candidates:
The Multinational Corps HQ North-East in Szczecin (Poland) sponsored by Denmark, Germany and Poland;

The Greek "C" Corps HQ near Thessaloniki (Greece).

High Readiness Forces (Maritime) Headquarters:
Headquarters and Commander Italian Maritime Forces on board of the Italian Naval Vessel GARIBALDI

Headquarters and Commander Spanish Maritime Forces (HQ COMSPMARFOR) on board of LPD CASTILLA

Headquarters and Commander United Kingdom Maritime Forces (HQ COMUKMARFOR) onboard a UK Aircraft Carrier

THE ALLIED RAPID REACTION CORPS (ARRC)
The concept of the Allied Rapid Reaction Corps was initiated by the NATO Defence Planning Committee in May 1991. The concept called for the creation of Rapid Reaction Forces to meet the requirements of future challenges within the alliance. The ARRC provides the Supreme Allied Commander Europe with a multinational corps sized grouping in which forward elements can be ready to deploy within 14 days (lead elements and recce parties at very short notice).

As stated by SHAPE the mission of the ARRC is: "HQ ARRC, as a High Readiness Force (Land) HQ, is prepared to deploy under NATO, EU or coalition auspices to a designated area, to undertake combined and joint operations across the operational spectrum as:

a Corps HQ

a Land Component HQ

a Land Component HQ in command of the NATO Response Force

a Joint Task Force HQ for Land-centric operations

These formations will enable crisis support management options or the sustainment of ongoing operations."

As NATO's first and most experienced High Readiness Force (Land) Headquarters the ARRC is actively engaged in the NATO Response Force (NRF) transformation initiative.

Currently the ARRC trains for missions across the spectrum of operations from deterrence and crisis management to regional conflict.

Headquarters ARRC is located in Rheindahlen, Germany with a peace-time establishment of 400 personnel. It comprises staff from all the contributing nations. A French liaison officer is officially accredited to the Headquarters. As the Framework Nation, the UK provides the infrastructure, administrative support, communications and 60% of the staff.

The Commander (COMARRC) and Chief of Staff are UK 3 Star and 2 Star generals and the Deputy Commander is an Italian 2 Star general. The other appointments, as with the training and exercise costs, are shared among the contributing nations.

During early 1996, HQ ARRC deployed to Sarajevo in the Former Yugoslavia to command the NATO Implementation Force (IFOR). In 1999 HQ ARRC was responsible for operations in Kosovo and Macedonia and in 2002 in Afghanistan. Once again HQ ARRC will deploy to Afghanistan in May 2006 to lead the NATO effort in the country.

Command Posts and Deployment: Due to the need to be able to respond flexibly to the whole range of potential operations, HQ ARRC has been developing the capability for rapidly deployable and modular HQs. Deployment will begin with the despatch of a Forward Liaison and Reconnaissance Group (FLRG) within 48 hours of the order being given which can then be quickly followed up.

Within four days the key enablers from 1 (UK) Signal Bde would be within theatre and three days later HQ ARRC Forward and HQ Rear Support Command (RSC) Forward – as required – could be established. The forward-deployed HQs are light, mobile and C-130 transportable. While there is a standard 'default' setting for personnel numbers, the actual staff composition is 'tailored' to the task and can vary from approximately 50 to 150 staff, depending on the requirement. The 'in-theatre' task would then be supported by the remainder of the staff, using sophisticated 'Reachback' techniques and equipment.

The Early Entry HQs are capable of sustained independent operations if required but can also be used as enablers if it is decided to deploy the full HQ ARRC. This deployment concept has been tested and evaluated on several exercises and has proven its worth. In parallel, HQ ARRC is continuously looking to make all of its HQs lighter and more survivable.

Outline Composition of the ARRC (ACE Rapid Reaction Corps)

For operations the ARRC might have some of the following formations under command:

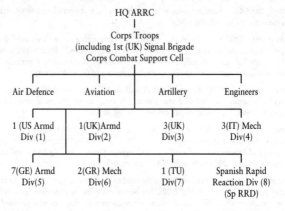

Notes: (1) United States; (2) Resident in Germany (3) Resident in the UK (4) IT – Italy (5) GE – Germany (6) GR – Greece (7) TU – Turkish.

The operational organisation, composition and size of the ARRC would depend on the type of crisis, area of crisis, its political significance, and the capabilities and availability of lift assets, the distances to be covered and the infrastructure capabilities of the nation receiving assistance. It is considered that a four-division ARRC would be the maximum employment structure.

The main British contribution to the ARRC is 1 (UK) Armoured Division that is stationed in Germany and there is also a considerable number of British personnel in both the ARRC Corps HQ and Corps Troops. In addition, in times of tension 3 (UK) Mechanised Division and 16 Air Assault Brigade will move to the operational area to take their place in the ARRC's order of battle. In total, we believe that if the need arose some 40,000 British soldiers could be assigned to the ARRC together with substantial numbers of Regular Army Reservists and formed TA Units.

European Union

This position of the UK Government (June 2005) is that NATO is the cornerstone of UK national defence, but that the EU can accomplish many tasks that are complementary to NATO.

The European Union (EU) consists of

Austria; Belgium; Cyprus (Greek part); Czech Republic; Denmark; Estonia; Finland; France; Germany; Greece; Hungary; Ireland; Italy; Latvia; Lithuania; Luxembourg; Malta; Netherlands; Poland; Portugal; Slovakia; Slovenia; Spain; Sweden; United Kingdom.

European Defence Agency

The European Defence Agency (EDA) was established on 12 July 2004 following a unanimous decision by European Heads of State and Government. It was established under the Council Joint Action 2004/5 51/CFSP on the basis of Article 14 of the treaty on the European Union (Maastricht).

The purpose of the European Defence Agency is to support the Member States and the Council of Europe in order to improve European defence capabilities in the field of crisis management, and to sustain and develop the European Security and Defence Policy.

The EDA has the following tasks:

To improve the EU's defence capabilities in the field of crisis management

To promote European armaments cooperation

To strengthen the European defence industrial and technological base and create a competitive European defence equipment market, in consultation with the Commission

To promote research, in liaison with Community research activities, with a view to strengthening Europe's industrial and technological potential in the defence field

In the longer term the EDA will achieve its goals by:

Encouraging EU governments to spend defence budgets on meeting tomorrow's challenges, not yesterday's threats

Helping them to identify common needs and promoting collaboration to provide common solutions.

The EDA is an agency of the European Union and therefore under the direction and authority of the Council, which issues guidelines to and receives reports from High Representative Janvier Solana (March 2006) as Head of the Agency. Detailed control and guidance, however, is the responsibility of the Steering Board.

EDA Organisation

Steering Committee

Chief Executive

Deputy Chief Executive

Media and Communications Unit ———— Planning and Policy Unit

Capabilities Directorate	Research & Technology Directorate	Armaments Directorate	Industry & Market Directorate	Corporate Services Directorate

Janvier Solana chairs the Steering Board, the principal decision-making body of the Agency, made up of Defence Ministers from 24 participating Member States (all EU members except Denmark) and a member of the European Commission. In addition to ministerial meetings at least twice a year, the Steering Board also meets at the level of national armaments directors, national research directors, national capability planners and policy directors.

The EDA budget from July 2004 to the end of 2004 was 1.8 million (£1.22 million)

The Agency has a budget of 19.9 million (£13.5 million) for 2005. For 2005 the United Kingdom will pay 3,596,803 (£2,446,804). This UK contribution will be paid from the budget of the UK MoD.

During 2005 the EDA had a budget to employ 80 staff. The EDA's chief executive is Nick Witney, a former UK Ministry of Defence civil servant.

EU Helsinki Headline Goal 2010
The European Union (EU) has adopted the following illustrative scenarios which form the basis for force planning to meet the EU Helsinki Headline Goal 2010:

♦ Stabilisation, reconstruction and military advice to third world countries
♦ Conflict Prevention
♦ Evacuation Operation in a non-permissive environment
♦ Separation of Parties by Force
♦ Assistance to Humanitarian Operations.

UK Commitment to the European Helsinki Goal 2010
In early 2005 the UK MoD confirmed a declaration of up to 12,500 troops towards the Helsinki Headline Goal on a voluntary case-by-case basis. Of this figure about 35% are infantry troops.

The UK currently offers three brigades which allows the UK to provide either an Armoured Brigade (based on Warrior Armoured Fighting Vehicles and Challenger 2 Main Battle Tanks), a Mechanised Brigade (based on Saxon Infantry Fighting Vehicles and Challenger 2 Main Battle Tanks) or an Air Assault Brigade consisting of lightly equipped infantry in the Air Manoeuvre role. An Amphibious Brigade (3 Commando Brigade) from the Royal Navy may also be available. Up to 18 UK warships and 72 UK combat aircraft are also available for EU operations.

However, these national forces are made available for EU operations on a voluntary, case-by-case basis, as for NATO or UN operations. UK contributions to such operations are provided from within existing forces.

As yet (early 2006) there is no standing European Rapid Reaction Force nor any EU agreement to create one. What has sometimes been referred to as a 'European Rapid Reaction Force' is, in fact, a catalogue of forces which member states could make available to the EU should they choose to participate in a particular EU-led operation. Any contribution to a particular EU-led operation would depend on the operation's requirements, the availability of forces at the time and the willingness of EU members to participate.

EU military plans

In the immediate future, the EU plans to be able to provide at least one coherent Battle Group package, to undertake single Battle Group-sized operations in support of the EU Helsinki Headline Goals

Three Battle Groups (UK, combined French/Belgian and Italian) are already operational.

Full Operational Capability (FOC) will be reached in 2007 when all Battle Groups will be available. The EU should then have the capacity to undertake at least two concurrent single Battle Group-size rapid response operations, including the ability to launch both such operations nearly simultaneously.

EU Member States have indicated that they will commit to Battle Groups, formed as follows by early 2007:

1	United Kingdom
2	France and Belgium
3	Italy
4	Spain
5	France, Germany, Belgium, Luxembourg and Spain
6	Germany, the Netherlands and Finland
7	Germany, Austria and Czech Republic
8	Italy, Hungary and Slovenia
9	Italy, Spain, Greece and Portugal
10	Poland, Germany, Slovakia, Latvia and Lithuania
11	Sweden, Finland and Norway
12	United Kingdom and the Netherlands

EU Military Structures

The following table sets out the main multilateral military structures outside NATO which include European Union members. A number of these also include non-EU countries. In addition, there are many other bilateral military agreements between individual EU member states.

The UK is a party to military agreements in respect of four of the structures listed in the following table. Military agreements between other EU members are a matter for those member states' governments.

Structure	EU participants
EAG—European Air Group	Belgium, France, Germany, Italy, Spain, UK
European Airlift Centre	Belgium, France, Germany, Italy, Netherlands, Spain, UK
Sealift Coordination Centre (Eindhoven)	Netherlands, UK
European Amphibious Initiative (including the UK/Netherlands Amphibious Force)	France, Italy, Netherlands, Spain, UK
SHIRBRIG—Stand-by High Readiness Brigade	Austria, Denmark, Finland, Ireland, Italy, Lithuania, Netherlands, Norway, Poland, Portugal, Slovenia, Spain, Sweden. (Observers: Czech Republic, Hungary)
SEEBRIG—South-Eastern Europe Brigade	Greece, Italy, Slovenia
NORDCAPS—Nordic Coordinated Arrangement for Military Peace Support	Finland, Sweden, Denmark
EUROCORPS	Germany, Belgium, Spain, France, Luxembourg
EUROFOR	France, Italy, Portugal, Spain
EUROMARFOR	France, Italy, Portugal, Spain

Eurocorps

The Eurocorps was created in 1992 and comprises military contributions from its five framework nations: Belgium, France, Germany, Luxembourg and Spain. The Headquarters is located in Strasbourg (France). Austria, Canada, Greece, Italy, Poland and Turkey have military liaison staff co-located at Eurocorps HQ.

The Common Committee, composed of the political directors of the foreign ministries and the chiefs of defence staffs of the nations providing Eurocorps contingents is the highest level of command level for the Eurocorps. The Common Committee meets once a year.

For coordination and day-to-day control, the Common Committee has established the POLMIL Group, which includes representatives at the military/political level from the framework nations' Ministries of Defence.

The Commander Eurocorps (COMEC) is a lieutenant general (3 stars). The Deputy Commander (DCOM) is a major general (2 stars). The staff is directed by the Chief of Staff (COS), also a major general and he is supported by two Deputy Chiefs of Staff (DCOS) for Operations and Support, both of whom are brigadier generals (1 star).

The posts of Commanding General, DCOM and the other general officers as well as some key functions are filled by EC framework nations on a rotational basis. COMEC, DCOM and COS are always of different nationalities. Their tour of duty generally lasts for two years.

The Eurocorps consists of formations under direct operational control and formations earmarked for assignment during an emergency:

Under direct operational control:

Franco German Brigade (GE-FR Bde)

Multinational Command Support Brigade (MNCS Bde)

Formations earmarked for assignment during an emergency:

French Contribution
Etat-Major de Force numéro 3 (EMF3) in Marseille (equivalent to a divisional HQ) composed of:

1 x Armoured Brigade

1 x Mechanised Infantry Brigade

Specialised support units

German Contribution
The 10th Armoured Division, with its HQ in Sigmaringen, composed of:

12th Armoured Brigade in Amberg

30th Mechanised Brigade in Ellwangen

Suport units

Belgian Contribution
Belgian Operational Command Land, with its HQ in Evere, composed of:

1st Mechanised Brigade in Leopoldsburg

7th Mechanised Brigade in Marche-en-Fammene

Support units

Spanish Contribution

1st Mechanised Division with its HQ in Burgos, composed of:

10th Mechanised Brigade in Cordoba

11th Mechanised Brigade in Badajoz

12th Armoured Brigade in Madrid

Luxembourg Contribution

Luxembourg assigns a reconnaissance company composed of about 180 personnel. During operations this unit would be integrated into the Belgian contingent.

During the past decade the Eurocorps has been involved in operations as follows:

SFOR (Bosnia) 1999-2000

KFOR III (Kosovo) 2000

ISAF IV (Afghanistan) 2004-2005

Note: If all earmarked national contributions were committed to operations, the Eurocorps would number approximately 60,000 personnel.

THE FINANCES OF DEFENCE

> "You need three things to win a war,
> Money, money and more money".

Trivulzio (1441-1518)

In general terms defence is related to money, and a nation's ability to pay for its defence is linked to its GDP (Gross Domestic Product) as measured by the sum of all economic activity within a country. Estimates for the world's top eight GDP rankings for 2004 (in billions of US$) and the latest year for which accurate figures are available are as follows:

United States	–	$11,700 billion
Japan	–	$4,660 billion
Germany	–	$2,570 billion
United Kingdom	–	$2,001 billion
France	–	$1,927 billion
China	–	$1,680 billion
Italy	–	$1,594 billion
Russia	–	$1,430 billion

Note: Above table at early 2006 exchange rates. The above figures are based on simple currency exchange totals. Under the purchasing power parity (PPP) measure the latest (2005) estimates suggest that the US and total EU figures are roughly similar at around $12.3 billion.

Finance – European Union – Top Five Nations (2004 Figures)

	GDP	Per Capita Income
Germany	Euro 2,160 bn (US$2,570 bn)	US$31,227
United Kingdom	£1,150 bn (US$2,001 bn)	US$33,898
France	Euro 1,620 bn (US$1,927 bn)	US$32,619
Italy	Euro 1,340 bn (US$1,594 bn)	US$27,540
Spain	Euro 799 bn (US$950 bn)	US$23,651

UK defence expenditure

In the 2005-2006 Financial Year (FY) the UK Government planned to spend £32,506 billion (Resource DEL) on defence. In Cash Limit terms the MoD budget for 2005/06 is £30.9 billion.

For comparison purposes defence expenditure is often expressed as a percentage of GDP. Expenditure in FY 2005-2006 represented about 2.4% of GDP having fallen from around 2.5% of GDP in FY 2001-02. In 1985 UK defence expenditure represented 5.2% of GDP.

The estimated total UK government expenditure for FY 2005-06 is £520.5 billion. Education, health, local government, defence, social security, Scotland, Wales and Northern Ireland constitute about 70 per cent of expenditure.

DEFENCE BUDGETS – NATO COMPARISON

The nations of the North Atlantic Treaty Organisation (NATO), spent some US$676 billion on defence during FY 2005 – 2006. Of this total the European members of NATO spent approximately US$200 billion.

Country	2005 Budget
United States	$465 billion
Canada	$10.9 billion
Belgium	$3.35 billion
Bulgaria	$0.630 billion
Czech Republic	$2.19 billion
Denmark	$3.17 billion
Estonia	$0.207 billion
France	$41.6 billion
Germany	$30.2 billion
Greece	$4.46 billion
Hungary	$1.43 billion
Iceland	No defence budget
Italy	$17.2 billion
Latvia	$0.278 billion
Lithuania	$0.333 billion
Luxembourg	$0.264 billion
Netherlands	$9.7 billion
Norway	$4.69 billion
Poland	$5.16 billion

Country	2005 Budget
Portugal	$2.43 billion
Romania	$2.10 billion
Slovakia	$0.828 billion
Slovenia	$0.580 billion
Spain	$8.8 billion
Turkey	$9.81 billion
United Kingdom	$51.1 billion
TOTAL	**$676.41 billion**

Note: Iceland has no military expenditure although it remains a member of NATO.

An interesting comparison is made by the total national defence budget divided by the total number of full time personnel in all three services. 2005 figures for the top five world defence spending nations are as follows:-

Ranking	Nation	2005 Defence Budget	Total Service Personnel	Cost per Serviceman
1	USA	US$465 billion	1,473,000	US$315,682
2	UK	US$51.1 billion	200,000	US$255,500
2	Japan	US$44.7 billion	239,000	US$187,029
4	France	US$41.6 billion	254,000	US$163,779
5	Germany	US$30.2 billion	284,000	US$106,330

Note: Figures are calculated on a direct currency exchange basis. For information, using direct currency exchange, Russia has a defence budget of US$18.8 billion and China a defence budget of US$29.5 billion. In our opinion the currency exchange figures are a more honest reflection of the actual situation than the purchasing power parity (PPP) figures.

UK DEFENCE BUDGET – TOP LEVEL BUDGET HOLDERS
For the past decade the UK defence budget has been allocated to a series of 'Top Level Budget Holders' each of whom were allocated a budget with which to run their departments. The money allocated to these Top Level Budgets (TLBs) constitutes the building bricks upon which the whole of the defence budget is based.

Top-Level Budgets 2005-2006 Resource DEL

Naval Operational Areas (C-in-C Fleet)	£3,524 million
Army Operational Areas (C-in-C Land Command)	£5,620 million
General Officer Commanding (Northern Ireland)	£609 million
Air Force Operational Areas (AOC RAF Strike Command)	£3,672 million
Chief of Joint Operations	£545 million
Chief of Defence Logistics	£7,600 million
Second Sea Lord/Naval Home Command	£729 million
Adjutant General (Army) Personnel & Training Command	£1,765 million
Air Officer Commanding RAF Personnel & Training Command	£911 million

Central			£3,201 million
Defence Procurement Agency			£2,805 million
Defence Estates			£974 million
Corporate Science and Technology			£504 million
		Total:	£32,461 million

Principal headings of the defence budget 2005-2006 (Resource basis)

Expenditure on Armed Forces personnel	£8,134 million
Expenditure on Civilian personnel	£2,770 million
Depreciation/impairments	£8,441 million
Cost of capital	£2,901 million
Equipment Support	£3,323 million
Stock Consumption	£1,172 million
Property Management	£1,589 million
Movements	£559 million
Accommodation & Utilities	£766 million
Professional Fees	£462 million
Fuel	£227 million
Other	£2,162 million
Total	£32,506 million

Note: Totals will differ from table to table because of the way in which the MoD recognises figures.

DEFENCE EQUIPMENT AND COLLABORATIVE EQUIPMENT PROGRAMMES

Battlespace manoeuvre

	Quantity	Cost	In service	Notes
Typhoon	232	£11,291 million*	2003	Fighter aircraft
Typhoon ASTA	1	£211 million	2005	Aircrew training system
BVRAAM	Classified	£1,204 million	2012	Air-to-air missile
A400M	25	£2,644 million	2011	Heavy transport aircraft
Support vehicle	5,324 units	£1,362 million	2008	4,851 cargo; 314 recovery & 69 trailers
C vehicle	n/a	£710 million	2006	Commercial provision of C vehicles
Terrier	65	£299 million	2008	Armoured engineer vehicle
LFATGW	378	£310 million	2005	Light Forces ATGW
NLAW	14,002	£365 million	2006	Short range anti-armour weapon

Precision attack

Type 45 Destroyer 6		£5,896 million	2009	Anti-air warfare vessel
Astute Class Submarine	3	£3,492 million	2009	Attack submarine
Sting Ray	Classified	£599 million	2006	Torpedo life extension and enhancement
Nimrod Mk 4	12	£3,808 million	2010	Reconnaissance and attack patrol aircraft
Future Joint Combat Aircraft	TBD	£1,914 million	TBD	Fighter and attack aircraft
Precision guided bomb	2,303	£352 million	2007	Air launched
GMLRS	6,204	£263 million	2007	Guided missile launched rocket system

Information superiority

ASTOR	5 aircraft 8 ground stations	£954 million	2006	Airborne stand off radar
Skynet	N/a	£2,775 million	2005	Satellite communications system
Bowman	47,000 radios	£2,000 million	2005	Tactical communications
Bowman hardware & software	N/a	£339 million	2005	Common equipment for a variety of roles

Notes; TBD – To be decided; N/a – Not applicable: Typhoon costs at £11,291 million are based on the unit cost of £49.1 million per aircraft as given in the MoD Major Projects Report 2004.

DEFENCE PERSONNEL TOTALS

Total Service and Civilian Personnel Strength (1 January 2006)

UK service personnel	200,940 (includes 3,350 Gurkhas)
UK civilian personnel	90,000
Locally entered/engaged service personnel	200
Locally entered/engaged civilian personnel	16,150
Royal Irish (Home Service)	3,130
Army reservists mobilised	1,270
RAF reservists mobilised	40
Royal Naval reservists mobilised	40
Total	**311,770**

For comparison: Total Service and Civilian Personnel Strength (1 April 1990)

UK service personnel	305,700
UK civilian personnel	141,400
Locally entered/engaged service personnel	9,000
Locally entered/engaged civilian personnel	30,900
Total	**487,000**

Note: In 1990, the figures for the then Ulster Defence Regiment (full time personnel) were included in the UK service personnel total.

STRENGTH OF UK REGULAR FORCES TRAINED AND UNTRAINED (1 JANUARY 2006)

Royal Navy	Officers	Other Ranks
Trained	6,780	28,800
Untrained	1,020	3,488

Army	Officers	Other Ranks
Trained	14,200	86,940
Untrained	780	12,400

Royal Air Force	Officers	Other Ranks
Trained	9,510	37,940
Untrained	1,000	1,100

Selected figures – deployment in budgetary areas (1 April 2005)

Naval Operational Areas	Officers	Other Ranks	Civilians
Consolidated Fleet Figure (1)	3,000	21,900	1,600
Royal Fleet Auxiliary – total personnel	2,300		

Note: (1) Consolidated figures are for: Naval Aviation, Fleet Infrastructure, Surface Fleet, Submarines and Royal Marines.

Army Operational Areas	Officers	Other Ranks	Civilians
Field Army	4,600	47,300	2,100
Joint Helicopter Command	1,400	11,200	500
Commander Regional Forces	1,300	9,900	5,200
Land Support	300	100	800
GOC Northern Ireland	600	5,200	3,100

Air Force Operational Areas	Officers	Other Ranks	Civilians
Strike Command Management Group	4,600	26,500	5,600

2nd Sea Lord/Commander-in-Chief Naval Home Command

	Officers	Other Ranks	Civilians
Flag Officer Training and Recruiting	600	1,800	1,000
Headquarters	1,000	2,000	800
Untrained personnel	900	2,600	–

Adjutant General (Personnel and Training Command)

	Officers	Other Ranks	Civilians
Army Personnel Centre	1,300	2,100	800
Army Training and Recruitment	1,100	5,300	4,000
Chief of Staff	300	600	900
General Staff	600	500	900
Untrained personnel	900	9,500	–

Air Officer Commander-in-Chief RAF Personnel and Training Command

	Officers	Other Ranks	Civilians
Personnel Management Agency	400	500	200
Training Group Defence Agency	1,100	2,500	2,200
Core Headquarters	500	900	3,000
Untrained personnel	1,000	2,000	–

Miscellaneous figures

	Officers	Other Ranks	Civilians
Central	4,000	6,800	17,400
Defence Logistics Organisation	1,900	4,400	20,600
Defence Procurement Agency	500	200	3,800
Permanent Joint Headquarters	400	400	200

Deployment Locations (1 April 2005)

United Kingdom
Service	171,870
Civilian	84,700

Mainland Europe

Germany
Service	22,170
Civilian	9,700

Balkans

Service	170
Civilian	660

Remainder

Service	1,200
Civilian	140

Mediterranean

Cyprus

Service	3,170
Civilian	2,790

Gibraltar

Service	360
Civilian	1,100

Middle East

Service	390
Civilian	1,650

Note: Above figures Include personnel based in Egypt, Iraq and Libya. but not those on temporary deployment in the region – especially Iraq.

Far East/Asia

Service	260
Civilian	730

Note: Above figures Include personnel based in Afghanistan on temporary deployment.

Africa

Sierra Leone

Service	100
Civilian	600

Elsewhere in Africa

Service	70
Civilian	170

North America

USA

Service	400
Civilian	200

Canada

Service	290
Civilian	20

Note: Excluding British troops training in Canada at the British Army Training Unit, Suffield.

Central and South America

Service	100
Civilian	150

Falkland Islands

Service	320
Civilian	50

Note: The figures for the Falkland Islands do not include personnel on temporary detachment.

Elsewhere

Service	230
Civilian	280

Intake – UK Regular Forces (2004-2005)

	Officers	Other Ranks
Royal Navy	370 (665)	3,320 (4,704)
Army	760 (1,525)	10,940 (18,743)
Royal Air Force	450 (936)	1,880 (6,078)

For Comparison – 1985-86 figures are in brackets.

Outflow – UK Regular Forces (2004-2005)

	Officers	Other Ranks
Royal Navy	510 (771)	4,130 (7,232)
Army	1,100 (1,985)	13,070 (19,316)
Royal Air Force	700 (983)	3,020 (6,234)

For Comparison – 1985-86 figures are in brackets.

Gender – UK Regular Forces (1 Jan 2006)

Royal Navy Officers	7,640
Male	6,980
Female	660
Royal Navy Other Ranks	31,780
Male	28,790
Female	2,990
Army Officers	14,600

Male	13,030
Female	1,570
Army Other Ranks	92,540
Male	86,010
Female	6,530
Royal Air Force Officers	10,350
Male	8,950
Female	1,400
Royal Air Force Other Ranks	39,040
Male	34,370
Female	4,660

Figures above exclude Full-Time Reserve Service personnel, Gurkhas, the Home Service battalions of the Royal Irish Regiment, mobilised reservists and Naval Activated Reservists – about 9,660 personnel. The figures above include trained and untrained personnel.

RESERVE FORCES

In an emergency the UK MoD could call upon a tri-service reserve component of some 235,000 personnel (early-2006 figure). This figure is composed of Regular Reserves and Volunteer Forces as follows:

Naval Regular Reserves	22,180
Naval Volunteer Reserves	3,610
University Units – Royal Navy	750
Regular Army Reserves	134,190
Territorial Army & Others	37,260
University Units – Army	4,760
Royal Air Force Regular Reserves	35,160
Royal Air Force Volunteer Reserves	1,450

Regular Reserves (191,000) comprise ex-service personnel who have completed regular service and have a reserve liability in civilian life. The Volunteer Forces (44,000) comprise volunteers who may not have had prior regular service and train on a part-time basis; generally at establishments close to their home.

In a National Audit Office (NAO) Report published in March 2006 the NAO reported that over 12,000 UK reservists have made a "very valuable contribution" to operations in Iraq since 2003, receiving particular praise for their adaptability and high skill levels.

The NAO report praised the successful development of a culture in which volunteer reservists expect and want to serve on operations. It highlights that the training between reservists and regular personnel will be brought even closer together as a result of recent restructuring. The report also acknowledges the improved management of reservists and the improved support given to them and to their families.

The NAO found that a majority of new recruits join the reserve forces because of "a desire to serve on operations" and that 76% of those who deploy on operations are satisfied with their overall experience. Around 70% of all reservists describe their overall experience as "challenging and worthwhile" and nearly half of all volunteer reservists remain in the service for over ten years. About 13% of those who choose to leave the reserve forces do so in order to join the regular forces.

Cadet Forces

In mid 2005 there were 153,000 in the cadet forces of the three services. Single service cadet force numbers (including officers and administrative staff) are as follows:

Royal Navy

Sea Cadets	16,350
Combined Cadet Force	5,560

Army

Army Cadets	52,010
Combined Cadet Force	28,910

Royal Air Force

Air Training Corps	40,170
Combined Cadet Force	10,130

IRAQ

British Forces are serving in Iraq as part of the Coalition Force authorised under United Nations Security Council Resolution 1546. This mandate will expire upon the completion of the political process or if requested by the Government of Iraq.

The UK Government has stated that it is committed to Iraq for as long as the Iraqi Government judge that the coalition is required to provide security and assist in the development of the Iraqi Security Forces.

On 1 January 2006, some 9,600 UK armed forces personnel were deployed on Operation Telic. Of this number approximately 8,000 were serving within Iraq. The majority of United Kingdom troops deployed to Iraq deploy for six-month tours and are in units commanded by the Multinational Division (South-East).

Over time the personnel deployed on Op Telic have declined as follows:

♦ Peak during Major Combat Operations (March/April 2003): 46,000
♦ At the end of May 2003: 18,000
♦ At the end of May 2004: 9,800
♦ At the end of May 2005: 9,700

The overwhelming majority of UK personnel in Iraq are based in South-East Iraq, with a small number based in Baghdad and around the country to liaise and coordinate with other Coalition and Iraqi forces.

Multinational Division (South-East) MND(SE)

The Headquarters of the MND(SE) is located at Basrah International Airport in Southern Iraq. This is a composite multinational headquarters with the majority of the personnel and infrastructure being provided by the UK.

MND(SE) covers four provinces in Iraq with subsidiary headquarters at: Shaibah (UK National Support Element) Maysan, Al Muthanna, Talil Airbase, As Samawah and Dhi Qar.

The primary activities of MND(SE) are:

♦ Supporting the ongoing political process in Iraq
♦ Security Sector Reform – Training the new Iraqi security Forces with partnership operations where MND(SE) forces back-up, assist and monitor these Iraqi Security Forces
♦ Normalisation – Helping to get society on its feet again by assisting in the restoration of water, power, health, education, judiciary, oil industry and heritage and encouraging commercial markets and the economy

The UK IFP (Integrated Force Package) is generally comprised of the following:

1 x Brigade Headquarters and Signal Squadron
1 x Armoured Regiment
1 x Artillery Regiment
3 x Infantry Battalions
1 x Engineer Regiment

A very high readiness reserve battalion (VHRR) is held in the UK at 10 days' readiness to deploy to Iraq.

In May 2006 HQ 7 Armoured Brigade will be replaced by HQ 20 Armoured Brigade

In addition to the UK personnel, in early 2006 MND(SE) had approximately 5,000 troops from countries that include: Australia, Czech Republic, Denmark, Italy, Japan, South Korea, Lithuania, Netherlands, Norway, Portugal, and Romania.

COSTS OF OPERATIONS IN IRAQ

	£ million
2002–03	
Operations in Iraq	629
Expenditure on capital equipment	218
Total	847
2003–04	
Operations in Iraq	1,051
Expenditure on capital equipment	260
Total	1,311

2004–05

Operations in Iraq	747
Expenditure on capital equipment	163
Total	910

Grand total	3,068

It is likely that the figure for FY 2005-2006 will be between £900 million and £1,000 million.

Reservists

During January 2006 Around 700 reservists were deployed in Iraq. This figure comprised more than 650 Army reserves, 28 Royal Air Force reserves, and 20 Royal Marine reservists. The majority of these reservists were serving on six-month tours.

NATO Support

At the ministerial meeting in Brussels on 9 December 2004, Foreign Ministers of the 26 NATO countries agreed to move ahead with expanding NATO's role in Iraq. Twenty three NATO countries have agreed to provide support to the NATO Training Mission-Iraq by providing personnel and equipment to train the Iraqi Security Forces in and outside of Iraq. Of these 23 countries, fifteen have agreed to deploy forces within Iraq. These are Bulgaria, Canada, Denmark, Hungary, Italy, Latvia, Lithuania, the Netherlands, Norway, Poland, Portugal, Romania, Turkey, the United Kingdom and the United States.

Iraqi National Guard

The mission of the Iraqi National Guard is to conduct internal security operations, including support to Ministry of Interior forces and constabulary duties.

The training process comprises three weeks' basic training for the individual, followed by four weeks' collective training. In late 2005, more than 50,000 personnel were assessed as being trained, equipped and operational in the Iraqi national guard. HQ Multinational Force Iraq assesses that the future strength of the Iraqi national guard will be more than 56,000 personnel.

During early 2006 there would appear to be approximately 190,000 Iraqi Security Force personnel available (50,000 National Guard and approximately 140,000 police associated personnel) but figures remain contradictory.

Awards for service in Iraq

As at 26 August 2005, the following medals had been issued to military personnel who have served or are serving in Iraq.

Medal	Number Awarded
Victoria Cross	1
George Cross	1
Distinguished Service Order	12
Conspicuous Gallantry Cross	8
Distinguished Service Cross	1
Military Cross	45
Distinguished Flying Cross	11
Bar to Distinguished Flying Cross	2
Air Force Cross	2
Queens Gallantry Medal	14
George Medal	1
Iraq Campaign Medal	72,000

Afghanistan

As of early 2006 the UK had approximately 500 armed forces personnel serving with the International Security Assistance Force (ISAF) in Afghanistan.

However, it is believed that the UK contribution in Afghanistan may number as many as 5,700 troops when the UK assumes command of the NATO peace support operation in the country in mid 2006. The majority of these troops will be sent to the volatile Helmand area in the south, which the UK MoD admits is "more demanding" than other regions in Afghanistan. The deployment will cost about £1 billion over three years.

The initial deployment would be 1,000 troops to the Headquarters Group of the Allied Rapid Reaction Corps (May 2006 to February 2007 only), with the main deployment of 3,300 (mainly combat personnel) heading to the south, including a Provincial Construction team. About 1,000 personnel would be involved in the construction of bases areas and would return to the UK as soon as their task was complete.

The summer 2006 deployment will see the creation of a new British-led Provincial Reconstruction Team (PRT) at Lashkar Gar, the capital of Helmand province. This PRT will be staffed and protected by 16 Air Assault Brigade.

The PRT will be based on a command and planning group consisting of the British military commander and officials from the Foreign and Commonwealth Office and the Department for International Development. These officials provide the area with a seamless package of political, democratic, developmental and military assistance in Helmand.

These UK troops will be supported by 6 x Harrier GR7 aircraft based at Kandahar. The task for these aircraft is to provide air reconnaissance and close air support to coalition forces engaged against the remnants of the Taliban and to ISAF.

UK operations in Afghanistan were costed at £35.9 million in FY2003-04. Estimates for FY2004-05 are in the region of £53 million.

Prior to this major deployment in early 2006 the UK presence in Afghanistan amounted to:

♦ Quick Reaction Force QRF*
♦ Kabul Patrols Company (KPC – withdrawn))
♦ Afghan National Army Training Team (ANATT)
♦ Provisional Reconstruction Teams (PRT) based in Mazer-e –Sharif **
♦ Harrier GR7 Detachment (6 x aircraft)

* Handed over to Norway in March 2006.
** Handed over to Sweden in March 2006.

NATO's International Security Assistance Force (ISAF) mission currently numbers about 9,200 troops. It is expected to increase the overall number to about 15,000 and it is believed that other countries – including Australia, New Zealand and the Netherlands will also contribute troops to strengthen the ISAF commitment.

As of January 2006 armed forces personnel from 35 nations were supporting ISAF. These nations include:

Albania; Austria; Azerbaijan; Belgium; Bulgaria; Canada; Croatia; Czech Republic; Denmark; Estonia; Finland; France; FYROM; Germany; Greece; Hungary; Iceland; Ireland; Italy; Latvia; Lithuania; Luxembourg; Netherlands; Norway; Poland; Portugal; Romania; Slovakia; Slovenia; Spain; Sweden; Switzerland; Turkey; United Kingdom and the United States of America.

CHAPTER 2 – THE ROYAL NAVY

Personnel Summary (at 1 January 2006)

		Trained Strength at 1 January 2006
Royal Navy	Trained Requirement	37,110
Officers		6,780
	Males	6,240
	Females	540
Other Ranks		28,880
	Males	26,170
	Females	2,710
	Total	**35,660**

Note: The above figures include some 7,200 Royal Marines but do not include the approximate figure of 1,600 personnel from the Army attached to 3 Commando Brigade.

Not included in the above figures are approximately 2,300 civilian personnel manning support ships operated by the Royal Fleet Auxiliary (RFA).

	Personnel in training at 1 January 2006
Officers	1,020
Other Ranks	3,480
Total	**4,500**

Estimated Fleet Strength

Submarines
In service:
4 x Nuclear Powered Ballistic Missile firing (UK Strategic Deterrent)
10 x Nuclear Powered Attack type

New construction:
3 x Nuclear Powered Attack type. Will displace 7,800 tons. Expected to enter service from 2008

Major surface vessels
In Service:
3 x Aircraft Carriers: Mix of fixed-wing Harriers and helicopters
1 x Helicopter Carrier
2 x Amphibious Assault Ships
3 x Amphibious Landing Ships

New construction:
4 x Landing Ships. Expected to enter service from 2006
2 x Aircraft Carriers. Planned to enter service from 2012

Destroyers and frigates
In Service:
8 x Destroyers
18 x Frigates

New Construction:
6 x Destroyers. Expected to enter service from 2008

Minewarfare vessels
In Service:
16 x Minehunters and minesweepers. Deployable worldwide

Survey Ships
In Service:
5 x Ocean survey vessels

Patrol vessels
In service:
1 x Antarctic patrol ship
5 x Patrol vessels. Fishery Protection and patrol duties
18 x Patrol craft

Fleet Support Ships
(Manned by Royal Fleet Auxiliary personnel. Supply fuel, stores and ammunition at sea to fleet units)

In Service:
2 x Fast fleet tankers
3 x Small fleet tankers
4 x Support tankers
4 x Replenishment ships
1 x Aviation training ship
1 x Forward repair ship
6 x Ro-Ro Ships (4 under civil management)

Naval Aircraft
8 x Sea Harrier. Air Defence and Recce/Attack (until March 2006)
38 x Merlin Helicopters. Anti-submarine warfare
12 x Sea King MK6. Anti-submarine warfare
23 x Lynx Helicopters. Anti-submarine warfare and missile armed for surface ship attack
11 x AEW Sea King Helicopters. Provide radar airborne early warning to fleet
41 x Sea King Commando Helicopters. Royal Marine Commando operations
6 x Lynx Helicopters. Anti-tank attack role. Part of Commando Force
8 x Gazelle Helicopters. Reconnaissance duties

Royal Marines Summary

1 x Commando Brigade Headquarters
3 x Royal Marine Commando (Battalion Size)
3 x Commando Assault Helicopter Squadrons
1 x Commando Light Helicopter Squadron
1 x Commando Regiment Royal Artillery
1 x Commando Squadron Royal Engineers
1 x Commando Logistic Regiment
1 Commando Assault Group (Landing-Craft)
1 x Fleet Protection Group
1 x Security Unit for National Strategic Deterrent
Royal Marines Training Establishment
Royal Marines Band Service
Reserve Units
4 x Special Boat Service Squadrons

Composition of the Fleet

Submarines			In Refit	Home Base
(Trident)	4	Vanguard, Victorious, Vigilant, Vengeance.	1	Faslane
(Fleet)	7	Tireless, Torbay, Trafalgar, Turbulent, Trenchant, Talent, Triumph	2	Devonport
	3	Sceptre, Superb, Sovereign.		Faslane
(Under construction)	3	Astute, Artful, Ambush (from 2008)		Faslane
Carriers	3	Invincible, Illustrious, Ark Royal	1	Portsmouth
Destroyers (Type 42)	8	Exeter, Manchester, York, Nottingham, Gloucester, Southampton, Liverpool, Edinburgh.	1	Portsmouth
Frigates (Type 23)	14	Sutherland, Monmouth, Northumberland, Somerset, Argyll, Montrose, Richmond, Lancaster, Iron Duke, Westminster, Grafton, Kent, Portland, St Albans.	2	Devonport/ Portsmouth
(Type 22)	4	Chatham, Campbeltown, Cornwall, Cumberland	1	Devonport
(Under construction)	6	Daring (launched February 2006), Dauntless, Diamond, Dragon, Defender, Duncan		
Assault Ships	2	Albion, Bulwark		Devonport
Helicopter Carrier	1	Ocean.		Devonport

Offshore Patrol

(Castle Class)	1	Dumbarton Castle		Portsmouth
(River Class)	3+1	Tyne, Mersey, Severn, Clyde		Portsmouth

Minehunters

(Hunt Class)	8	Brocklesby, Chiddingfold, Ledbury, Middleton,	2	Portsmouth
		Atherstone, Cattistock, Quorn, Hurworth		
(Sandown Class)	8	Walney, Penzance, Pembroke, Grimsby, Bangor,	2	Faslane/
		Blythe, Ramsay, Shoreham.		Portsmouth

Coastal	16	Biter, Blazer, Archer, Charger, Dasher, Smiter, Puncher,
Training		Pursuer, Example, Explorer, Express, Exploit, Tracker,
Craft		Raider, Ranger, Trumpeter.

Two of these craft (Dasher and Pursuer) act as the Cyprus Squadron. The remaining 14 are employed as University Naval Units (URNU) for training. The Gibraltar Squadron has 2 x 16 m patrol craft.

Ice Patrol	1	Endurance		Portsmouth
Survey Ships	5	Scott, Roebuck, Echo, Enterprise, Gleaner	2	Devonport

Note: Numbers of surface ships and submarines worked up and fully operational can vary greatly, due to refit, repair or other problems. The Royal Navy has very high standards of both operational efficiency and safety. The Fleet is worked hard.

Royal Fleet Auxiliary

Fast Fleet Tankers	2	Wave Knight, Wave Ruler
Small Fleet Tankers	3	Black Rover, Gold Rover, Grey Rover.
Support Tankers	4	Bayleaf, Brambleleaf, Oakleaf, Orangeleaf.
Replenishment Ships	4	Fort George, Fort Austin, Fort Rosalie, Fort Victoria.
Aviation Training Ships	1	Argus.
Landing Ships	3	Sir Galahad, Sir Bedivere, Sir Tristram.
	4	Cardigan Bay, Largs Bay, Lyme Bay, Mounts Bay (entering service in 2006)
Forward Repair Ships	1	Diligence.
Roll-on Roll-off Vessels	2	Sea Crusader, Sea Centurion (available when required)
	4	Hurst Point, Harland Point, Eddystone, Longstone, Beachy Head (Four available at any one time from AWSR Ltd)

Fleet Air Arm

Sea Harrier Force (1)

	Number	Type
Air Defence / Attack	8	Sea Harrier FA-2 (until March 2006 – see note 2)

Note 1. The Joint Force Harrier (JFH) was established on 1 April 2000 and brought together the Sea Harrier FA.2 squadrons, previously under Naval Air Command, with the RAF's Harrier GR.7 squadrons in a new command within RAF Strike Command. See 'Fleet Air Arm' section later for more details.

Note 2. Sea Harrier FA-2 and Harrier T Mk8 were decommissioned in March 2006 and replaced by Harrier GR 7/GR 9. There will be 2 x Fleet Air Arm Squadrons, each with 9 x aircraft.

Naval Helicopters

Anti-Submarine	38	Merlin HM Mk1
Anti-Submarine	12	Sea King HAS MK6
Anti-Submarine / Anti-Ship	23	Lynx MK8
Airborne Early Warning	13	11 x Sea King AEW2, 2 x AEW MK7
Commando Helicopter Force (See Note 3 below)		
Commando Assault	41	Sea King HC4
Ground Attack	6	Lynx AH MK7
Reconnaissance	8	Gazelle (AH MK1)

Note 3. As from 1 October 1999 the Commando Helicopter Force joined with the support and battlefield helicopters of the Army Air Corps and the Royal Air Force in the new Joint Helicopter Command (JHC). See 'Fleet Air Arm' section later for more details.

Aircrew Training

Observer Training	13	Jetstream T2 /T3
Fleet Training & Support	14	Hawk T MK1

HIGHER MANAGEMENT OF THE ROYAL NAVY

The Ministry of Defence (MoD) is a Department of State, headed by the Secretary of State for Defence (SofS) who implements national defence policy and plans the expenditure of the defence budget. The MoD is the highest level of headquarters for the Armed Forces, both administrative and operational. All major issues of policy are referred to the SofS or to one of his three Ministerial colleagues:

♦ Minister of State for the Armed Forces
♦ Parliamentary Under-Secretary of State for Defence Procurement
♦ Parliamentary Under-Secretary of State for Veterans Affairs

Under the direction of the Defence Council (described in Chapter 1) management of the Services is the responsibility of the Service Boards, in the case of the Royal Navy the Admiralty Board is the senior management directorate.

The Admiralty Board

The routine management of the Royal Navy is the responsibility of The Admiralty Board, the composition of which is as follows:

The Secretary of State for Defence
Minister of State for the Armed Forces
Parliamentary Under-Secretary of State for Defence Procurement
Parliamentary Under-Secretary of State for Veterans Affairs
Parliamentary Under-Secretary of State for Defence
Chief of the Naval Staff and First Sea Lord
Commander-in-Chief Fleet
Second Sea Lord and Commander-In-Chief Naval Home Command
Naval Member for Logistics
Controller of the Navy
Second Permanent Under-Secretary of State and Secretary of the Admiralty Board
Assistant Chief of Naval Staff

The Admiralty Board meets formally twice a year

The Navy Board

The First Sea Lord's responsibilities (delivery of naval capabilities, maintaining the strategic deterrent, planning and operational advice, management, overall efficiency and morale of the service) are exercised through the Service Executive Committee of the Admiralty Board, known as the Navy Board (NAVB). The First Sea Lord is the chairman of NAVB; its membership is the same as the Admiralty Board, but without Ministers. NAVB meets formally on a regular basis.

Sub-Navy Board Committee

Many pan Navy decisions are taken by the Sub-Navy Board Committee (SNBC) which is chaired by the Assistant Chief of Naval Staff (ACNS) with the NAVB members' deputies; Deputy Commander in Chief Fleet (DCINCFLEET), COS/2SL/CNH, Chief of the Strategic Systems Executive (CSSE), Capability Manager (Strategic Deterrent CM(SD) and Director General Resources and Plans (DGRP).

Admiral Sir Jonathon Band KCB ADC

Born in 1950, Jonathon Band spent much of his early childhood abroad before returning to England for schooling at Brambletye and Haileybury. He joined the RN in 1967 and, having trained at BRNC Dartmouth, underwent Fleet training in ships in the Far East. This was followed by three years at Exeter University as an undergraduate.

After graduation he served in junior officer appointments in Her Majesty's Ships Lewiston and Rothesay and on exchange with the United States Navy in USS Belknap. This period saw service throughout the world. Following junior officer staff and warfare training in 1976-1977 he served for two years as Principal Warfare Officer and Operations Officer in the Frigate HMS Eskimo. This appointment included deployments to the West Indies and South Atlantic.

Subsequently he commanded the minesweeper HMS Soberton for nearly two years in the Fishery Protection Squadron around the UK coast. Between 1981 and 1983 Jonathon Band served as Flag Lieutenant to Commander-in-Chief Fleet, a period which included the Falklands Campaign. Promoted Commander in 1983, he assumed command of the frigate HMS Phoebe, operating in the NATO area, at the time of the RN's first operational experience with surface ship towed passive sonar. This was followed at the end of 1985 by attendance at the Joint Services Defence College and a subsequent appointment to the Defence Staff in the Ministry of Defence in the Directorate of Defence Policy.

Promoted Captain in 1988, he commanded HMS Norfolk and established the first Type 23 Frigate Squadron. Thereafter, in 1991, he became the Assistant Director Navy Plans and Programmes in the Ministry of Defence, a period that saw the implementation of the 'Options for Change' Review. In 1994 he was a member of the Defence Costs Study (Front Line First) Secretariat and, prior to returning to command at sea, attended the Higher Command and Staff Course. His last Sea Command between 1995 and 1997 was the aircraft carrier HMS Illustrious. The period included two operational deployments to the Adriatic in support of United Nations, and then NATO operations in Bosnia.

Promoted Rear Admiral in May 1997, he returned to the Ministry of Defence as Assistant Chief of Naval Staff. This appointment included the period of the Strategic Defence Review, the subsequent significant change programme that resulted from it and the Kosovo Campaign. He left this appointment in December 1999 and assumed the position of Team Leader of the Defence Education and Training Study in January 2000 on promotion to Vice Admiral. He became the Deputy Commander-in-Chief Fleet in May 2001 and was appointed a Knight Commander of the Most Honourable Order of the Bath in the 2002 New Year's Honours List.

He was promoted Admiral on 2 August 2002 on becoming Commander-in-Chief Fleet and Commander Allied Maritime Component Command – Northwood. This period in Command saw the 2003 Iraq Campaign, the major reorganisation of the Fleet Command and subsequent changes in NATO. He was appointed First Sea Lord and Chief of Naval Staff in February 2006

Jonathon Band is the President of the Royal Navy Volunteer Band Association, the Royal Navy Rugby Union and the Royal Naval and Royal Albert Yacht Club. The Patron of the MTB 102 Trust, he is also a Younger Brother of Trinity House.

Admiral Sir Jonathon Band

The First Sea Lord maintains effective command and control of the Royal Navy by means of three principal headquarters:

- Fleet Headquarters
- Naval Home Command
- Defence Logistics Organisation (via Director General Logistics Fleet)

FLEET COMMAND AND ORGANISATION

Fleet Headquarters

The Commander-in-Chief, Fleet (CINCFLEET) is Admiral Sir James Burnell-Nugent KCB CBE(appointed November 2005). Admiral Burnell-Nugent has full command of all deployable UK Fleet units, including the Royal Marines. As the sole UK based four star NATO Commander (JFCC Maritime – Northwood), he is the maritime advisor to the NATO Joint Force Commander (Brunssum) and has to be prepared in all respects to participate in joint and combined operations. He is also responsible for key maritime elements of the Standing NATO Response Force

Fleet HQ Portsmouth at Portsmouth has three major roles:

- The generation of maritime forces to match the operational requirement. Forces generated have to be manned, equipped and trained to the appropriate readiness states.

- Management of the resources provided to the Fleet and the monitoring of resourses and assets thus employed to ensure operational effectiveness and value for money.

- The Commander-in-Chief Fleet manages maritime operations by delegating operational command and control to the Commander Operations (located at Northwood). Commander Operations has the majority of Fleet units under his command.

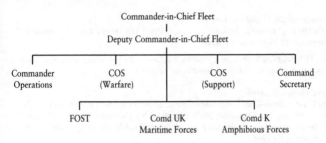

Note: COS – Chief of Staff; FOST – Flag Officer Sea Training; Comd – Commander

Deputy Commander-in-Chief Fleet

Is the deputy for the Commander and is a member of the Sub-Navy Board Committee. The Deputy Commander directs the staff work of Fleet Headquarters.

Commander (Operations)

Is the officer who directs all maritime and amphibious forces and associated operations under the command of the CINCFLEET. In addition he is the commander of the submarine arm and is the NATO Commander Submarines East Atlantic and Commander Submarines Allied Naval Forces North.

Chief of Staff (Warfare)

This officer and his staff are responsible for delivering the operational capability to match the perceived short and longer-term requirement.

Chief of Staff (Support)

Is responsible for sustaining the Fleet and ensuring that the required vessels and units are available for operations. His responsibilities include personnel administration, the Maritime Warfare Centre, communications systems, engineering and some aspects of the Fleet Air Arm support.

The Command Secretary

Is the senior civilian in Fleet Headquarters responsible for civilian personnel, external accountability, resource management and some aspects of planning.

Flag Officer Sea Training
Is the officer responsible for training on all Royal Naval and Royal Fleet Auxiliarry vessels.

Commander UK Maritime Forces
Commander of the United Kingdom Task Group and Commander of the Amphibious Task Group

Commander UK Amphibious Forces
Is the Head of Service for the Royal Marines, Commandant General Royal Marines and commander of 3 Commando Brigade.

Fleet HQ maintains Waterfront organisations at Devonport and Faslane and is responsible for Naval Air Stations at Culdrose, Prestwick and Yeovilton.

Naval Home Command
The Commander-in-Chief Naval Home Command and Second Sea Lord Vice Admiral Adrian Johns CBE (appointed November 2005) is the Royal Navy's Principal Personnel Officer. He has the responsibility for maintaining operational capability by providing the correctly trained manpower to the Fleet.

Vice-Admiral Johns is responsible for all naval manpower matters. With a nation having no serious current unemployment problems, the Royal Navy is competing for high grade people against attractive other careers. The key word is 'quality' as highly intelligent officers and ratings are essential to man the ships – and the same applies to the Royal Marines and the Royal Fleet Auxilliary.

'Stretch' (long periods away from UK) is a matter of some importance as, though sailors and marines will respond to good leadership, they can be pushed (stretched) too far regarding separation from families – good pay or even Financial Retention Incentives (FRIs) are not enough. The Fleet has been stretched for many years and has continued to perform satisfactorily but personnel numbers have been falling with the Royal Navy having even more operational tasks to complete. Naval Home Command has the responsibility for ensuring that outflow figures do not exceed the inflow totals.

Defence Logistics Organisation
Separate logistic support for the three Services ended in 2000 with the establishment of the Defence Logistics Organisation (DLO). The DLO's mission is to provide joint logistic support to the UK Armed Services and employs about 20,000 personnel, of whom about 5,000 are uniformed (approximately 1,000 Royal Navy).

The DLO is led by a four star officer Chief of Defence Logistics, General Sir Kevin O'Donoghue.(appointed January 2005) and the organisation has an annual spend ot £8 billion (20 per cent of the defence budget). Royal Naval logistics are the responsibility of the Director General Logistics Fleet, a two star naval officer.

Royal Naval logistic support is provided by the DLO's one star cluster groups as follows:

- DG Logistics (Fleet)
    - Maritime Platform
    - Waterfront Operations
    - Maritime Equipment
- DG (Nuclear)
    - Nuclear-related items
- DG Logistics (Land)
    - Manoeuvre/Strike
    - Rotary Wing
    - Combat Service Support
- DG Logistics (Strike)
    - RAF Groups
- DG Logistics (Supply Chain)
    - Commodities
    - Munitions Group

Logistics support for maritime or amphibious operations may come from one or more of the above cluster groups.

ROYAL NAVY SHORE ESTABLISHMENTS AND RESERVE UNITS

Major Bases

HM Naval Base, Portsmouth
Home base to surface ships, notably Carriers, Type 42 Destroyers and Type 23 Frigates. Also home to Fleet Headquarters and Comander-in-Chief Home Command organisation

HM Naval Base, Devonport (Plymouth)
Largest naval base in Western Europe. Home port for nuclear Attack submarines (SSNs), Large Assault Ships, Type 22 and 23 Frigates, Hydrographic Ships. There are over 5,000 ship movements annually. Also home to Flag Officer Sea Training and the RN Hydrographic School

HM Naval Base, Clyde
Home base to UK's nuclear deterrent ballistic missile submarines (SSBNs). Also base to SSNs and minewarfare vessels. HMS Caledonia at Rosyth provides support for naval personnel standing by ships and submarines in refit at HM Naval Base , Clyde.

RN Air Station, Yeovilton
Home base to RN, naval helicopter squadrons and other fixed-wing aircraft. Yeovilton operates over 100 aircraft of different types. Nearly 4,000 uniformed and civilian personnel work at RNAS Yeovilton. Also training of aircrew and engineers of resident aircraft types. RN Fighter Controller School trains ground and airborne AEW controllers.

RN Air Station, Culdrose

RNAS Culdrose supports the Anti-Submarine Warfare and Airborne Early Warning helicopter squadrons of the Royal Navy. Eight Naval Air Squadrons are based at RNAS Culdrose, both front line and training Squadrons. Responsible for the operational and advanced flying training of helicopter pilots, observers and aircrewmen.

HMS Caledonia

As a DLO facility HMS Caledonia's role is to provide support services to both the Royal Navy and the MoD in the East of Scotland. As stated previously HMS Caledonia supports the requirements of personnel operating on RN vessels from HM Naval Base Clyde.

Training Establishments

BRNC (Dartmouth)

The principal function of the College is the training of young officers for service in the Royal Navy. A large number of students from friendly Navies are also trained here.

A variety of other courses are undertaken including leadership and teambuilding Programmes, seamanship, navigation and other naval subjects.

HMS Collingwood (Fareham)

HMS Collingwood is the lead establishment of the Maritime Warfare School (MWS) and the largest naval training centre in Western Europe . The MWS is a federated training establishment incorporating HMS Excellent, the Defence Diving School , the RN Physical Training School, the School of Hydrography and Meteorology in Plymouth and the Royal Marines School of Music in Portsmouth Naval Base. At any one time the MWS is training about 10% of the Royal Navy and has an annual throughput of over 30,000 Officers and Ratings, both regular and reserve.

HMS Dryad (Portsmouth)

Dryad provides training to over 5000 students a year, attending over 265 different types of courses. An annual budget of some £36 million is required to manage assets which include an estate of some 300 acres. Within the framework of the Naval Recruiting and Training Agency (NRTA), the primary aim of the Maritime Warfare School (MWS) is to deliver outstanding Maritime Warfare Training, providing the required number of Warfare Personnel appropriately trained for their individual tasks. The Maritime Warfare School currently consists of HMS Collingwood, Dryad and Excellent.

HMS Excellent (Portsmouth)

HMS Excellent has proud and important traditions but is also one of the newest establishments, having been recommissioned in 1994 to deliver a wide range of different training functions. These include damage control and fire fighting and harbour training on board HMS Bristol for RNR personnel, cadet forces and youth organisations. HMS Excellent provides support for a number of lodger units, most notably the Headquarters of Commander-in-Chief Fleet, and the UK's Operational Battle Staffs.

HMS Raleigh (Torpoint)

HMS Raleigh is the initial entry training establishment for all junior ratings entering the Royal Navy and the Royal Naval Reserve. About 2,500 people work in the Establishment and a New Entry of up to some 100 ratings joins most weeks of the year.

HMS Raleigh also provides professional courses in military training, seamanship, logistics and submarine operations as well as vital training for ships' team preparing for operational deployments. Raleigh is also home to the band of Her Majesty's Royal Marines Plymouth.

HMS Sultan (Gosport)

HMS Sultan is the school of Marine and Air Engineering for the Royal Navy. Training of Marine and Air Engineers of Foreign and Commonwealth Navies is also undertaken. Large numbers of officer and rating students are trained annually e.g. the Ship Systems Group alone has a throughput of some 1,000 students per year. There are five other similar training groups

HMS Sultan is also home to the Admiralty Interview Board, and other lodger units including the Central Air and Admiralty Medical Board.

HMS Temeraine (Portsmouth)

HMS Temeraine houses the staff of the Directorate of Naval Physical Training and Sport (DNPTS), the Royal Navy School of Physical Training and the Fleet Recreation Centre.

Royal Naval Reserve (RNR) Units

The RNR is a part-time organisation, which complements the Royal Navy in times of war, conflict and in peacetime when there is a requirement. Entry into the RNR is the same as for the regular service. Training takes place on evenings and at weekends at the units listed below:

HMS Calliope	Gateshead	HMS Cambria	Penarth
HMS Caroline	Northern Ireland	HMS Dalriada	Greenock
HMS Eaglet	Liverpool	HMS Ferret	Chicksand
HMS Flying Fox	Bristol	HMS Forward	Birmingham
HMS King Alfred	Portsmouth	HMS President	London
HMS Scotia	Pitreavie	HMS Sherwood	Nottingham
HMS Vivid	Devonport	HMS Wildfire	Northwood

Current (January 2006) RNR numbers are estimated at 3,620 (1,100 officers and 2,520 other ranks).

University Royal Naval Units are located as follows:

Aberdeen	HMS Archer	Oxford	HMS Tracker
Birmingham	HMS Exploit	London	HMS Puncher
Bristol	HMS Trumpeter	Manchester	HMS Biter
Cambridge	HMS Raider	Northumbrian	HMS Example
Glasgow	HMS Smiter	Sussex	HMS Ranger
Liverpool	HMS Charger	Southampton	HMS Blazer
Wales	HMS Express	Yorkshire	HMS Explorer

Current (January 2006) numbers at University Naval Units are estimated at 750.

In the following paragraphs we comment briefly on the significant classes of warship currently in service with the Royal Navy, together with those under construction and projected. The most important units are those with which we open our remarks, the four units which provide the UK's strategic nuclear deterrent.

Strategic Deterrent

The United Kingdom's Strategic Deterrent is undertaken by the Royal Navy and submarine launched ballistic missiles (SLBM) have been installed in Royal Naval submarines since the late 1960s. Operational patrols commenced in 1969 with US Polaris missiles embarked. The first class of UK SSBN (Nuclear Powered Ballistic Missile Submarine) was the Resolution Class with four boats – this class has now been replaced by the larger Vanguard class armed with 16 x US Trident II D5 missiles. Each missile has the capability of carrying up to 12 x MIRV (Multiple Independently Targeted Re-entry Vehicles) warheads, making a possible total of 192 warheads per submarine. The UK is believed to have purchased 58 x Trident 2D-5 missile bodies from the United States and the range of the missile is believed to be in excess of 9,000 km with a CEP (Circular Error of Probability) of about 100 metres. It is believed that in UK service the Trident II D5 carry eight warheads per missile.

These large submarines displace over 16,000 tonnes and have a length of 150 metres. The three decks offer accommodation for the crew of 130 which is unusually spacious for a submarine. Good domestic facilities are provided for the crew and the air purification system enables them to remain submerged for long periods without any outside support. Each submarine has two crews known as Port and Starboard – when one crew is away on patrol the other crew is training or taking leave.

Following the 1998 Strategic Defence Review (SDR), the UK MoD revealed that it was no longer necessary to have a stockpile of 300 warheads and that the stockpile was being reduced to 200 operationally available warheads. In addition, the 58 missile bodies already purchased would be sufficient to maintain a credible deterrent. The MoD confirmed that there would be one SSBN on patrol at any one time but carrying a reduced load of 48 warheads. In order to ensure one ship of a class to be available for operations, it is normally reckoned that three should be in service – one in repair or refit, one preparing for operations or working up and one fully operational. Four submarines provide a guarantee of one operational at all times. The four submarines of the Vanguard class commissioned as follows:

- ♦ HMS Vanguard   1993
- ♦ HMS Victorious   1995
- ♦ HMS Vigilant   1996
- ♦ HMS Vengeance   1999

In October 2005 HMS Vanguard successfully launched an unarmed Trident II D5 ballistic missile during a naval exercise in the Atlantic Ocean. HMS Vanguard had completed a period of routine maintenance and this test launch was the final part of the trials package prior to her return to operational service. HMS Vanguard is the first of the Royal Navy's Trident class submarines to complete a Long Overhaul Period.

This was the 8th occasion on which a Royal Navy submarine has test-fired a Trident II D5 missile, and the first for a Trident boat on completion of a Long Overhaul Period. The firing marks the final stage of the re-qualification of the submarine crew, and provides reliability and accuracy data which confirms the effectiveness of the strategic weapon system.

In January 2005 the Secretary of State for Defence stated that the total cost of the Trident programme (with payments already made expressed at the prices and exchange rates actually incurred and future spend at the current financial year exchange rate) was £9,8 billion.

Details of the replacement for the current strategic deterrent are up for debate and as yet (March 2006) no decision has been taken. However, a recent announcement by the UK MoD has confirmed that the service life of HMS Vanguard has been extended to 2024-25. We would assume that the service life for the other three submarines will be similarly extended.

Fleet Submarines

The Royal Navy operates a total of 10 Nuclear Powered Attack Submarines (SSNs) in two classes – the Swiftsure and Trafalgar classes. Both classes are capable of continuous patrols at high underwater speed, independent of base support, and can circumnavigate the globe without surfacing. By 2007 six of these submarines will be capable of firing the Tomahawk Land Attack Cruise missile.

The first of an initial three new Astute class SSNs is planned to enter service in 2009.

Armament: The boats of the Swiftsure and Trafalgar classes are armed with a mix of the following:

Submarine Launched Cruise Missiles (SLCM). Tomahawk Block IIIC, range 1,700 km: Anti-Ship Missiles: UGM-84B Sub Harpoon Block 1C; range 130 km

Wire-guided Anti-ship/submarine torpedoes: Range to 30 kms.

Swiftsure Class
Dates of Service Entry:

- Sovereign   1973
- Superb   1974
- Sceptre   1976

Key specifications are as follows:
Length 82.9 m
Displacement 4,200 tons surfaced and 4,500 tons dived
Max Speed 20 knots surfaced and over 30 knots dived
Diving depth 400m (operational) and 600m maximum
Complement 12 officers and 85 ratings

Trafalgar Class
Dates of Service Entry:

- Trafalgar   1981
- Turbulent   1982
- Tireless   1984
- Torbay   1985
- Trenchant   1986
- Talent   1988
- Triumph   1991

Key specifications are as follows:
Length 85.4 m
Displacement 4,700 tons surfaced and 5,200 tons dived
Max Speed 20 knots surfaced and 32 knots dived
Diving depth 400 m (operational) and 600 m maximum
Complement 12 officers and 85 ratings

Astute Class
Possible Dates of Service Entry for first three projected vessels:

- Astute   2009
- Ambush   2010
- Artful   2012 (Keel laid in March 2006)

Likely key specifications are as follows:
Length 97.0m
Displacement 6,500 tons surfaced and 7,800 tons dived
Max Speed 29 knots dived
Complement 12 officers and 86 ratings
Armament likely to be as for Swiftsure and Trafalgar classes with 6 x torpedo tubes

With improved communications, a greater capacity for joint operations and the ability to carry more weaponry, the Astute Class submarines will become a cornerstone of UK defence capability until at least 2035.

The Astute submarine programme is expected to have a total cost to the MoD of about £3.5 billion. Around 5,500 people are employed on the project for the first three Astute class submarines.

Astute Class submarines will have massively increased firepower compared with earlier attack submarines and can dive to depths in excess of 300 metres with a complement of 98 men. They are to be powered by a Pressurised Water Reactor 2, equipped with Core H, which will fuel the reactor for the submarine's full service life, ending the need for costly reactor refuelling.

Orders for the procurement of further Astute boats are being considered and according to the MoD, announcements will be made at the appropriate time. Astute class submarines will be based at Faslane on the Clyde and will undergo refits at Devonport.

SURFACE FLEET

During 2002 the Royal Naval surface fleet was reorganised into two flotillas, one based at Portsmouth and the other at Devonport. There are four major fleet elements:

Aircraft carriers – the largest ships in the fleet with their embarked air carrier groups providing the main armament for expeditionary operations.

Destroyers and frigates – as always, the workhorses of the fleet. Destroyers concentrate on air defence and frigates concentrate on surface and sub-surface warfare. The MoD's longer term intention (post 2012) is to operate a fleet of 25 destroyers and frigates.

Smaller fighting vessels – which include include mine countermeasures vessels (MCM). Neutralisation of mines is a vital task if sea lanes are to be kept open and the Royal Navy is an acknowledged world leader in mine countermeasures operations.

Offshore patrol vessels – these continue to play an important role in UK home waters by enforcing fishery laws and providing protection to UK oil and gas facilities.

Aircraft Carriers

Invincible Class

The primary task of this class of ship is to act as the command ship for a small task force and provide organic air power against limited opposition. Since entering service in the early 1970s, the ships of this class have proved vital in projecting UK interests overseas from the Falklands conflict of 1982 through to the amphibious assault on Iraq in the spring of 2003. Lessons have been learned over the years and the vital importance of 'an eye in the sky' has been recognised by developing Sea King helicopters for Airborne Surveillance and Control. The problem with the ships is, of course, their small size for air operations at sea and the typical Air Group below has been augmented by adding additional RAF Harriers and helicopters for specific operations. There is a longer term possibility that RAF Longbow Apache attack helicopters will be configured for operations from the Invincible Class Carriers.

Key specifications are as follows:
Length: 209.1m
Displacement: 20,600 tons full load
Max Speed: 28 knots. Range 7,000 n.miles at 19 knots.
Complement: 685 (60 officers) plus 366 (80 officers) air group plus up to 600 marines if
          required
Armament:
Aircraft. A typical embarked air group could consist of: 6 x Harrier GR 7, 6 x Merlin Mk 1 (Anti-Submarine), 3 x Sea King ASaC (Airborne Surveillance & Control).
Guns: 3 x Close-in Weapon Systems (Goalkeeper or Vulcan Phalanx) anti-aircraft or anti-missile.

Dates of Service Entry:

♦ Invincible   1977
♦ Illustrious   1978
♦ Ark Royal   1981

HMS Invincible is now in reserve (March 2006) and will be withdrawn from the fleet in 2010; HMS Illustrious is to be decommissioned in 2012; and HMS Ark Royal is to be decommissioned in 2015. Carrier operations will then be the responsibility of the Future Carrier (CVF) details of which follow.

The Future Carrier (CVF)

Following the 1998 Strategic Defence Review (SDR), the UK MoD announced its intention to replace the Royal Navy's current carrier force with two larger vessels once the current vessels have reached the end of their planned lives. The intention is to acquire two CVFs, with the vessels entering service in 2012 and 2015 respectively (the MoD has yet to announce a final in-service date). Each carrier would be capable of operating up to 50 aircraft (implying a displacement of at least 40,000 tonnes) and would have a crew of about 1,000 officers and ratings, including the Air Group. In addition to strike aircraft belonging to the RN/Royal Air Force, the CVF will be required to support helicopter and UAV (unmanned aerial vehicle) operations. The short take-off and vertical landing (STOVL) variant of the US JSF (Joint Strike Fighter) has been the UK's preferred choice for its Future Carrier Borne Aircraft requirement, to replace the Harriers but as of March 2006 there appear to be problems associated with technology transfer and it is possible that another aircraft solution will have to be found. The Carrier project will provide the UK Armed forces with the largest and most powerful warships ever constructed in the UK and should create or sustain over 10,000 UK jobs.

In January 2006 the MoD stated that the plans to acquire two new aircraft carriers were progressing well following the transition into the Demonstration Phase announced on 14 December 2005. The Demonstration Phase will deliver a mature design, provide more detailed cost definition, reduce risk and produce a contractual framework that will allow a decision to be made to commit to manufacture. In March 2006 an agreement was signed by UK and French Governments where France and the UK will co-operate on the demonstration phase work to produce a Common Baseline Design that will meet requirements for both the UK CVF and French requirements for its carrier, PA2. The French have agreed to pay an initial £100 million in recognition of the investment already made by the UK in the design of the ships. France will also contribute one third of the demonstration phase costs of the common baseline design.

Projections of the costs vary but most analysts agree on a demonstration and manufacture cost for both carriers of between £3 and £4 billion. Both carriers are expected to have a 50 year service life. CVF will be based at Portsmouth.

It is likely that these new carriers will be designated as the Queen Elizabeth Class and the two vessels will be named 'Queen Elizabeth' and 'Prince of Wales'.

Helicopter Carrier

Ocean (LPH)

HMS Ocean, an LPH (Landing Platform Helicopter) was built by Kvaerner Govan, on the Clyde, taking advantage of commercial build methods and facilities, before sailing for Barrow-in-Furness for fitting out prior to acceptance into service with the Royal Navy. The hull of the ship was built to Merchant Navy standards at a cost of some £170 million. The ship is capable of carrying an air group of 12 x Sea King troop lift helicopters, 6 x Lynx attack helicopters and 4 x Landing Craft Vehicle Personnel (LCVP). The vessel's secondary roles include afloat training, with a limited anti-submarine warfare capability and the possibility of being used as an afloat base for anti-terrorist operations.

Key specifications are as follows:
Length: 203.4 m
Displacement: 21,758 tons full load
Max Speed: 19 knots. Range 8,000 n.miles at 15 knots.
Complement: 285, 206 Air Group, plus up to 830 marines (Marine Commando Group)
Military lift: 4 LCVP Mk 5 (on davits); 2 Griffon hovercraft; 40 vehicles
Aircraft. Helicopters: 12 Sea King HC Mk 4/Merlin plus 6 Lynx (or navalised variants of WAH-64 Apache).
Guns: 8 Oerlikon/BMARC 20 mm GAM-B03 (4 twin). 3 Vulcan Phalanx Mk 15 Close-in Weapon Systems

Date of Service Entry:
♦ Ocean   1998

Assault Ships

Albion Class (LPD)

The contract (worth £449 million) to build the two LPDs (Landing Platform Docks) was awarded on 18 July 1996 and first steel was cut 17 November 1997. There are two helicopter landing spots and the configuration includes a well dock and stern gate together with side ramp access. Substantial command and control facilities are included within a large combined Operations Room. The ships are being built to military damage control standards. Though conceived under the previous Conservative government this class fits in well with the current government's concept of expeditionary activities worldwide. The UK is developing a useful amphibious capability with the new Assault ships and other new Landing Ships coming along.

Both vessels are capable of carrying 305 troops, with an overload of a further 405 for short periods. There is a vehicle deck capacity for up to 6 x main battle tanks or up to 30 x armoured all-terrain vehicles. In addition, there is a floodable well dock, with the capacity to take either four utility landing craft (each capable of carrying a main battle tank or a

71

hovercraft landing craft. There are 4 x smaller landing craft on davits, each capable of carrying 35 troops.

Key specifications are as follows:
Length: 176 m
Displacement: 19,560 tons full load
Max Speed: 20 knots. Range 8,000 n.miles at 15 knots.
Complement: 325. Military lift: 305 x troops; 67 x support vehicles; 4 x LCU Mk 10 or 2 x LCAC (dock); 4 x LCVP Mk 5 (davits)
Guns: 2-20 mm (twin). 2 Goalkeeper Close-in Weapon Systems (CIWS)
Helicopters: Platform for 3 Merlin EH 101. Chinook capable.

Date of Service Entry:
♦ Albion   2003
♦ Bulwark   2004

Destroyers

By 2014 the MoD expects to be operating 5 x Type 45 Destroyers (HMS Daring, Dauntless, Diamond, Dragon, and Defender). In addition, the period 2012-2015 is expected to see the withdrawal from service of the last three Type 42 Destroyers, HMS Edinburgh, HMS Nottingham and HMS York, and their replacement by three further Type 45 Destroyers, the first being HMS Duncan.

Type 42 Class

The ships of this class are armed with the ageing Sea Dart medium-range air defence missile system, which also has a limited anti-ship capability. In addition they have a useful gun armament. They have been useful work horses of the fleet for many years and are equipped with the latest communication and sensor equipments. In addition to their air defence role, the Type 42 Class vessels have an extensive general purpose capability as patrol vessels, capable of a wide range of maritime enforcement and humanitarian assistance operations.

Batch 2 key specifications are as follows:
Length:125.0 m
Displacement: 4,200 tons full load
Max Speed: 29 knots. Range 4,000 n.miles at 18 knots.
Complement: 253 (24 officers)
Missiles: SAM: British Aerospace Sea Dart twin launcher, radar/semi-active radar guidance to 40 km; limited anti-ship capability
Guns: 1 x 4.5 in (25 rounds/min. Range 22 km). 2 or 4 x 20 mm (Range 2kms). 2 x 20 mm Phalanx Close-in Weapon Systems (Range 1.5kms)
Modern above and under water sensors and decoys
Helicopter: Lynx Mk 8 (Missile and torpedo armed)

Date of Service Entry

Batch 2
- Exeter   1980
- Southampton   1981
- Nottingham   1982
- Liverpool   1982

Batch 3
- Manchester   1982
- Gloucester   1985
- Edinburgh   1985
- York   1985

Type 45 – Daring Class.

The first Type 45 (HMS Daring) is expected to enter service during 2009. Subsequent vessels of a planned eight ship class (six ordered) are expected to follow at regular intervals between that point and around 2015. The current estimated unit production cost of each Type 45 is £561.6 million, based on the currently approved programme of six ships. This estimate includes the cost of the principal surface-to-air missile system (PAAMS), which is the primary weapons system for the Type 45 destroyer. Within the figure of £561.6 million overall cost, the cost of the PAAMS system is approximately one third or about £187 million.

In addition to its role as an air defence vessel the Type 45 destroyer will be a versatile platform that is planned to deliver a number of capabilities. These include naval gunfire support and, through its embarked helicopter, anti-submarine and anti-surface warfare. Vessels will be capable of employment in a full range of tasks including maritime force protection, interdiction and peace support operations.

With eight Type 45 destroyers in service, a minimum of five units would be available to the Fleet for deployment at various states of readiness.

During 2004 the Defence Procurement Agency conducted an assessment of the potential to fit tactical Tomahawk missiles to the Type 45 destroyer. Although this assessment confirmed the practicability of either fitting or retro-fitting Tomahawk missiles it remains the position that there is currently no requirement for the Type 45 to be fitted with them.

Key specifications are as follows:
Length: 152.4 m
Displacement: 7,350 tons full load
Max Speed: 29 knots. Range 7,000 n miles at 18 knots
Complement: 187
Armament (Estimated).

Missiles: SSM: 8 x Harpoon (2 quad)
Surface-to-Air (SAM): 6 x DCN Sylver A 50 VLS PAAMS (principal anti-air missile system);
16 x Aster 15 and 32 Aster 30 weapons or combination
Guns: 1 x Vickers 4.5 in (114 mm)/55 Mk 8 Mod 1; 2 x 20 mm Vulcan Phalanx Close-in
Weapon Systems: Helicopters: Lynx or Merlin

Date of Service Entry (Projected):
- Daring   2009
- Dauntless   2010
- Diamond   2010
- Dragon   2011
- Defender   2012
- Duncan   2012

Frigates

By 2014 the MoD expects to be operating a frigate force consisting of 4 x Type 22 Frigates
(HMS Cornwall, Cumberland, Chatham and Campbeltown) and 13 x Type 23 Frigates (HMS
Argyll, Lancaster, Iron Duke, Monmouth, Montrose, Westminster, Northumberland,
Richmond, Somerset, Sutherland, Kent, Portland and St. Albans).

OUTLINE ORGANISATION OF A FRIGATE

The organisation of a typical RN frigate is the result of hundreds of years of evolution and
above all, the ship is organised to fight. The six major departments in a modern frigate are the
following:

Executive Department

The Executive Department is responsible for the command of the ship with the First
Lieutenant (Executive Officer) having overall responsibility for the Department. The Executive
Department has the overall responsibility for the medical, chaplaincy, physical training and
seamanship aspects of the ship. In addition discipline and routines in the ship are maintained
by the Master At Arms and Leading Regulator.

Warfare Department – This department basically 'fights' the ship and is the direct descendant
of the Seaman Branch which manned the guns in earlier generations.

Marine Engineering Department – Runs the machinery of the ship ie. the main propulsion units that drive the vessel (gas turbines or diesels), the electrical power supplies and all of the ancillary machinery required.

Weapons Engineering Department – Responsible for the efficient functioning of all of the ship's highly complex sensors and weapons.

Supply Department and Logistics Department – Responsible for the logistic arrangements in the ship ie. catering, spares for all of the weapons, general stores, sensors and machinery spares and for all pay and accounting matters.

Flight

The ship's helicopter is arguably the most potent weapon platform available and can generally carry Stingray torpedoes and depth charges for use against submarines, and Sea Skua missiles for engaging surface targets. The Flight Team is usually composed of a small group of aircrew supported by a team of skilled flight engineers.

Departments

All of the departments are inter-dependent and each has a head of department – known collectively as 'the HODs'. These HODs meet at regular intervals and agree such matters as programmes, training and the efficient administration of everything on board. Whilst each HOD is responsible directly to the commanding officer for the efficiency of his department. HODs are likely to be Lieutenant Commanders and, even if senior to the First Lieutenant, are subordinate to him – the First Lieutenant is the man who takes over if the Commanding Officer is unable to perform his duties.

The cleaning of the ship and all of the general tasks are shared by the departments, and the HODs would discuss these matters at their meetings – for example, they would agree how many sailors would be required from each department for a storing at sea operation. A recent development is the presence on board many RN ships of female personnel. These females share all the duties of their male counterparts but, of course, have separate living quarters.

The Commanding Officer is usually a Commander RN (with a background in the Warfare/Operations Department) and he is known as 'The Captain'. In command of a squadron of frigates an officer with the rank of Captain RN will be found who doubles the duties both of 'Captain' of his ship and Captain (F) to whom the 'Captains' of the frigates in his squadron report.

The complement of a frigate relates to the requirement to man the ship for battle. A Batch 3 Type 22 has a total of 232 (13 officers) and a newer Duke Class Type 23 has a complement of 169 (12 officers).

Type 23 (Duke Class)

The first of class was ordered from Yarrows on 29 October 1984 at the height of the Cold War. Further batches of three were ordered in September 1986, July 1988, December 1989, January 1992 and February 1996. The class is now completed. There were some early problems, e.g. the Comand System was not operational as quickly as had been planned, but these have been overcome and the RN has made steady improvements to weapons and sensors in the ships over the years since first introduction. From 1999, the Lynx helicopter was replaced on some of the vessels by the EH 101 Merlin helicopter. These ships are powered by a CODLAG system (Combined diesel-electric and gas-turbine propulsion) and the diesel-electric is used for minimum underwater noise during ASW operations.

Key specifications are as follows:
Length: 133.0 m
Displacement: 4,200 tons full load
Max Speed: 28 knots. Range 7,800 n.miles at 15 knots
Complement: 181 (13 officers)
Armament:
Missiles: Surface-to-Surface (SSM). 8 x Harpoon (130 km range). Surface-to-Air (SAM). Sea Wolf (Range 6 kms)
Guns: 1 x 4.5 in (25 rounds/min. Range 22kms). 2 x 30mm twins (Range 10kms)
Modern above and under water sensors and decoys
Helicopter: Lynx or Merlin (Missile and Torpedo armed)

Date of Service Entry:

♦ Argyll	1989
♦ Lancaster	1990
♦ Monmouth	1991
♦ Iron Duke	1991
♦ Westminster	1992
♦ Northumberland	1992
♦ Montrose	1992
♦ Richmond	1993
♦ Somerset	1994
♦ Grafton	1994
♦ Sutherland	1996
♦ Kent	1998
♦ Portland	1999
♦ St Albans	2000

Type 22 (Broadsword) Class

The remaing four ships of this class have a useful armament and sensor fit and, by the standards of some Navies, at 20 years of age are still quite youthful. The above water armament reflects the lessons of the Falklands conflict – plenty of guns and missiles. The earlier ships have either been sold to Brazil (the Batch 1 frigates) or scrapped.

Key specifications are as follows:
Length:148.0 m
Displacement: 5,300 tons full load
Max Speed: 30 knots (18knots on Tynes). Range 4,500 n miles at 18 knots
Complement: 250 (31 officers)
Armament:
Missiles:Surface-to-Surface (SSM). 8 x Harpoon (130km range). Surface-to-Air (SAM). Sea
Wolf (Range 6 kms)
Guns: 1 x 4.5 in (25 rounds/min. Range 22 kms); 1 x Goalkeeper 30 mm Close-in Weapon
System; 2 x 20mm twins (Range 10kms)
Modern above and under water sensors and decoys.
Helicopter: 2 Westland Lynx HMA 3/8; or 1 Westland Sea King HAS 5 (Missile and Torpedo
armed)

Date of Service Entry:

♦ Cornwall	1988
♦ Cumberland	1988
♦ Campbeltown	1989
♦ Chatham	1989

Mine Warfare Vessels

Hunt Class (Minesweepers/Minehunters – Coastal)
The first of this advanced class of GRP-built mine countermeasures vessels, HMS Brecon
(decommissioning) entered service in 1979. The Royal Navy has a small but highly efficient
mine warfare force and the Hunts were regarded as very costly when first entering service.
However they have proved their value repeatedly and modernisation proceeds. Hunt Class
vessels have recently been fitted with Sonar 2193 which has replaced the older Sonar 193M. In
addition, the command system has been replaced with a newer system developed from the
NAUTIS system already fitted in Sandown class vessels.

When deployed operationally Hunt Class vessels are fitted with additional weapon systems
and communications. Also used for Fishery Protection duties.

Key specifications are as follows:
Length: 57.0 m
Displacement: 750 tons full load
Max Speed: 15 knots. Range 1,500 n miles at 12 knots
Complement: 45 (5 officers)
Armament: 1 x 30 mm (650 rounds/min. Range 10 km). For operational deployments also
fitted with 2 x 20 mm (900 rounds/min to 2 km) and 2 x 7.62 mm MGs
Full range of sensors and systems for dealing with all types of ground and moored mines.

Date of Service Entry:

- ♦ Ledbury   1979
- ♦ Cattistock   1981
- ♦ Brocklesby   1982
- ♦ Middleton   1983
- ♦ Chiddingfold   1983
- ♦ Hurworth   1984
- ♦ Atherstone   1986
- ♦ Quorn   1988

Sandown Class (Minehunters)

HMS Sandown, the first of the new Single-Role Minehunter class, entered service in 1988 (since decommissioned), and HMS Blythe, the latest, entered service in January 2001. Of Glass Reinforced Plastic (GRP) construction, they are capable of operating in deep and exposed waters, e.g. the approaches to the Clyde where the ballistic missile armed submarines are based. Sandown Class vessels are equipped with a mine-hunting sonar and mine-disposal equipment, making them capable of dealing with mines at depths of up to 200 m.

Key specifications are as follows:

Length: 52.2 m
Displacement: 450 tons full load
Max Speed: 13 knots. Range 2,500 n miles at 12 knots
Complement: 34 (5 officers)
Armament: 1 x 30 mm (650 rounds/min. Range 10 km)
Full range of sensors and systems for undertaking any minehunting task.

Date of Service Entry:

- ♦ Walney   1991
- ♦ Penzance   1997
- ♦ Pembroke   1997
- ♦ Grimsby   1998
- ♦ Bangor   1999
- ♦ Ramsey   1999
- ♦ Blythe   2001
- ♦ Shoreham   2001

Antarctic Patrol Ship.

Endurance
HMS Endurance (previously MV Polar Circle) entered service with the Royal Navy in 1991 and supports British interests in the South Atlantic and Antarctic waters. The ship works alongside members of the British Antarctic Survey Team, carrying out hydrographic surveying, meteorological work and research programmes. The hull is painted red for easy recognition in ice and the vessel has importance as a political presence in the Southern Ocean and Antartica

Key specifications are as follows:
Length: 57.0 m
Displacement: 6,500 tons full load
Max Speed: 15 knots. Range 6,500 n miles at 12 knots
Complement: 112 (15 officers) plus 14 Royal Marines
Helicopters: 2 Westland Lynx HAS 3
Range of Sensors.

Survey Ships

Scott
This ship was ordered in January 1995 and entered service in June 1997. She is equipped with an integrated navigation suite for surveying operations, together with a Sonar Array Sounding System (SASS) and data processing equipment. She also has gravimeters, a towed proton magnetometer and the Sonar 2090 ocean environment sensor. The ship is planned to remain at sea for 300 days per year with a crew of 42, 20 personnel being rotated from shore to allow leave and recreation.

Key specifications are as follows:
Length: 131.1 m
Displacement: 13,500 tons full load
Max Speed: 17.5 knots
Complement: 62 (12 officers)
Hydrographic sensor fit (See above)
Helicopters: Platform for 1 light helicopter

Echo Class
An order was placed with Vosper Thornycroft in 2000 for two new Hydrographic Vessels. This is a 'through life contract' covering support for 25 years. The ships will work with the fleet worldwide, supporting mine warfare and amphibious tasks besides carrying out specialist

hydrographic activities. As with Scott (see previous entry) the ships are planned to work over 300 days per year at sea.

Key specifications are as follows:
Displacement, tons: 3,470 full load
Dimensions, feet (metres): 295.3 x 55.1 x 18 (90 x 16.8 x 5.5)
Main machinery: Diesel electric; 4 MW; 2 azimuth thrusters
Speed, knots: 15. Range, miles: 9,000 at 12 kt
Complement: 46 with accommodation for 81
Hydrographic Sensor fit.

Date of Service Entry:
- Echo   2003
- Enterprise   2004

Roebuck

Commissioned in 1986 HMS Roebuck is designed for hydrographic surveys to modern commercial standards and is fitted with a Differential Global Positioning Systems and integrated digital navigation and survey system. The ship also carries a survey motor boat which is fitted with similar sonar suites to the mother ship. Warfare capability has recently been enhanced by the fit of additional upper deck weapons.

Key specifications are as follows:
Length: 64 m
Displacement: 1,350 tons full load
Max Speed: 16 knots
Survey Speed: 8 knots
Complement: 52
Hydrographic sensor fit (See above)
Armament: 1 x GAMBO 20 mm canon; 2 x M323 Mk44 7.62 mm Miniguns and 4 x 7.62 mm General Purpose Machine Guns

Gleaner

Commissioned in 1983 HMS Gleaner is the smallest commissioned vessel in the Royal Navy and has been designed to conduct inshore surveys around the coast of the United Kingdom.

Key specifications are as follows:
Length: 16 m
Complement: 8

Patrol Vessels

Patrol Vessels are used for fishery protection and patrolling Britain's offshore gas and oilfield installations. In addition these useful ships can be used further afield, e.g. Castle class vessels have been used in the Falklands patrol role.

Castle Class

These ships were started as a private venture and ordered in August 1980. The design includes an ability to lay mines. Inmarsat commercial communications terminals are fitted. Two Avon Sea Rider high-speed craft are embarked. HMS Leeds Castle was 'paid off' in August 2005 leaving only one vessel of this class remaining.

Key specifications are as follows:
Length: 81.0 m
Displacement: 1,427 tons full load
Max Speed: 19.5 knots. Range 10,000 n miles at 12 knots
Complement: 45 (6 officers) plus austerity accommodation for 25 Royal Marines
Armament: 1 x 30 mm, range 10 kms; Sensors and Combat Data System
Helicopters: Platform for operating Sea King or Lynx.

Date of Service Entry:
♦ Dumbarton Castle   1982

River Class.

Vosper Thornycroft contracted in May 2001 for the construction, lease and support of four vessels over an initial five-year period to replace the ships of the Island Class (see previous entry). Each vessel has a large working cargo deck that allows the vessel to be equipped for a specific role such as disaster relief, anti-pollution, fire fighting, rescue work or interception of other vessels. Standard containers can be handled using a fitted 25-ton crane.

Key specifications are as follows:
Length: 79.75 m
Displacement: 1,700 tons full load
Max Speed: 20 knots. Range 5,500 n miles at 15 knots
Complement: 30 (plus 18 Boarding Party)
Armament: 1 x 20 mm
Sensors and Combat Data System
Small helicopter deck.

Date of Service Entry:
♦ Tyne   2003
♦ Severn   2003
♦ Mersey   2004
♦ Clyde   2006

The Royal Fleet Auxiliary Service

The Royal Fleet Auxiliary Service (RFA) is a civilian manned fleet, owned by the Ministry of Defence. Its main task is to replenish the warships of the Royal Navy at sea with fuel, food, stores and ammunition. Thus it fills a vital role that is becoming increasingly important as the current UK government has worldwide ambitions which demand the services of the Royal Navy. Other RFA tasks include amphibious support and sea transport for the Army. The RFA is managed by the Commodore RFA who is directly responsible to Commander-in-Chief Fleet for the administration and operation of the organisation.

The RFA employs over 2,300 civilian officers and ratings, and is one of the larger employers in the UK shipping industry. Replenishment of warships at sea requires specialist knowledge and training, and RFA personnel are on terms of service that take account of both of these activities and of being directed to possible operational areas. Many RFA ships carry naval or military parties for tasks such as the operation and maintenance of helicopters.

The RFA boasts a significant number of large ships, especially in comparison with the warships it supports. The largest ship in the present Royal Navy is HMS Ocean, displacing 21,758 tons full load. In the RFA there are 10 vessels (the largest at 49,000 tons) that are larger. Though many of these ships are ageing, the UK MoD has made fair provision for realistic support of a global reach for the Royal Navy.

The UK MoD believes that the RFA average cost of maintenance is estimated at £3.5 million per annum for each vessel. This includes maintenance on operational vessels, defect rectification, post design work, stock consumption and small packages of upkeep. In addition an element has been included to reflect the cost of scheduled refits, which are generally undertaken on a five-yearly basis for each vessel.

Tankers

Wave Class (Large Fleet Tankers)

Following a tendering process, contracts to build two ships were placed with VSEL (BAE Systems) on 12 March 1997. There had been many delays in the construction of the two vessels but the first, Wave Knight, entered service in March 2003, two years later than originally planned. Wave Ruler entered service in 2004. The ships have a one spot flight deck with full hangar facilities for a Merlin helicopter. There are three replenishment rigs and one crane.

Key specifications are as follows:
Length: 196.5 m
Displacement: 31,500 tons full load
Max Speed: 18 knots. Range 10,000 n miles at 15 knots
Complement: 80 plus 22 helicopter personnel
Cargo capacity 16,000 metric tons
Helicopters: 1 x Merlin helicopter
Guns: Fitted for 2 x Phalanx Close-in Weapon Systems; 2 x BMARC 30 mm

Date of Service Entry:
- Wave Knight   2003
- Wave Ruler   2004

Appleleaf Class (Support Tankers)

Support Tankers have the dual role of both replenishing warships and fleet tankers at sea and undertaking the bulk movement of fuels between naval supply depots. Specifications for each ship differ somewhat, therefore figures below are illustrative.

Key specifications are as follows:
Length: 170.0 m
Displacement: 38,000 tons full load
Speed: 15.5 knots
Complement: 56 (19 officers)
Cargo capacity 25,000 metric tons
Guns: 2 x 20 mm Oerlikon. 4 x 7.62 mm MGs.

Date of Service Entry:
- Brambleleaf   1980
- Orangeleaf   1982
- Bayleaf   1982
- Oakleaf   1981

Rover class (Small Fleet Tankers)

These small tankers have proved most valuable over many years in supplying HM ships at sea with fuel, fresh water, limited dry cargo and refrigerated stores in all parts of the world. There is no hangar but a helicopter platform is served by a stores lift, to enable stores to be transferred at sea. Two of the class (five originally constructed) have been sold on, one to Portugal and one to Indonesia.

Key specifications are as follows:
Length: 140.6 m
Displacement: 11,522 tons full load
Speed: 19 knots. Range 15,000 at 15 knots
Complement: 50 (17 officers)
Cargo capacity 6,600 metric tons
Guns: 2 x 20 mm Oerlikon. 4 x 7.62 mm MGs

Date of Service Entry:
- Grey Rover   1970
- Gold Rover   1974
- Black Rover   1974

Fleet Replenishment Ships

Fort Victoria Class (Fleet Replenishment Ships)

These ships provide fuel and stores support to the Fleet at sea. The original plan was to build six of the class but the diminishing requirement and undoubted budget problems have meant that only two of these large and excellent ships have been constructed. There are four dual-purpose abeam replenishment rigs for simultaneous transfer of liquids and solids, besides stern refuelling. There are repair facilities for Merlin helicopters.

Key specifications are as follows:
Length: 203.5 m
Displacement: 36,580 tons full load
Speed: 20 knots
Complement: Ships crew 134 (95 RFA plus 15 RN plus 24 civilian stores staff)
Embarked Air Group up to 150 personnel (includes 28 officer air crew)
Cargo capacity 12,500 metric tons liquids. 6,200 metric tons solids
Helicopters: 5 x Sea King or Merlin helicopters
Guns: 2 x 30 mm. 2 x Phalanx Close-in Weapon Systems
Sensor fit appropriate for aircraft control

Date of Service Entry:
- Fort Victoria   1994
- Fort George   1993

Fort Grange Class (Fleet Replenishment Ships)

These ships were ordered in 1971 and after valuable service are over 25 years old. Usually a single helicopter is embarked and ASW armaments for helicopters are carried on board. There are six cranes, three of 10 tons lift and three of 5 tons.

Key specifications are as follows:
Length: 183.9m
Displacement: 23,384 tons full load
Speed: 22 knots. Range 10,000 n. miles at 20 knots
Complement: 114 (31 officers) plus 36 RNSTS (civilian supply staff) plus 45 RN aircrew
Cargo capacity 3,500 tons of ammunition and stores
Helicopters: Up to 4 x Sea King
Guns: 2 x 20 mm

Date of Service Entry:
- Fort Rosalie   1978
- Fort Austin   1979

Landing Ships

Sir Bedivere Class (Landing Ships Logistic)
By the end of 2006 only one of these vessels (Sir Bedivere) will remain in service, Sir Galahad
and Sir Tristram having been decommissioned in earlier in 2006. Although this class is being
replaced by the Landing Ship Dock (Auxiliary) vessels Sir Bedivere is programmed to remainin
in service until 2011.

Key specifications are as follows:
Length: 125.6 m
Displacement: 6,700 tons full load (After Service Life Extension Programme – SLEP)
Speed: 17 knots. Range 8,000 n.mile at 15 knots
Complement: 51 (18 officers); 49 (15 officers) (SLEP)
Military Lift: 340 troops (534 hard lying); 17 or 18 (SLEP) MBTs; 34 mixed vehicles; 120 tons
POL; 30 tons ammunition; 1-25 ton crane; 2-4.5 ton cranes. Increased capacity for 20
helicopters (11 tank deck and 9 vehicle deck) after SLEP
Guns: 2 or 4 x 20 mm. 4 x 7.62 mm MGs
Helicopters: Platforms to operate Gazelle, Lynx, Chinook (SLEP) or Sea King
Sensor fit appropriate for aircraft control

Date of Service Entry:
♦ Sir Bedivere   1967
♦ Sir Galahad   1968 (decommissioned 2006)
♦ Sir Tristram   1965 (decommissioned 2006)

Bay Class – Landing Ship Dock (Auxiliary)
These ships will displace over double the figure of the class they are replacing. Two ships were
ordered in 2000 and contracts for two further ships of the class were placed in November
2001. The design is based on the Dutch LPD Rotterdam and Bay Class vessels and they are
designed to transport troops, vehicles, ammunition and stores as a follow-up to an amphibious
assault. Offload is carried out by a flight deck capable of operating heavy helicopters, an
amphibious dock capable of operating one LCU and mexeflotes which can be hung on the
ships' sides. There is no beaching capability.

Key specifications are as follows:
Length: 176.0 m
Displacement: 16,160 tons full load
Speed: 18 knots. Range 8,000 n.mile at 15 knots
Complement: 60, plus 356 troops
Military Lift: Space for vehicles equating to 36 Challenger MBTs or 150 light trucks plus 200
tons ammunition
Helicopters: Platform capable of operating Chinook
Armament: 1 x 30 mm cannon; CIWS Phalanx

Projected Date of Service Entry:
- Largs Bay   2006
- Lyme Bay   2007 (estimated)
- Mounts Bay   2007 (estimated)
- Cardigan Bay   2008 (estimated)

Miscellaneous RFA Vessels

Argus – Aviation Training Ship

Argus was procured for a helicopter training role. This former Ro-Ro container ship was converted for her new task by Harland and Wolf, completing in 1988. The former Ro-Ro deck is used as a hangar with four sliding WT doors able to operate at a speed of 10 m/min. Argus can replenish other ships underway. There is one lift port midships and one abaft the funnel. Domestic facilities are somewhat limited if she is used in the Command support role. She was the first RFA to be fitted with a command system. Argus has a subsidiary role as a Primary Casualty Receiving Ship – facilities were improved significantly following an upgrade period completed in late 2001. This included conversion of three decks into a permanent 100-bed hospital with three operating theatres.

Studies are underway relating to a Joint Casualty Treatment Ship programme intended to replace the capability currently provided by RFA Argus. This programme would aim to deliver a ship-borne medical facility broadly similar in scope to a field hospital, capable of treating a full range of casualties, whether from sea, land or air environments.

Key specifications are as follows:
Length: 175.1 m
Displacement: 26,421 tons full load
Speed: 18 knots. Range 20,000 n.mile at 15 knots
Complement: 80 (22 officers) plus 35 permanent RN plus 137 RN Aviation personnel
Military lift: 3,300 tons dieso; 1,100 tons aviation fuel; 138 x 4 ton vehicles in lieu of aircraft
Guns: 4 x 30 mm. 4 x 7.62 mm MGs
Combat Data System and Sensor fit appropriate for aircraft control
Fixed-wing aircraft: Provision to transport 12 x BAe Harrier
Helicopters: 6 Westland Sea King HAS 5/6 or similar

Diligence – Forward Repair Ship

This ship was originally the Stena Inspector, designed as a Multipurpose Support Vessel for North Sea oil operations, and completed in 1981. She was chartered on 25 May 1982 for use as a fleet repair ship during the Falklands War and purchased from Stena (UK) Line in October 1983. She was then converted in 1984 for use as Forward Repair Ship in the South Atlantic (Falkland Islands).

The vessel has four 5-ton anchors for a four-point mooring system and is strengthened for operations in ice. In addition to supporting the Royal Navy in the Falklands and the Balkans she has also been used as an support ship in the Gulf.

Key specifications are as follows:
Length: 112.0 m
Displacement: 10,765 tons full load
Speed: 12 knots. Range 5,000 n.mile at 12 knots
Complement: 38 (15 officers) plus accommodation for 147 plus 55 temporary
Cargo capacity: Long-jib crane SWL 5 tons; maximum lift, 40 tons
Guns: 4 x 20 mm. 4 x 7.62 mm MGs

Military Afloat Reach and Sustainability project (MARS)
During February 2006 the UK MoD chose three companies to work on the next (assessment) stage of a project (MARS) to provide a new fleet of naval support vessels. In time we would expect one of these companies to become the programme integrator. The overall budget for the complete assessment programme is £44 million.

The MARS vessels are intended to provide fuel, food and stores to units afloat and a new seabasing facility to support forces ashore. These MARS vessels will have some military equipment and will be technically similar to specialist merchant ships.

The project is expected to provide for replacement of some classes of Royal Fleet Auxiliary vessels, including Rover and Leaf class tankers and Fort class support. We would expect to see the first of the MARS vessels entering service by around 2012.

RFA decommissioning programme
Current plans for the decommissioning of RFA vessels are as follows:

Grey Rover 2006; Sir Tristram 2006; Sir Galahad 2006; Orangeleaf 2009; Brambleleaf 2009; Gold Rover 2009; Bayleaf 2010; Oakleaf 2010; Black Rover 2010; Sir Bedivere 2011; Fort Rosalie 2013; Fort Austin 2014; Diligence 2014; Fort Victoria 2019; Fort George 2019; Argus 2020; Wave Ruler 2028; Wave Knight 2028.

Two of these vessels, Orangeleaf and Bayleaf, are chartered.

Harbour Services
Historically, all waterborne harbour services and some others (e.g. Mooring and Salvage Vessels) were operated by the personnel of the Royal Maritime Auxiliary Service (RMAS) under the direction of the local Captain of the Port or Queen's Harbourmaster. However in 1996 the majority of harbour services, particularly in the Dockyard ports of Devonport, Portsmouth and The Clyde, were awarded to Serco Denholm Ltd under a Government Owned/Commercially Operated (GOCO) contract.

Fleet Air Arm
The Fleet Air Arm numbers just over 6,000 personnel and operates about 200 aircraft. Operating fixed wing Harrier aircraft and Merlin, Sea King and Lynx helicopters from ships at sea and two main Naval Air Stations at Yeovilton and Culdrose, the Fleet Air Arm provides the Royal Navy with the aviation support required to conduct maritime operations.

Current Naval Aircraft Inventory

(Aircraft figures are estimates)

Role	Total	Type	Squadron
Harrier Force – See following remarks about Joint Force Harrier (JFH)			
Air Defence / Attack	36	Harrier GR 7/7A	
Naval Helicopters			
Anti-Submarine	8	Merlin HM Mk1	814 Sqn Culdrose
Anti-Submarine	9	Merlin HM Mk 1	820 Sqn Culdrose
Anti-Submarine	9	Merlin HM Mk1	829 Sqn Culdrose
Anti-Submarine (IFTU)	6	Merlin HM Mk1	700 Sqn Culdrose
Anti-Submarine / Anti-Ship	36	Lynx HAS 3, HMA 8	815 Sqn (See Note 1) Yeovilton
Anti-Submarine / Anti-Ship	12	Lynx HAS 3, HMA 8 (OCU)	702 Sqn Yeovilton

Note 1: The total for 815 Squadron includes 6 aircraft with Squadron HQ. The remaining aircraft are mostly dispersed in flights of one or two aircraft amongst the ships of the Fleet.

Airborne Early Warning	8	Sea King AEW 2	849 Sqn Culdrose
Commando Helicopter Force (See remarks above about Joint Helicopter Command)			
Commando Assault	10	Sea King HC4	845 Sqn Yeovilton
Commando Assault	10	Sea King HC4	846 Sqn Yeovilton
Commando Assault	9	Sea King HC4	848 Sqn Yeovilton
Ground Attack	6	Lynx AH7	847 Sqn Yeovilton
Aircrew Training			
ASW Training	6	Merlin HM Mk1	824 Sqn Culdrose
OEU	4	Merlin HM Mk1	700M Sqn Culdrose
Observer Training	9	Jetstream T2 /T3	750 Sqn Culdrose
Search & Rescue Training	5	Sea King HAS Mk5	771 Sqn Culdrose
Air Defence Training (Drone)	37	Mirach 100/5	792 Sqn Culdrose
Elementry Flying Training	8	Firefly	703 Sqn Barkstone Heath
Fleet Training & Support	12	Hawk	Culdrose

Joint Force Harrier

The Joint Force Harrier (JFH) was established on 1 April 2000 and brought together the Sea Harrier FA.2 squadrons, previously under Naval Air Command, with the RAF's Harrier GR 7/7A squadrons in a new command within RAF Strike Command. However, less than two years later, it was announced that the Sea Harrier FA.2 was to be retired early from the JFH under a development that will see the JFH standardise on the RAF's Harrier GR 9/9A. Announcing the move in 2002, UK MoD officials said the type rationalisation was in preparation for the introduction of the Future Joint Combat Aircraft and the Future Aircraft Carrier in 2012.

The MoD explained that the optimum development of the JFH is to support only one Harrier type to its end of service life, the 'more capable GR 9'. The Sea Harrier FA.2 was therefore withdrawn from service between 2004 and March 2006.

The JFH received its first upgraded Harrier GR 9 from BAE Systems' Warton facility in November 2005. Under the terms of a £500 million programme the avionics of some 60 x Harrier GR 7/7A will be upgraded to GR 9 standard and 11 x Harrier T 10 will be upgraded to T 12 standard.

From 1 April 2006 the JFH will consist of 4 x squadrons as follows:

800 Naval Air Squadron	9 x Harrier GR 7/7A	Cottesmore
801 Naval Air Squadron	9 x Harrier GR 7/7A	Cottesmore
1 Squadron RAF	9 x Harrier GR 9/9A	Cottesmore
4 Squadron RAF	9 x Harrier GR 7/7A	Cottesmore

All four squadrons should have 12 pilots and eventually all will operate the Harrier GR 9/9A and T 12.

Joint Helicopter Command

As from 1 October 1999 the Commando Helicopter Force joined with the support and battlefield helicopters of the Army Air Corps and the Royal Air Force in a new Joint Helicopter Command (JHC). The JHC is a single authority under Commander-in-Chief Land. The Fleet Air Arm contribution consisted of all the aircraft (plus about 1,000 personnel) of 845, 846, 847 and 848 Naval Air Squadrons plus 9 further aircraft from an attrition reserve.

Naval Aircraft

Harrier GR 7/7A

Crew (GR 7, GR 7A, GR 9, GR 9A) 1; (T Mark 10, T Mark 12) 2; Length (GR 7, GR 7A, GR 9) 14.1 m; Length (T10, T12) 17 m; Wingspan (normal) 9.2 m; Height (GR 7) 3.45 m; Height (T10) 4.17 m; Max Speed 1,065 k/ph (661mph) at sea level; All Up Operational Weight approx 13,494 kg; Engine (GR 7, GR 9, T10, T12) 1 x Rolls-Royce Pegasus Mk 105 (GR 7A, GR 9A) 1 x Rolls-Royce Pegasus Mk 107; Ferry Range 5,382 km (3,310 miles) with 4 x drop tanks. Armament on seven available wing stations: 2 x 30 mm Aden guns, 4 x wing weapon pylons and 1 x under-fuselage weapon pylon, conventional or cluster bombs; 2 x Sidewinder AIM-9L AAM, ASRAAM; up to 16 x Mk 82 or six Mk 83 bombs; 4 x Maverick air-to-ground anti-armour missiles, Paveway II and III laser-guided bombs; Brimstone anti-armour missiles, CRV-7 rocket pods; 2 x Storm Shadow CASOM

The Harrier GR 7 (two seat variant T-10) is the majority of in-service of Harrier 'Jump Jets' originating from the 1960s. Capable of taking off and landing vertically, the Harrier is not tied to airfields with long concrete runways but can be dispersed to sites in the field close to the forward edge of the battle area. The normal method of operation calls for a short take-off and vertical landing (STOVL), as a short ground roll on take-off enables a greater weapon load to be carried. The second-generation GR 5 and GR 7 versions replaced the original Harrier GR3s in the late 1980s/early 1990s in the offensive support role. First flight of the Harrier GR 7 was in 1989, and deliveries to RAF squadrons began in 1990. A total of 96 aircraft were ordered, including 62 interim GR 5s which were later modified to GR 7 standard.

The Harrier GR 7 has received a number of upgrades which include the fitting of new Pegasus 107 engines (giving more thrust at higher temperatures as well as reduced maintenance costs) having been fitted to 30 aircraft, these becoming Harrier GR 7As.

In addition, a major upgrade to the aircraft's avionics and weapons systems is under way (March 2006) that will enable the Harrier to carry a variety of current and future weapons. These include Maverick air-to-surface missiles, Brimstone anti-armour missiles and AIM-9L Sidewinder air-to-air missiles for self-defence. A new, stronger composite rear fuselage will also be fitted. These aircraft will become Harrier GR 9s, whilst those with the uprated engines and weapons systems will be Harrier GR 9As. The programme also includes an upgrade of the two-seater T10 aircraft to the equivalent GR 9 standard known as the Harrier T12.

No 800 and 8001 Naval Air Squadrons operate Harrier GR 7/7A from RAF Cottesmore. Eventually both squadrons will be equipped with Harrier GR9/9A.

Sea King

Principal Characteristics: HC4: Crew: 1 x pilot and 1 x aircrewman: Fuselage Length 22 m: Width 3.78 m: Height 4.72 m: Weight (empty) 6201 kg: Max Take-Off Weight 9525 kg: Rotor Diameter 18.9 m: Cruising Speed 208 km/h (129mph) at sea level: Service Ceiling 1,220m

The Westland Sea King is a licence-built version of the US Sikorsky S-61. The Royal Navy's HAS Mark 1 aircraft's first flight was in 1969. Since that time, the aircraft has been extensively upgraded and passed through a series of Marks.

The AEW 2 is used for airborne early-warning and is a Sea King HAS Mark 2 fitted with a Thorn EMI Search Water Radar carried in a radardome that can be swivelled down underneath the aircraft for operational searches. A detachment of 3 x AEW 2 aircraft generally deploys with each aircraft carrier.

The Sea King HC4 (Commando) is a tactical military helicopter capable of transporting 28 fully equipped troops or 6,000 lbs (2,720 kg) as an internal load. Carrying 28 troops the aircraft has a range of about 246 miles (396 km). The first HC4 deliveries were made to the Royal Navy in 1979.

The Mk 5 aircraft in service with 771 Sqn are SAR aircraft (Search & Rescue). RN SAR aircraft are stationed at Prestwick and Culdrose.

Lynx

Principal Characteristics: Crew 2 on the flight-deck and up to 2 mission crew in the fuselage. Length: Fuselage 11.92 m: Height 3.2 m: Rotor Diameter 12.8 m: Max Speed 144 mph (232 km/h) at sea level: Ferry Range 1,046 km (650 miles) with max internal and external fuel tanks: Weight (max take-off) 4,876 kg (10,750 lbs).

Lynx aircraft are at sea with all frigates and destroyers, to provide anti-surface surveillance, anti-submarine warfare (ASW) capabilities and anti-ship attack capabilities. With the introduction into service of the first of the upgraded 44 x HAS 3, HMA 8 aircraft in late 1994, the Lynx in Royal Naval service has been turned from an anti-submarine helicopter into a dedicated maritime attack aircraft. Capable of carrying anti-submarine torpedoes (range 10 km) and anti-ship Sea Skua missiles (range 20km), the HMA 8 is capable of integrating its navigational, communications and fighting systems through a 1553B databus.

Typical combat mission profiles in the anti-submarine role could be a patrol out to 60 miles, a two-hour loiter in the search area carrying torpedoes and smoke markers etc and return.

EH101 Merlin HM Mk1

Principal Characteristics: Service Ceiling 4,572 m; Range 550 n miles (1,019 km); Top Speed 167 knots; All Up Weight 14,600 kg; Sensors: GEC-Marconi Blue Kestrel 5000 radar, Thomson Marconi Flash AQS 960 dipping sonar, GEC-Marconi sonobuoy acoustic processor AQS-903, Racal Orange Reaper ESM: Weapons; ASW 4 x Stingray torpedoes or Mk 11 Mod 3 depth bombs plus anti-ship missiles

Merlin was ordered in the early 1990s in a contract worth £1.5 billion and the first of 44 production aircraft appeared in 1996 and Merlin was accepted into service in 1999. The Royal Navy currently operates 38 x aircraft (with four in reserve) in the anti-submarine and anti-surface warfare role in 5 x squadrons (814, 820, 824, 829 and 700 Sqns). All are based at RNAS Culdrose. When embarked the aircraft can operate from almost any capable flight deck.

The aircraft has a state of the art mission system, which processes data from an extensive array of on-board sensors, giving Merlin an independent capability to search for, locate and attack submarine targets. It is this autonomous capability which makes Merlin almost unique among Anti-Submarine Warfare helicopters.

Merlin's operational debut came during operations in the Northern Gulf and Southern Iraq during 2003. The planned out of service date for the Merlin Mk 1 is 2029.

New Carrier-borne Fixed Wing Aircraft

Enhanced operational flexibility, an earlier in-service date and greater industrial benefits for UK industry have emerged as the key factors leading to the UK's selection of the short-take off/vertical landing (STOVL) variant of Lockheed Martin's F-35 Joint Strike Fighter (JSF) to fulfil its Future Joint Combat Aircraft (FJCA) requirement. The procurement of 150 of the Joint Combat Aircraft is currently estimated to cost about £10 billion. The Minister for Defence Procurement said in September 2002 that the STOVL variant of JSF would fully meet the UK's military needs and build on the RAF's and RN's "unique and valuable knowledge of STOVL aircraft, acquired during nearly four decades of operations of Harrier on land and sea." The initial cost of construction of the two new carriers is expected to be between £3 billion and £4 billion.

In January 2006 the UK MoD stated that "It remains our plan to operate the F-35B (Short Take-Off Vertical Landing variant) Joint Strike Fighter aircraft from the future carrier. We also retain the option to deploy Harrier GR 9 initially. However, the design has the flexibility to be adapted to operate conventional take-off and landing aircraft if we decide to do so in the future."

Naval Missiles

Trident D-5

The UK Strategic deterrent (US Trident D-5) is deployed in the four Vanguard class Ballistic Missile Nuclear-Powered Submarines (SSBNs). The Trident D-5 missile is a three-stage, solid propellant Submarine Launched Ballistic Missile (SLBM) – it is 13.42 m long and has a body diameter of 2.11 m. It has a launch weight of 59,090 kg and a maximum range of 12,000 km. The minimum range is believed to be about 2,500 km.

It has been stated that the UK missiles will carry up to eight warheads each, but it is expected that there will be between one and four warheads fitted to most missiles. The UK plans to use some Trident D-5 missiles in a 'sub-strategic' role, with a single warhead set to produce a smaller yield, believed to be around 10 kT. A statement in 1999 clarified the situation with regard to the maximum number of warheads to be carried by each of the UK's SSBNs, which will be limited to 48.

SLCM: Hughes Tomahawk Block IIIC/Block IV

US-built Tomahawk is being deployed in all RN Attack submarines. In 1995, the first export order for Tomahawk missiles was announced, with the UK ordering 65 missiles, Advanced Tomahawk Weapon Control Systems for seven boats, and a shore-based mission planning system. The missiles are UGM-109C TLAM-C versions to the Block 3 build standard, to be launched from standard torpedo tubes. Two unguided test rounds and one guided flight were made from a 'Swiftsure' class boat in 1998. The UK fired 20 missiles against targets in Serbia in early 1999, with more missiles fired against Afghanistan in 2001 and Iraq in 2003. Tomahawk has a range of up to 1,700 kms.

In February 2006 it was disclosed that Tomahawk missiles had been purchased as follows: 1997 – 48; 1998 – 17; 1999 – 0; 2000 – 0; 2001 – 20; 2002 – 0; 2003 – 22. During early 2006 64 x Block IV Tomahawk cruise missiles are currently on order..

Harpoon

Harpoon, manufactured by McDonnel-Douglas of the USA, is an extremely powerful anti-shipping missile that is fitted to the Type 22 and Type 23 Frigates. The Sub-Harpoon (UGM-84A) is also deployed in Trafalgar and Swiftsure Class submarines. The latest versions of this missile have extremely sophisticated electronic counter measures (ECM), and the ability to fly a sea-skimming course on a dog-leg path through three pre-programmed way points. The warhead is extremely powerful and a hit from Harpoon is almost certain to result in the destruction or disablement of a major surface vessel.

Principal Characteristics: Length 3.84 m; Diameter 0.343 m; Total Weight 526 kg; Warhead Weight 225kg; Range 110 kms

PAAMS (Aster)

The PAAMS (Principal-Anti-Air-Missile System) surface-to-air missile system will equip the Type 45 Destroyers. Two versions will be in service, the Aster 15 (short range) and the Aster 30 (long-range). PAAMS is the only available system that can integrate three operational naval missions: self-defence, local area defence of nearby vessels and fleet area defence. The complete system consists of the missiles, missile launchers, command and control (C2) system and the associated radars.

Within the figure of £561.6 million overall cost for a Type 45 Destroyer, the cost of the PAAMS system is approximately one third or about £187 million.

PAAMS is also being purchased by France and Italy.

Aster 15 – Principal characteristics: Range 30 kms (in excess of): Weight 310 kg; Length: 4.2 m; Diameter 0.18 m; Speed Mach 3; Aster 30 – Principal characteristics; Range 100 kms (in excess of); Weight 450 kg; Length 4.9 m; Diameter 0.18 m; Speed Mach 4.5

Sea Dart

Sea Dart is a surface-to-air missile system with a long range (probably in excess of 80 kms) and employs a two-stage system with a primary booster rocket powering the warhead and ramjet on their way to the target. There is a limited surface-to-surface capability out to a range of about 28 km and the guidance system is a semi-active homing radar. It is installed in Type 42 destroyers.

Principal Characteristics: Length 4.40 m; Diameter 0.42 m; Total Weight 549 kg;

Range 80 km+ approx

Sea Wolf

Sea Wolf is a ship-based, surface-to-air missile designed for the defence of point targets. This is a highly efficient system thought to be capable of dealing with aircraft, missiles and even artillery rounds. The guidance system is semi-automatic command to line of sight with radar and/or infra-red missile and target tracking.

Principal Characteristics: Length 1.91m; Diameter 0.18 m; Total Weight 79.8 kgs; Range 6/7,000 m; Altitude 3/4000 m

Sea Skua

Sea Skua is a short-range, anti-ship missile that has been in Royal Naval service since 1982. The missile is currently carried as the main armament of the Lynx aircraft flying from RN destroyers / frigates. The guidance system is semi-active terminal homing.

Sea Skua is currently planned to leave service from around the 2012 to 2014 period. It is intended to be replaced by the Future Anti-Surface Guided Weapon.

Principal Characteristics: Length 2.85 m; Diameter 0.22 m; Total Weight 147 kg;

Range 20 km approximately

Other Missiles

Other air-launched missiles in RN service may be found in relevant entries in the RAF Section.

The Royal Marines

The Royal Marines (RM) are an elite Corps and specialists in Amphibious Warfare – and wherever there is action, the Royal Marines are likely to be involved. They were prominent, for example, in the Falklands campaign, and they can be found wherever the UK Armed Services are actively involved e.g. Northern Ireland, the Balkans, Sierra Leone, Afghanistan and Iraq. The Royal Marines number approximately 7,200 men and, since the end of the Cold War, and especially in recent years, the Corps appears to have reverted to its traditional role of being ready for operations anywhere in the world.

All Royal Marines, except those in the Royal Marines Band Service, are first and foremost, commando soldiers. They are required to undergo what is recognised as one of the longest and most demanding infantry training courses in the world. This is undertaken at the Commando Training Centre Royal Marines at Lympstone in UK's West Country, not far from Dartmoor.

The titular head of the Royal Marines is always a Major General – Commandant General Royal Marines (CGRM). There have been significant recent structural changes in the higher management of the Royal Navy recently and this has added to the responsibilities and raised the profile of CGRM.

The Royal Marines have small detachments in ships at sea and other units worldwide with widely differing tasks. However, the bulk of the manpower of the Royal Marines is grouped in battalion-sized organisations known as Commandos (Cdo). There are 3 Commando Groups and they are part of a larger formation known as 3 Commando Brigade (3 Cdo Bde).

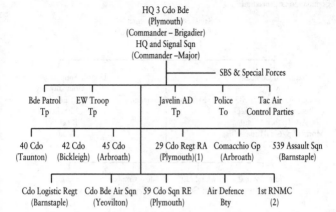

HQ 3 Cdo Bde
(Plymouth)
(Commander – Brigadier)
HQ and Signal Sqn
(Commander –Major)

SBS & Special Forces

Bde Patrol Tp — EW Troop Tp — Javelin AD Tp — Police To — Tac Air Control Parties

40 Cdo (Taunton) — 42 Cdo (Bickleigh) — 45 Cdo (Arbroath) — 29 Cdo Regt RA (Plymouth)(1) — Comacchio Gp (Arbroath) — 539 Assault Sqn (Barnstaple)

Cdo Logistic Regt (Barnstaple) — Cdo Bde Air Sqn (Yeovilton) — 59 Cdo Sqn RE (Plymouth) — Air Defence Bty — 1st RNMC (2)

Notes:

(1) 29 Cdo Regt RA has one battery stationed at Arbroath with 45 Cdo.

(2) 1st Bn The Royal Netherlands Marine Corps is part of 3 Cdo Bde for NATO assigned tasks. The Air Defence troop is equipped with Rapier. There are three regular Tactical Air Control Parties and one reserve. 539 Assault Squadron has hovercraft, landing craft and raiding craft.

(3) It is likely that a proposed Army Commando Battalion (1st Battalion The Rifles) will join 3 Commando Brigade to provide a fourth Commando Group in 2007.

Commando Organisation

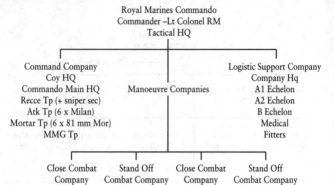

Note: There are 4 x Manoeuvre Companies:

♦ 2 x Close Combat Companies each with 3 x Fighting Troops (5 officers and 98 other ranks).

♦ 2 x Stand Off Combat Companies one of which is tracked (Viking armoured vehicle) and the other wheeled. Each Stand Off Combat Company has 1 x Heavy Machine Gun Troop with 6 x 0.5 HMG, 1 x Anti-Tank Troop with 6 x Milan and 1 x Close Combat Fighting Troop (5 officers and 78 other ranks).

♦ Total personnel strength is 692 all ranks.

♦ A troop (Tp) roughly equates to an army platoon and consists of about 30 men.

Locations.

Headquarters Royal Marines	(Portsmouth)
HQ 3 Commando Brigade Plymouth	(Stonehouse)
3 Commando Bde HQ & Signal Squadron	(Stonehouse)
3 Commando Bde Air Sqn	(RNAS Yeovilton)
40 Commando	(Taunton)
42 Commando	(Bickleigh)
45 Commando	(Arbroath)
Commando Logistic Regiment	(Barnstaple))
539 Assault Sqn Plymouth	(Barnstaple)
Fleet Protection Group	(Clyde)
Commando Training Centre	(Lympstone)
Royal Marines Stonehouse	(Plymouth)
Royal Marines Poole	(Poole)

| Amphibious Training & Trials Unit | (Bideford) |
| 1 Assault Group | (Poole) |

Royal Marines Reserve (RMR)

The RMR consists of about 600 personnel based around the following locations:

RMR London: The detachment is in London and is located alongside the HQ. The three remaining detachments are based in Chatham, Henley and Portsmouth.

RMR Merseyside: The Headquarters is in Liverpool were there is a detachment. The other two detachments are based in Birmingham and Manchester.

RMR Scotland: HQ is in Glasgow with the five remaining detachments based in Greenock, Edinburgh, Dundee, Aberdeen and Inverness.

RMR Tyne: A single location at Newcastle-on-Tyne

RMR Bristol: The main detachment is in Bristol which is located alongside the HQ. The four remaining detachments are based in Poole, Plymouth, Cardiff and Lympstone.

Special Boat Service

This organisation is the Naval equivalent of the Army's SAS (Special Air Service). Personnel are all volunteers from the mainstream Royal Marines and vacancies are few with competition for entry fierce.

Generally speaking only about 30% of volunteers manage to complete the entry course and qualify. The SBS specialises in mounting clandestine operations against targets at sea, in rivers or harbours and against occupied coastlines.

Comacchio Group/Fleet Protection Group Royal Marines (FPGRM)

This specialist company was formed in 1980, and has the task of guarding the UK's oil rigs and other associated installations from a variety of threats – in particular terrorist attacks.

During 2001 Comacchio Group was renamed as the Fleet Protection Group Royal Marines (FPGRM) and the unit moved from RM Condor to HMNB Clyde.

FPGRM is structured around 3 x rifle companies and 1 x headquarters company. Personnel strength is in the region of 533 personnel.

CHAPTER 3 – THE BRITISH ARMY

Personnel Summary (at 1 February 2006)

		Trained Strength at 1 January 2006 (Trained and Untrained)
Army	Trained Requirement	101,800
Officers	13,630	
Other Ranks	83,270	
Gurkhas	3,360	
	Total	100,260

Note: The above figures do not include 3,100 Royal Irish Regiment (Home Service). 1,270 Mobilised Army Reservists and 200 Gibraltar Regiment Permanent Cadre.

From August 2005 the Army Trained Strength Requirement has been reduced from 106,970 in 2002 to the current 101,800.

Personnel in training (at 1 February 2006)

		Personnel in training
Officers		1,020
Other Ranks		10,070
	Total	11,090

BRITISH ARMY STATISTICS

Strength of The Regular Army (1 Jan 2006)

Armour	10 x Regiments (1)
Royal Artillery	15 x Regiments (2)
Royal Engineers	11 x Regiments
Regular Infantry Battalions	40 x Battalions (3)
Home Service Battalions	4 x Battalions
Army Air Corps	5 x Regiments
Signals	11 x Regiments
Equipment Support	7 x Battalions (4)
Logistics	22 x Regiments
Medical	8 x Major Units (5)

Notes: (1) Excludes Joint NBC Regiment. (2) Includes 1 x Training Regiment and 29 Commando Regiment. (3) Excludes 1 x battalion of the Royal Gibraltar Regiment (4) Includes 1 x Equipment Support (Aviation) Battalion. (5) Includes 5 x Medical Regiments and 3 x Hospitals.

In general these Battalions/Regiments are commanded by Lt Colonels and have a strength of between 500 and 800 personnel.

Strength of the Territorial Army (1 January 2006)

Armour	4 x Regiments (1)
Royal Artillery	7 x Regiments (2)
Royal Engineers	5 x Regiments
Infantry	15 x Battalions
Signals	11 x Regiments
Equipment Support	4 x Battalions
Logistics	15 x Regiments
Intelligence	1 x Battalion
Medical	11 x Hospitals; 4 x Field Ambulances and 2 x Regiments

Notes: (1) 4 x Regional National Defence Reconnaissance Regiments.(2) Includes Honourable Artillery Company (HAC).

Joint Units (1 January 2006)

Special Air Service	1 x Regular Regiment
Special Air Service	2 x Territorial Army Regiments
Special Reconnaissance Regiment	1 x Regiment
Special Boat Service (RM)	4 x Squadrons
Joint Nuclear Biological & Chemical	1 x Regiment

Joint Helicopter Command

Regular Army Air Corps Regiments	5 x Regiments
Territorial Army Aviation	1 x Regiment

BRITISH ARMY EQUIPMENT SUMMARY

Armour: 386 x Challenger 2; 137 x Sabre (approx); 60 x Striker; 325 x Scimitar; 1,100 x FV 432; 575 x MCV 80 Warrior; 585 x Spartan; 640 x Saxon; 11 x Fuchs NBC recce vehicles; 10 x Stormer.

Artillery: 179 x AS 90; 64 x 227mm MLRS ; 48 x FH 70; 165 x 105mm Light Gun; 470 x 81 mm Mortar (including 112 SP); 2,093 x 51 mm Light Mortar.

Air Defence: 98 x Rapier Fire Units (24 SP); 330 x Javelin Launchers; 147 x Starstreak LML; 135 x HVM (SP).

Army Aviation: 108 x Lynx (some armed with TOW); 133 Gazelle; 7 x BN-2; 67 x Apache on order (possibly 20 in service in mid 2003); Helicopters available from RAF – 38 x Chinook; 39 x Puma; 22 x Merlin.

Personnel Strength – Arm of Service

Comparison of liability to full-time trained strength of the Army as at 1 January 2006. This table includes FTRS (Full Time Reserve Service personnel).

	Liability	Strength
Staff	720	810
The Household Cavalry/ Royal Armoured Corps	5,790	5,560
Royal Regiment of Artillery	7,480	7,410
Corps of Royal Engineers	9,460	8,780
Royal Corps of Signals	8,440	8,640
The Infantry	24,620	24,520
Others	—	650
Army Air Corps	2,010	1,980
Royal Army Chaplains Department	130	140
The Royal Logistics Corps	15,700	15,680
Royal Army Medical Corps	3,270	2,810
Royal Electrical and Mechanical Engineers	9,680	9,730
Adjutant General's Corps (Provost Branch)	1,800	2,010
Adjutant Generals Corps (Staff and Personnel Support Branch)	4,040	4,440
Adjutant Generals Corps (Educational and Training Services Branch)	290	340
Adjutant Generals Corps Royal (Army Legal Service)	120	100
Royal Army Veterinary Corps	190	190
Small Arms School Corps	140	150
Royal Army Dental Corps	420	370
Intelligence Corps	1,550	1,440
Army Physical Training Corps	420	440
Queen Alexandra's Royal Army Nursing Corps	1,080	840
Corps of Army Music	880	940
Long Service List	480	620
Unallocated	—	10
Total trained regular Army and FTRS	98,710	97,940
Gurkhas	3,090	3,360
Full-time trained Army	**101,800**	**101,300**

HIGHER MANAGEMENT OF THE ARMY

The Ministry of Defence (MoD) is a Department of State, headed by the Secretary of State for Defence (SofS) who implements national defence policy and plans the expenditure of the defence budget. The MoD is the highest level of headquarters for the Armed Forces, both administrative and operational. All major issues of policy are referred to the SofS or to one of his three Ministerial colleagues:

- Minister of State for the Armed Forces
- Parliamentary Under-Secretary of State for Defence Procurement
- Parliamentary Under-Secretary of State for Veterans Affairs

Under the direction of the Defence Council (described in Chapter 1) management of the Services is the responsibility of the Service Boards, in the case of the Army, the Army Board is the senior management directorate.

The Army Board

The routine management of the Army is the responsibility of The Army Board the composition of which is as follows:

- The Secretary of State for Defence
- Minister of State for the Armed Forces
- Parliamentary Under-Secretary of State for Defence Procurement
- Parliamentary Under-Secretary of State for Veterans Affairs
- Parliamentary Under-Secretary of State for Defence
- Chief of the General Staff
- Assistant Chief of the General Staff
- Adjutant General
- Quartermaster General
- Master General of the Ordnance
- Commander-in-Chief (Land Command)
- Commander UK Support Command (Germany)

Executive Committee of the Army Board (ECAB)

Attended by senior UK Army commanders, ECAB dictates the policy required for the Army to function efficiently and meet the aims required by the Defence Council and government. The Chief of the General Staff is the chairman of the Executive Committee of the Army Board.

Army Board and ECAB decisions are acted upon by the military staff at the various headquarters worldwide.

The Chief of the General Staff (CGS) is the officer responsible for the Army's contribution to the national defence effort and he maintains control through the commanders and the staff branches of each of the various army headquarters organisations.

CHIEF OF THE GENERAL STAFF (AS AT 29 AUGUST 2006)

General Sir Richard Dannatt KCB CBE MC

General Sir Richard Dannatt was commissioned into The Green Howards from Sandhurst in 1971 and has served with 1st Battalion The Green Howards in Northern Ireland, Cyprus and Germany. He commanded the Battalion in the Airmobile role from 1989 – 1991. In tours away from Regimental Duty he has been a Company instructor at Sandhurst, Chief of Staff of the 20th Armoured Brigade, Military Assistant to the Minister of State for the Armed Forces and Colonel Higher Command and Staff Course/Doctrine at the Staff College.

From 1994-1996 he commanded 4th Armoured Brigade. During this period he was deployed from Germany to Bosnia as Commander Sector South West in the final months of the United Nations Protection Force (UNPROFOR) and then commanding his Brigade at the start of the Implementation Force (IFOR) with Multinational Division (South West). From 1996-1998 he was Director of Defence Programmes in the Ministry of Defence. He took command of 3rd (United Kingdom) Division in January 1999, and served that year in Kosovo as Commander British Forces. In November 2000 he was appointed Deputy Commander Operations of the

Stabilisation Force (SFOR) in Bosnia. He was the Assistant Chief of the General Staff in the UK Ministry of Defence from April 2001 to October 2002, and assumed the command of the Allied Rapid Reaction Corps on the 15th January 2003. In March 2005 he was appointed as the Commander-in-Chief Land Command and he assumed the appointment of Chief of the General Staff on 29 August 2005.

In addition to his current appointment, General Sir Richard Dannatt is Colonel Commandant of The King's Division, The Royal Military Police and Army Air Corps. He is President of the Army Rifle Association, and the Soldier's and Airmen's Scripture Readers Association, and Vice-President of The Officers Christian Union.

General Sir Richard Dannatt

Note; General Sir Richard Dannatt's predecessor as CGS was General Sir Mike Jackson MBE CBE CB KCB DSO ADC Gen.

CHAIN OF COMMAND

The Army is controlled from the MoD via the above three subsidiary headquarters and a number of smaller headquarters worldwide. The diagram illustrates this chain of command as at 1 Jan 2006.

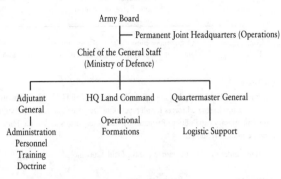

Note: * The Quartermaster General will operate with support from the Director General Logistics (Land) and Director General Logistics (Supply Chain). Both of these organisations are part of the joint Defence Logistics Organisation (DLO).

HQ LAND COMMAND

HQ Land Command is located at Erskine Barracks, Wilton near Salisbury and controls about 80% of the troops in the British Isles and almost 100% of its fighting capability. HQ Land Command replaced HQ United Kingdom Land Forces (HQ UKLF) in 1995.

Land Command's role is to deliver and sustain the Army's operational capability, whenever required throughout the world, and the Command comprises all operational troops in Great Britain, Germany, Nepal and Brunei, together with the Army Training Teams in Canada, Belize and Kenya.

Land Command has almost 76,000 trained Army personnel – the largest single Top Level Budget in Defence, with a budget of over £5.6 billion. It contains all the Army's fighting equipment, including attack helicopters, Challenger 2 tanks, Warrior Infantry Fighting Vehicles, AS90 and the Multi-Launched Rocket System (MLRS).

Land Command is one of the three central command agencies in the British Army, the other two being the Adjutant General (with responsibility for administration, personnel and training) and Director General Logistics (Land) responsible for supply and logistics. The Command is responsible for providing all the Army's fighting troops throughout the World. These are organised into eight formations and are commanded by Major Generals.

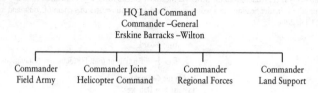

HQ Land Command
Commander –General
Erskine Barracks –Wilton

| Commander Field Army | Commander Joint Helicopter Command | Commander Regional Forces | Commander Land Support |

FIELD ARMY

The Commander Field Army has operational command of all Field Army Formations. This includes training designated forces for all types of military operations and providing appropriate military capability to Permanent Joint Headquarters and/or the Joint Rapid Reaction Forces as required.

Major units under the direct command of the Field Army include:

- ♦ 1 (UK) Division   (Ready Division)
- ♦ 3 (UK) Division   (Ready Division)

- ♦ Combat Service Support Group (United Kingdom)
- ♦ Combat Service Support Group (Germany)

Service personnel total for the Field Army at 1 April 2005 was 51,900.

Joint Helicopter Command (JHC)

The Joint Helicopter Command's primary role is to deliver and sustain effective Battlefield Helicopter and Air Assault assets, operationally capable under all environmental conditions, in order to support UK's defence missions and tasks. JHC major formations are as follows:

- ♦ All Army Aviation Units
- ♦ RAF Support Helicopter Force
- ♦ Commando Helicopter Force
- ♦ Joint Helicopter Force (Northern Ireland)
- ♦ 16 Air Assault Brigade
- ♦ Combat Support Units
- ♦ Combat Service Support Units
- ♦ Joint Helicopter Command and Standards Wing

Service personnel total for the Joint Helicopter Command at 1 April 2005 was 12,600 (includes RAF and Royal Navy personnel).

Commander Regional Forces

The Commander Regional Forces maintains, and where possible, enhances the provision of the military capability and infrastructure support required to meet Land Command's operational requirements.

In addition, Commander Regional Forces at HQ LAND is the Inspector General of the Territorial Army, with additional responsibilities for Cadets and the University Officer Training Corps (UOTC).

Major units that assist Commander Regional Forces are amongst the following:

♦ 2 Division   (Regenerative Division)
♦ 4 Division   (Regenerative Division)
♦ 5 Division   (Regenerative Division)

♦ United Kingdom Support Command (Germany)
♦ London District
♦ Land Support Management Group

Service personnel total for the Commander Regional Forces at 1 April 2005 was 11,200.

Commander Land Support

The Defence Supply Chain provides a range of support functions to enable the British armed forces to carry out operations. These include storing and distributing all the supplies needed by the forces, such as equipment, mail, medical supplies, fuel, clothing, food and ammunition, as well as transporting personnel and freight anywhere in the world.

Personnel total for the Commander Land Support grouping at 1 April 2005 was 400 service and 800 civilian personnel.

Ready Divisions

There are two 'Ready' Divisions: the 1st (UK) Armoured Division, based in Germany, and the 3rd (UK) Division in the United Kingdom. Both of these divisions are earmarked to form part of the Allied Command Europe Rapid Reaction Corps (ARRC), NATO's premier strategic formation; but they also have the flexibility to be employed on rapid reaction tasks or in support of other Defence Roles.

In addition to their operational roles, these divisions also command the Army units in specified geographic areas: in the case of the 1st Division, this area is made up of the garrisons in Germany where the Division's units are based; and in the case of the 3rd Division the area of the South West of England.

Combat Service Support Group (United Kingdom) consists of a supply regiment, two transport regiments, a general support medical regiment which has both regular and territorial army squadrons, three field hospitals, and a field medical equipment depot. For operations, the group may have assigned to it two Territorial Army transport regiments, five Territorial Army field hospitals, and a Territorial Army Royal Electrical and Mechanical Engineers maintenance battalion.

Combat Service Support Group (Germany) consists of a supply regiment; two transport regiments, and a general support medical regiment which has both Regular and Territorial Army squadrons. For operations, the group may have assigned to it a Territorial Army transport regiment, six Territorial Army field hospitals, a Territorial Army field medical equipment depot, and a Territorial Army Royal Electrical and Mechanical Engineers maintenance battalion.

Regenerative Divisions

There are three Regenerative Divisions, based on old Military Districts of the United Kingdom. These are the 2nd Division with its Headquarters at Edinburgh, the 4th Division with its Headquarters at Aldershot, and the 5th Division with its Headquarters at Shrewsbury. These Regenerative divisions are responsible for all non-deployable Army units within their boundaries, and could provide the core for three new divisions, should the Army be required to expand to meet a major international threat.

Districts

Two Districts remain: London District (although subordinated to 4th Division for budgetary purposes), and the United Kingdom Support Command (Germany). London District is responsible for all Army units within the M25 boundary. The United Kingdom Support Command (Germany) with its Headquarters at Rheindahlen has similar responsibilities, but also provides essential support functions for 1 (UK) Armoured Division and the Headquarters of the ARRC.

These divisional and district areas are further sub-divided into brigades and garrisons, which also have a varying mix of operational and infrastructure support responsibilities. As a result of the Defence Costs Studies, some brigade headquarters, which previously had purely operational functions, have been amalgamated with garrison headquarters to achieve savings and greater efficiency.

EMBEDDED FORMATIONS/UNITS

Other formations/units embedded in the Land Command Order of Battle include:

1 Artillery Brigade which consists of two artillery regiments, equipped with the multiple launch rocket system, and a surveillance and target acquisition regiment, equipped with the Phoenix remotely piloted vehicle, radar and sound-ranging equipment. For operations, the brigade may have assigned to it a Territorial Army artillery regiment, equipped with the multiple launch rocket system, and a Territorial Army observation post regiment.

7 Air Defence Brigade which consists of two air defence artillery regiments equipped with Rapier surface-to-air missile systems. For operations, the brigade may have three Territorial Army air defence artillery regiments assigned to it, each equipped with Javelin close air defence systems.

1 Signal Brigade consisting of two signal regiments and the Allied Command Europe Rapid Reaction Corps support battalion.

2 (NC) Signal Brigade provides information and communications systems support to the army and government in times of crisis. In the main TA signal regiments and squadrons are used to achieve this aim.

11 Signal Brigade consisting of a strategic communications signal regiment and a trunk communications signal regiment. For operations, the brigade may have five Territorial Army signal regiments assigned to it.

29 (Corps Support) Engineer Brigade may have two Territorial Army engineer regiments assigned to it.

12 (Air Support) Engineer Brigade could consist of an air support engineer regiment and two independent air support squadrons. For operations, the brigade may have two Territorial Army air support engineer regiments assigned to it.

1 Military Intelligence Brigade has the responsibility for 3 x regular and 1 x TA intelligence battalions. Under the Future Army Structure proposals 1 Military Intelligence Brigade is to be enhanced. It is possible that the tri-service 15 (UK) Psychological Operations Group is also under the command of this brigade.

Composition of 1(UK) Armoured Division

1 (UK) Armoured Division has its headquarters at Herford in Germany (about 50 kms from Hanover) and the three Armoured Brigades under command are located at Osnabruck, Bergen-Hohne and Paderborn.

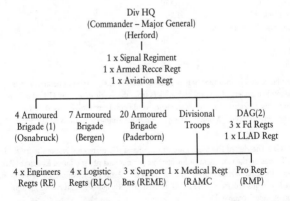

Note:
(1) Under Future Army Structure (FAS) proposals 4 Armoured Brigade will re-role to become a mechanised brigade. Restructuring should be complete by 2008 and 4 Armoured Brigade will move from Germany to Catterick in Yorkshire. 1 (UK) Armoured Division will then

consist of 7 Armoured and 20 Armoured Brigades. (2) DAG (Divisional Artillery Group) This DAG could be reinforced by Rapier Air Defence and MLRS units from the UK as necessary. (3) Personnel total in Germany is approximately 21,000 with about 17,000 in 1 (UK) Armoured Division. During early 2006 this Division could provide the Headquarters (HQs) for up to nine Battlegroups.

Non-UK brigades

For non-national operations such as NATO military tasks in support of the Allied Rapid Reaction Corps (ARRC), 1 (UK) Armoured Division could have two extra brigades available for deployment. These two brigade could be the Danish Reaction Brigade and 4 (Czech) Reaction Brigade.

102 Logistics Brigade

This brigade provides third line combat service support wherever this is required army wide but is the first 'port of call' for combat service support to 1 (UK) Armoured Division. The Brigade Headquarters is at Gutersloh in West Germany, reasonably close to the Headquarters of 1 (UK) Armoured Division in Herford.

Estimate of Force Levels in 1 (UK) Armoured Division (1 Jan 2006)

Army Personnel	17,000
Challenger 2 MBT	150
Warrior AIFV	450
Other Tracked Vehicles	1,100
Helicopters (Army Aviation)	24
Artillery Guns	66
MLRS	0
AVLB	18

It is probable that in the event of hostilities (as was the case in recent operations in Iraq) considerable numbers of officers and soldiers from the Territorial Army (TA) would be used to reinforce this division. These reinforcements would consist of individuals, drafts of specialists, or by properly formed TA units varying in size from Mobile Bath Units of 20 men, to Major Units over 500 strong.

UKSC(G) – The United Kingdom support Command (Germany) has responsibility for British Army Troops on the Continent of Europe that are not part of 1st (United Kingdom) Armoured Division. Its headquarters replaces that of the British Army of the Rhine, whose sign it has adopted. The headquarters of UKSC(G) is located at Rheindahlen and has about 600 personnel under command.

Armoured Brigade Organisation

The following diagram illustrates the possible composition of an Armoured Brigade in 1(UK) Armoured Division on operations.

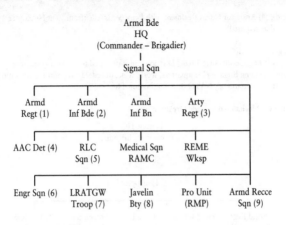

```
                          Armd Bde
                            HQ
                 (Commander – Brigadier)
                            |
                        Signal Sqn
```

Armd Regt (1)	Armd Inf Bde (2)	Armd Inf Bn	Arty Regt (3)	
AAC Det (4)	RLC Sqn (5)	Medical Sqn RAMC	REME Wksp	
Engr Sqn (6)	LRATGW Troop (7)	Javelin Bty (8)	Pro Unit (RMP)	Armd Recce Sqn (9)

Totals: 58 x Challenger MBT (Possibly)
         145 x Warrior AIFV
         340 x AFV 432/Spartan Armoured Vehicles
         24 x AS 90 SP Gun
         Approx 5,000 personnel

Notes: (1) Armoured Regiment with approx 58 x Challenger MBT; (2) Armoured Inf
Battalion with approx 52 x Warrior (with rifle coys) and approx 40 x FV432; (3) Artillery
Regiment with 24 x AS90 SP Guns; (4) Army Air Corps Detachment (possibly 9 x Lynx & 4 x
Gazelle); (5) Transport Squadron RLC with approximately 60 –70 trucks; (6) Engineer
Squadron with 68 vehicles but depending upon the task could involve a complete engineer
battalion; (7) Long-Range Anti-Tank Guided Weapon Troop (Swingfire) but due to be
replaced in the longer term; (8) RA Bty with possibly 36 x HVM AD missiles; (9) Armoured
Recce Squadron.

This Brigade could provide the HQs for three Battlegroups

COMPOSITION OF 3 (UK) MECHANISED DIVISION

The 3rd (United Kingdom) Division is the only operational (Ready) Division in the UK. The
Division has a mix of capabilities encompassing armoured and wheeled elements in its three
brigades.

Note: (1) 1 Mechanised Brigade; (2) 19 Brigade has started to re-role to become a light brigade
and should be ready for deployment in late 2006 when it will serve as the contingent NATO
response force; The Headquarters of 19 Light Brigade will probably be in Scotland with some
units in Northern Ireland; (3) Artillery Regiment with Multi Launch Rocket System (if

allocated); (4) Army Air Corps Regiment with Lynx & Gazelle (from Joint Helicopter Command as required).

101 Logistic Brigade

101 Logistic Brigade supports 3 (UK) Division and is prepared to deploy logistic force elements, including Brigade Headquarters, world wide, in order to support the UK's military contribution to a national, NATO or a multinational force

3 (UK) Div – Mechanised Brigade Organisation

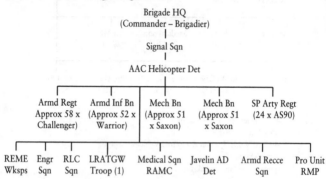

Note: (1) Long-Range Anti-Tank Guided Weapons – Currently Striker/Swingfire. (2) Both brigades have 1 x armoured infantry battalion.

THE BATTLEGROUP

A division usually consists of 3 x brigades. These brigades are further sub divided into smaller formations known as battlegroups. The battlegroup is the basic building brick of the fighting formations.

A battlegroup is commanded by a Lieutenant Colonel and the infantry battalion or armoured regiment that he commands provides the command and staff element of the formation. The battlegroup is then structured according to task, with the correct mix of infantry, armour and supporting arms.

The battlegroup organisation is very flexible and the units assigned can be quickly regrouped to cope with a change in the threat. A typical battlegroup fighting a defensive battle might be composed of one armoured squadron and two armoured infantry companies, containing about 600 men, 12 tanks and about 80 armoured personnel carriers.

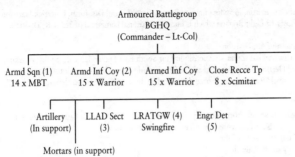

(1) Armoured Squadron
(2) Armoured Infantry Company
(3) LLAD-Low-Level Air Defence – Javelin
(4) LRATGW – Long-Range Anti-Tank Guided Weapon – Swingfire.
(5) Engineer Detachment

The number of battlegroups in a division and a brigade could vary according to the task the formation has been given. As a general rule you could expect a division to have as many as 9 x battlegroups and a brigade to have up to three. The above diagram shows a possible organisation for an armoured battlegroup in either 1(UK) Armd Div or 3(UK) Div.

REGENERATIVE DIVISIONS

There are three Regenerative Divisions, based on older UK military districts. These are the 2nd Division with its Headquarters at Edinburgh, the 4th Division with its Headquarters at Aldershot, and the 5th Division with its Headquarters at Shrewsbury. These Regenerative divisions are responsible for all Army units within their boundaries and could provide the core for three new divisions, should the Army be required to expand to meet a major international threat.

Composition of 2nd Division

The 2nd Division has responsibility for the whole of Scotland and Northern England. The Divisional Headquarters is in Edinburgh. The 2nd Division comprises four brigades and a garrison:

- 15 (North East) Brigade, with its HQ in York, responsible for units in the North East of England
- 42 (North West) Brigade, with its HQ in Preston, responsible for units in the North West of England
- 51 (Scottish) Brigade, with its HQ in Perth, responsible for all units north of Stirling including Shetland and the Western Isles
- 52 (Infantry) Brigade, with its HQ in Edinburgh, with light role infantry battalions at Edinburgh, Chester and Preston under command.

- Catterick Garrison, including units in Ripon, Topcliffe and Dishforth. Catterick Garrison also hosts 19 Light Brigade which is under operational command of 3rd (UK) Division.

Composition of 4th Division

The 4th Division has military responsibility for South East England, including Bedfordshire, Essex and Hertfordshire and its headquarters is in Aldershot. It was previously based in Germany until 1992 as an armoured division. The division now has four brigades under command:

- 2 Brigade based in Shorncliffe. This is a light infantry brigade with battalions based in Chepstow, North Luffenham and Tern Hill under command.
- 49 (East) Brigade in Chilwell
- 145 Brigade in Aldershot
- 16 Air Assault Brigade in Colchester. Administered by 4th Division but under the operational command of HQ Land Command and the Joint Helicopter Command.

Composition of 5th Division

The 5th Division has responsibility for military units and establishments in Wales, the West Midlands and the South West. The Division has its Headquarters is in Shrewsbury and the divisional area of responsibility covers about one third of Great Britain. The following brigades are under command:

- 143 (West Midlands) Brigade based at Shrewsbury
- 160 (Wales) Brigade based at Brecon
- 43 (Wessex) Brigade in Exeter

Northern Ireland

The military presence in support of the civilian authorities in Northern Ireland is controlled by HQ Northern Ireland (HQNI) which is located at Lisburn, just outside Belfast.

The number of armed forces personnel (Army, Navy and RAF), under the command of the General Officer Commanding Northern Ireland (GOC NI), stationed in Northern Ireland at 1 January 2006 was around 7,000 Regular Armed Forces personnel (Excludes Royal Irish Regiment). Since 1969 more than 300,000 soldiers have served in the Province at a cost of 651 dead and 6,116 wounded

The GOC NI also has under his command troops that are rear based in Great Britain that can be called forward to the Province as and when required.

HQNI is responsible for military operations in support of the Police Service of Northern Ireland (PSNI). For command purposes Northern Ireland is subdivided into the following brigade areas:

- 39 Brigade
- 8 Brigade
- 107 (Ulster) Brigade

39 Brigade area corresponds with the PSNI Urban Region and includes Belfast City, the province's two main airports and the seaport of Belfast. In addition 39 Brigade is responsible for half of Lough Neagh, the largest body of inland water in the UK.

8 Brigade area corresponds with the PSNI's Rural Region and includes Londonderry (the second largest city in the Province). The Brigade area includes areas of Antrim, Fermanagh, South Armagh, County Londonderry, mid-Tyrone and Strangford Lough.

107 (Ulster) Brigade supports the Territorial Army in the Province and provides a contingent for the UK's Civil Contingencies Reaction Force Reserve.

Under the operational command of 8 Brigade and 39 Brigade (during early 2006) were:

Army:	4 x Resident Infantry Battalions on roughly two-year tours
	2 x Infantry Battalions on short six-month tours
	1 x Engineer Regiment
	1 x Royal Signals Regiment
	1 x Army Air Corps Regiment
	1 x RLC Logistic Support Regiment
	1 x REME Workshop
	1 x RMP Regiment
	3 x Home Service Battalions of the Royal Irish Regiment
RAF:	1 x Puma Squadron
	1 x RAF Regiment Field Squadron
Navy:	1 x Support and Liaison Detachment

Royal Irish Regiment

During August 2005 the announcement of the disbandment of the three Royal Irish Regiment (Home Service) battalions was made by the Secretary of State for Defence. Disbandment will take place by 1 August 2007, and some 3,000 personnel will be affected.

In mid 2005 there were three home service battalions of the Royal Irish Regiment with a total strength of about 3,400. This figure of 3,400 was made up of about 2,100 full time personnel and 1,300 part time personnel.

Until August 2007 battalion headquarters locations are as follows:

♦ 2nd Battalion The Royal Irish Regiment   –   Holywood
♦ 3rd Battalion The Royal Irish Regiment   –   Armagh
♦ 4th Battalion The Royal Irish Regiment   –   Omagh

The worst year for terrorist violence was in 1972 when 131 service personnel were killed and 578 injured. At one stage in 1972 there were over 30,000 service personnel in the Province supported by another 10,000 police.

Districts

From 1 April 2000 two Districts remain: London (although subordinated to 4th Division for budgetary purposes), and the United Kingdom Support Command (Germany). London is responsible for all Army units within the M25 boundary. The United Kingdom Support Command (Germany) with its Headquarters at Rheindahlen has similar responsibilities, but also provides essential support functions for the 1st Division and the Headquarters of the ARRC.

Activities outside the United Kingdom

The overseas detachments in Canada, Belize, Brunei and Nepal are commanded directly from Headquarters Land Command at Wilton.

Garrisons in Northern Ireland, Cyprus and the Falkland Islands are commanded from the MoD via PJHQ. Operations in Afghanistan, Bosnia, Iraq, Kosovo and Sierra Leone are also commanded by PJHQ.

16 Air Assault Brigade

Nearly 10,000 personnel form the personnel component of 16 Air Assault Brigade. Using everything from the latest Apache helicopter to air-mobile artillery equipment and high velocity air defence missiles, this Brigade has marked a considerable leap forward in Britain's defence capability.

The Brigade capitalises on the combat capabilities of the former 24 Airmobile Brigade and 5 Airborne Brigade, including two parachute battalions with an increase in combat service support. The introduction of the Apache Attack Helicopter has provided a new generation of weapons systems bringing major improvements in military capability. This brigade is under the operational command of the JHC (Joint Helicopter Command) and could be assigned to other formations for operations. On a daily basis the brigade falls under the administrative command of 4th Division.

Until late 2005 the Brigade core group was based around the three battalions of the Parachute Regiment. Under the Future Army Restructuring plans 1 Para will re-role as a 'Ranger' type or Special Forces Support Group available for operations from 2008. It is believed that the Special Forces Support Group will be located at St Athan, in South Wales, close to the SAS headquarters in Hereford.

The other two Parachute Regiment battalions will remain with 16 Air Assault Brigade and continue to provide the lead airborne battlegroup in rotation.

It would appear that 16 Air Assault Brigade will retain 4 x infantry battalions with (possibly) two non Parachute Regiment battalions assigned to the Brigade.

Support helicopters are provided by the RAF (from the Joint Helicopter Command) and the Brigade would normally expect to operate with 18 x Chinook and 18 x Puma. An air assault infantry battalion can be moved by 20 x Chinook equivalents lifts. Each air assault infantry battalion has a personnel strength of 687 and is equipped with 12 x Milan firing posts.

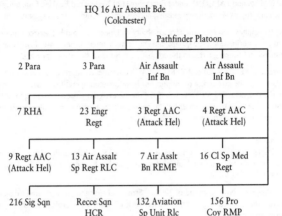

HQ 16 Air Assault Bde
(Colchester)

Pathfinder Platoon

2 Para	3 Para	Air Assault Inf Bn	Air Assault Inf Bn
7 RHA	23 Engr Regt	3 Regt AAC (Attack Hel)	4 Regt AAC (Attack Hel)
9 Regt AAC (Attack Hel)	13 Air Assault Sp Regt RLC	7 Air Asslt Bn REME	16 Cl Sp Med Regt
216 Sig Sqn	Recce Sqn HCR	132 Aviation Sp Unit Rlc	156 Pro Coy RMP

Note: At this stage (early 2006) it is unclear how many non Parachute Regiment Air Assault Battalions will be in the Brigade. In the above diagram we are showing two battalions but it is possible that the final total will be one.

Background to the Future Army Structure (FAS)

During December 2004 the UK MoD made the following announcement regarding FAS.

"The current structure of the Army is based on the most demanding tasks it has to be able to conduct, namely large-scale war-fighting. Experience in the way that the Field Army has been structured in the last seven years has shown that this does not suit the pattern of concurrent medium and small-scale operations that it has been routinely exposed to, particularly for key enablers. FAS will ensure that the Army is structured for the most likely tasks with a true war-fighting capability at its core, whilst retaining the ability to generate for the most demanding tasks.

The requirement to mount expeditionary operations at medium and small scale more rapidly requires a re-balancing from heavy forces to a lighter, more deployable structure. The three mechanised brigades will take on a rapid intervention medium weight role, although it is recognised that they will not achieve the full level of deployability required until the introduction of new air-portable platforms, particularly the Future Rapid Effect System (FRES).

In addition to FRES, the Army's contribution to effects-based warfare will be enhanced by the introduction of the Apache attack helicopter as well as long range precision attack munitions from 155 mm guns and rockets and improved Intelligence, Surveillance, Target Acquisition and Reconnaissance (ISTAR) capabilities. These are in addition to digitised communications

(BOWMAN and FALCON), under the umbrella of Networked Enabled Capability (NEC), which aim to link more closely sensors, decision-makers and weapons systems.

Greater emphasis on expeditionary capability will mean that combat service support units will form robust brigade logistic groups and ensure more force elements are closely matched in readiness and training terms to the combat elements that they are supporting.

Operations TELIC (Iraq) and VERITAS (Afghanistan) have marked the emergence of the TA as the reserve of first choice to support our land forces on operations. Greater integration into the restructured FAS Army will make the TA even more useable and deployable. TA personnel will continue to contribute to enduring commitments on a voluntary basis as they have been doing so effectively over the last few years".

Timetable
FAS Implementation will not happen overnight. FAS has been in the planning stages for several months and a detailed implementation plan has been endorsed by the Army Board and its timetable is as follows:

a.   Phase 1.   Now until end of 2008.   Structural changes. 4 Armoured Brigade will re-role to a mechanised brigade and 19 Mechanised Brigade will re-role to a light brigade via an interim structure.

b.   Phase 2.   2008-2012.   Infrastructure adjustments in place.   FRES experimentation carried out.

c.   Phase 3.   Beyond 2012.   FRES and full range of ISTAR, NEC, deep target attack and Air Manoeuvre capabilities delivered.

Summary
FAS aims to produce a war-fighting Army, geared for expeditionary operations, structured for the most likely tasks at brigade level but able to generate forces for less frequent but larger deployments.   It will be balanced in combat capability, able to deploy, support and maintain forces on operations, with integrated reserves and more predictable tour intervals.

FAS will produce an agile, balanced, intervention capability consisting of medium and light forces underpinned by effective, capable heavy forces able to conduct operations across the full spectrum of conflict.

Details of how FAS will affect the Household Cavalry and the Royal Armoured Corps, Infantry, Artillery, Army Air Corps, Engineers, Communications and Combat Service Support are included within the next section.

UNITS OF THE ARMY (SITUATION AT 1 JANUARY 2006)

THE CAVALRY
Apart from the Royal Tank Regiment, which was formed in the First World War with the specific task of fighting in armoured vehicles, armoured forces (main battle tank and force reconnaissance) in the British Army are provided by the regiments which formed the cavalry

element of the pre-mechanised era. In January 2006 there were 11 x regular armoured regiments and 4 TA Yeomanry Regiments. One of these regiments forms The Household Cavalry and the remaining regiments are known collectively as The Royal Armoured Corps (RAC).

Following FAS changes we believe that the 11 regular field force units of the RAC will be deployed as follows:

♦ <u>In Germany</u>. Three Armoured Regiments and one Force Reconnaissance (FR) Regiment.
♦ <u>In the UK</u>. Two Armoured Regiments, four FR Regiments and the Joint NBC Regiment.

Note: The Household Cavalry Mounted Regiment is permanently stationed in London. The Territorial Army has four Yeomanry Regiments. These units are national defence regiments with a reconnaissance role.

In January 2006 the personnel strength of the The Household Cavalry/ Royal Armoured Corps 5,560

Regimental Titles are as follows:

The Household Cavalry
The Household Cavalry Regiment	HCR
The Household Cavalry Mounted Regiment	HCMRD

The Royal Armoured Corps
1st The Queen's Dragoon Guards	QDG
The Royal Scots Dragoon Guards	SCOTS DG
The Royal Dragoon Guards	RDG
The Queen's Royal Hussars	QRH
9th/12th Royal Lancers	9/12L
The King's Royal Hussars	KRH
The Light Dragoons	LD
The Queen's Royal Lancers	QRL
1st Royal Tank Regiment	1 RTR
2nd Royal Tank Regiment	2 RTR

Armoured Regiment Wiring Diagram

Regiments equipped with Challenger 2 are equipped with 58 tanks and have 600 personnel.

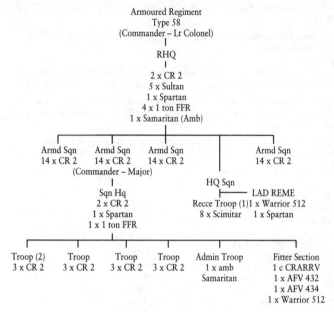

Armoured Regiment
Type 58
(Commander – Lt Colonel)

RHQ

2 x CR 2
5 x Sultan
1 x Spartan
4 x 1 ton FFR
1 x Samaritan (Amb)

| Armd Sqn 14 x CR 2 | Armd Sqn 14 x CR 2 (Commander – Major) | Armd Sqn 14 x CR 2 | | Armd Sqn 14 x CR 2 |

Sqn Hq
2 x CR 2
1 x Spartan
1 x 1 ton FFR

HQ Sqn ── LAD REME
Recce Troop (1) 1 x Warrior 512
8 x Scimitar 1 x Spartan

| Troop (2) 3 x CR 2 | Troop 3 x CR 2 | Troop 3 x CR 2 | Troop 3 x CR 2 | Admin Troop 1 x amb Samaritan | Fitter Section 1 c CRARRV 1 x AFV 432 1 x AFV 434 1 x Warrior 512 |

Notes:

(1) Recce Troop under direct command of CO in the field.

(2) Tank Troop commanded by 2Lt/Lt with Troop Sergeant as 2ic in own tank. The third tank is commanded by a Corporal.

(3) Totals: 58 x CR2, 8 x SCIMITAR, 4 x CRARV. Total strength for war is approx 550.

(4) A Challenger 2 has a crew of 4 – Commander, Driver, Gunner and Loader/Operator.

The Infantry

The British Infantry is based on the well tried and tested Regimental System that has been justified regularly on operational deployment. It is based on battalions, which (with the exception of the Foot Guards) are generally part of larger regiments. Most regiments have both Regular (active) battalions and Territorial Army (reserve) battalions. Regiments are generally grouped together within Divisions, which provide a level of administrative command.

The Division of Infantry is an organisation that is responsible for all aspects of military administration, from recruiting, manning and promotions for individuals in the regiments under its wing, to the longer term planning required to ensure continuity and cohesion. Divisions of Infantry have no operational command over their regiments, and should not be confused with the operational divisions such as 1(UK) Armd Div and 3 (UK) Div.

At the end of 2005 the Divisions of Infantry were as follows:

The Guards Division	–	5 regular battalions
The Scottish Division	–	5 regular battalions
The Queen's Division	–	6 regular battalions
The King's Division	–	5 regular battalions
The Prince of Wales Division	–	5 regular battalions
The Light Division	–	5 regular battalions

Not administered by Divisions of Infantry but operating under their own administrative arrangements are the following:

The Parachute Regiment	–	3 regular battalions
The Brigade of Gurkhas	–	2 regular battalions
The Royal Irish Regiment	–	1 regular battalion

TA battalions are under the administrative command (from early 2007) of the following:

The Guards Division	–	Possibly 1 TA Battalion (LONDONS)
The Scottish Division	–	2 TA battalions
The Queen's Division	–	3 TA battalions
The King's Division	–	2 TA battalions
The Prince of Wales Division	–	2 TA battalions
The Light Division	–	2 TA battalions
The Parachute Regiment	–	1 TA battalion
The Royal Irish Regiment	–	1 TA battalion

At the beginning of 2006 the British Army had 37 regular battalions available for service and this total combined with the 14 TA battalions could give a mobilisation strength of 51 infantry battalions.

Outside of the listed Regiments of the Guards Division, are three companies of guardsmen each of 110 men, who are provided to supplement the Household Division Regiments while on public duties in London. This allows the battalions on public duties to continue to carry out normal training on roulement from guard duties.

Gibraltar also has its own single battalion of the Royal Gibraltar Regiment comprising one Regular and two volunteer companies.

During mid 2006 the infantry were grouped as follows:

United Kingdom	–	28 x battalions (including 4 Resident in Northern Ireland)
Germany	–	6 x battalions

Cyprus	–	2 x battalions
Falkland Islands	–	1 x company group on detachment
Balkans	–	1 x composite battalion on detachment
Brunei	–	1 x battalion (Gurkha)
Iraq	–	2 x battalion groups (on detachment from UK/Germany)
Afghanistan	–	2 x battalions (on detachment from UK/Germany)

As explained previously, it would be most unusual for the Infantry to fight as battalion units especially in armoured or mechanised formations. The HQ of an infantry battalion will generally be the HQ of a battle group, and the force will be provided with armour, artillery, engineers, and possibly aviation to enable it to become a balanced all arms grouping.

Infantry personnel strength in January 2006 was 24,520.

UK Infantry Battalions (From early 2007)

Current title	New title

The Guards Division

1st Bn Grenadier Guards	1st Bn Grenadier Guards	1 GREN GDS
1st Bn Coldstream Guards	1st Bn Coldstream Guards	1 COLDM GDS
1st Bn Scots Guards	1st Bn Scots Guards	1SG
1st Bn Irish Guards	1st Bn Irish Guards	1 IG
1st Bn Welsh Guards	1st Bn Welsh Guards	1 WG

The Scottish Division

The Royal Regiment of Scotland (from March 2006)

Regular Bns

1st Bn The Royal Scots (The Royal Regiment)	On merger becomes The Royal Scots Borderers, 1st Bn The Royal Regiment of Scotland	1 SCOTS
1st Bn The King's Own Scottish Borderers	On merger becomes The Royal Scots Borderers, 1st Bn The Royal Regiment of Scotland *as above*	1 SCOTS (as above)
1st Bn The Royal Highland Fusiliers (Princess Margaret's Own Glasgow and Ayrshire Regiment)	The Royal Highland Fusiliers, 2nd Bn The Royal Regiment of Scotland	2 SCOTS
1st Bn The Black Watch (Royal Highland Regiment)	The Black Watch, 3rd Bn The Royal Regiment of Scotland	3 SCOTS
1st Bn The Highlanders (Seaforth, Gordons and Camerons)	The Highlanders, 4th Bn The Royal Regiment of Scotland	4 SCOTS

1st Bn The Argyll and Sutherland Highlanders (Princess Louise's)	The Argyll and Sutherland Highlanders, 5th Bn The Royal Regiment of Scotland	5 SCOTS

Territorial Army Bns

52nd Lowland Regiment	52nd Lowland, 6th Bn The Royal Regiment of Scotland	6 SCOTS
51st Highland Regiment	51st Highland, 7th Bn The Royal Regiment of Scotland	7 SCOTS

The Queen's Division
The Princess of Wales's Royal Regiment (Queen's and Royal Hampshires)

Regular Bns

1st Bn The Princess of Wales's Royal Regiment (Queen's and Royal Hampshires)	1st Bn The Princess of Wales's Royal Regiment (Queen's and Royal Hampshires)	1 PWRR
2nd Bn The Princess of Wales's Royal Regiment (Queen's and Royal Hampshires)	2nd Bn The Princess of Wales's Royal Regiment (Queen's and Royal Hampshires)	2 PWRR

Territorial Army Bn

3rd Bn The Princess of Wales's Royal Regiment (Queen's and Royal Hampshires)	3rd Bn The Princess of Wales's Royal Regiment (Queen's and Royal Hampshires)	3 PWRR

The Royal Regiment of Fusiliers
Regular Bns

1st Bn The Royal Regiment of Fusiliers	1st Bn The Royal Regiment of Fusiliers	1 RRF
2nd Bn The Royal Regiment of Fusiliers	2nd Bn The Royal Regiment of Fusiliers	2 RRF

Territorial Army Bn

The Tyne Tees Regiment	5th Bn The Royal Regiment of Fusiliers	5 RRF

The Royal Anglian Regiment
Regular Army Bns

1st Bn The Royal Anglian Regiment	1st Bn The Royal Anglian Regiment	1 R ANGLIAN
2nd Bn The Royal Anglian Regiment	2nd Bn The Royal Anglian Regiment	2 R ANGLIAN

Territorial Army Bn

The East of England Regiment	3rd Bn The Royal Anglian Regiment	3 R ANGLIAN

The King's Division
The Duke of Lancaster's Regiment (King's, Lancashire and Border) (from July 2006)

Regular Bns

Elements of 1st Bn The King's Own Royal Border Regiment; 1st Bn The King's Regiment and 1st Bn The Queen's Lancashire Regiment	1st Bn The Duke of Lancaster's Regiment (King's, Lancashire and Border)	1 LANCS
Elements of 1st Bn The King's Own Royal Border Regiment; 1st Bn The King's Regiment and 1st Bn The Queen's Lancashire Regiment	2nd Bn The Duke of Lancaster's Regiment (King's, Lancashire and Border)	2 LANCS

Territorial Army Bn

The Lancastrian and Cumbrian Volunteers	4th Bn The Duke of Lancaster's Regiment (King's, Lancashire and Border)	3 LANCS

The Yorkshire Regiment (from June 2006)

Regular Bns

1st Bn Prince Of Wales's Own Regiment Of Yorkshire	1st Bn The Yorkshire Regiment (Prince Of Wales's Own)	1 YORKS
1st Bn The Green Howards (Alexandra, Princess of Wales's Own Yorkshire Regiment)	2nd Bn The Yorkshire Regiment (Green Howards)	2 YORKS
1st Bn The Duke Of Wellington's Regiment (West Riding)	3rd Bn The Yorkshire Regiment (Duke of Wellington's)	3 YORKS

Territorial Army Bn

The East and West Riding Regiment	4th Bn The Yorkshire Regiment	4 YORKS

The Prince of Wales's Division
The Mercian Regiment (from August 2007)

Regular Bns

1st Bn The Cheshire Regiment	1st Bn The Mercian Regiment (Cheshire)	1 MERCIAN
1st Bn The Worcestershire and Sherwood Foresters Regiment (26th/45th Foot)	2nd Bn The Mercian Regiment (Worcesters and Foresters)	2 MERCIAN

1st Bn The Staffordshire Regiment (The Prince of Wales's)	3rd Bn The Mercian Regiment (Staffords)	3 MERCIAN

Territorial Army Bn

The West Midlands Regiment	4th Bn The Mercian Regiment	4 MERCIAN

The Royal Welsh (from March 06)

Regular Bns

1st Bn The Royal Welch Fusiliers	1st Bn The Royal Welsh (The Royal Welch Fusiliers)	1 R WELSH
1st Bn The Royal Regiment of Wales (24th/41st Foot)	2nd Bn The Royal Welsh (The Royal Regiment of Wales)	2 R WELSH

Territorial Army Bn

The Royal Welsh Regiment	3rd Bn The Royal Welsh	3 R WELSH

The Light Division

The Rifles (from early 2007)

Regular Bns

1st Bn The Devonshire and Dorset Light Infantry and 1st Bn The Royal Gloucestershire, Berkshire and Wiltshire Light Infantry	1st Bn The Rifles	1 RIFLES
Elements from 1st Bn The Royal Green Jackets; 2nd Bn The Royal Green Jackets; 1st Bn The Light Infantry and 2nd Bn The Light Infantry	2nd Bn The Rifles	2 RIFLES
Elements from 1st Bn The Royal Green Jackets; 2nd Bn The Royal Green Jackets; 1st Bn The Light Infantry and 2nd Bn The Light Infantry	3rd Bn The Rifles	3 RIFLES
Elements from 1st Bn The Royal Green Jackets; 2nd Bn The Royal Green Jackets; 1st Bn The Light Infantry and 2nd Bn The Light Infantry	4th Bn The Rifles	4 RIFLES

Elements from 1st Bn The Royal Green Jackets; 2nd Bn The Royal Green Jackets; 1st Bn The Light Infantry and 2nd Bn The Light Infantry	5th Bn The Rifles	5 RIFLES

Territorial Army Bns

The Rifle Volunteers	6th Bn The Rifles	6 RIFLES
The Royal Rifle Volunteers	7th Bn The Rifles	7 RIFLES

The Royal Irish Regiment

Regular Bns

1st Bn The Royal Irish Regiment	1st Bn The Royal Irish Regiment	1 R IRISH

Territorial Army Bn

The Royal Irish Rangers	The Royal Irish Rangers	RANGERS

The Parachute Regiment

Regular Bns

1st Bn, The Parachute Regiment	1st Bn The Parachute Regiment	1 PARA
2nd Bn, The Parachute Regiment	2nd Bn The Parachute Regiment	2 PARA
3rd Bn, The Parachute Regiment	3rd Bn The Parachute Regiment	3 PARA

Note: 1 PARA will form the core element of the new Special Forces Support Group and be removed from the formal Infantry structure

Territorial Army Bn

4th Bn, The Parachute Regiment	4th Bn The Parachute Regiment	4 PARA

The Brigade of Gurkhas

1st Bn The Royal Gurkha Rifles	1st Bn The Royal Gurkha Rifles	1 RGR
2nd Bn The Royal Gurkha Rifles	2nd Bn The Royal Gurkha Rifles	2 RGR

The London Regiment

Territorial Army Bn

The London Regiment	The London Regiment	LONDONS

Note: We await an announcement from the UK MoD that would place The London Regiment under the administrative arrangements of the Household Division

From April 2002 there are four infantry training battalions at the Infantry Training Centre (ITC Catterick).

Special Forces

The Special Air Service: Although not strictly part of the Infantry, the SAS (Special Air Service) has a single regular battalion established to carry out special operations. SAS soldiers are selected from other branches of the Army after exhaustive selection tests. There are two regiments of TA SAS.

Special Reconnaissance Regiment (SRR): This Regiment was declared operational on 6 April 2005 and has been formed to meet a growing worldwide demand for a special reconnaissance capability.

The SRR will ensure improved support to international expeditionary operations and will provide a wide range of specialist skills and activities related to covert surveillance. The SRR will draw personnel from existing capabilities and recruit new volunteers from serving members of the Armed Forces where necessary. Due to the specialist nature of the unit it will come under the command of Director Special Forces and be a part of the UK Special Forces group.

Special Forces Support Group: Under the Future Army Structuring plans 1 Para will re-role as a 'Ranger' type or Special Forces Support Group available for operations from 2008.

It is believed that the Special Forces Support Group will be located at St Athan, in South Wales, close to the SAS headquarters in Hereford. The force will be composed of around 450 Parachute Regiment soldiers and 200 personnel from both the Royal Marines and the RAF Regiment.

Soldiers wishing to become part of the Special Forces Support Group will need to be able to offer more than the average infantryman but the entrance requirements will be different from those of the SAS.

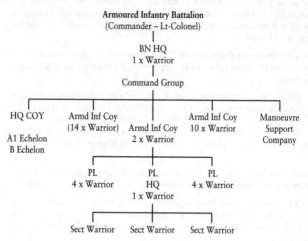

Armoured Infantry Battalion
(Commander – Lt-Colonel)

BN HQ
1 x Warrior

Command Group

HQ COY

A1 Echelon
B Echelon

Armd Inf Coy
(14 x Warrior)

Armd Inf Coy
2 x Warrior

Armd Inf Coy
10 x Warrior

Manoeuvre
Support
Company

PL
4 x Warrior

PL
HQ
1 x Warrior

PL
4 x Warrior

Sect Warrior   Sect Warrior   Sect Warrior

Totals:

52 x Warrior, 12 x Milan (or LF ATGW), 21 x AFV 432, 8 x Sabre, 6 x 81 mm Mortar, 741 All Ranks.

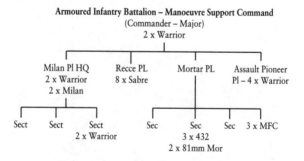

Armoured Infantry Battalion – Manoeuvre Support Command
(Commander – Major)
2 x Warrior

Milan Pl HQ
2 x Warrior
2 x Milan

Recce PL
8 x Sabre

Mortar PL

Assault Pioneer
Pl – 4 x Warrior

Sect   Sect   Sect
2 x Warrior

Sec   Sec   Sec   3 x MFC
3 x 432
2 x 81mm Mor

Note:

(1) There are 9 x Armoured Infantry Battalions, six of which are in Germany with 1 (UK) Armoured Division and the remaining three in the UK with 3 (UK) Division.

(2) There are plans to replace the AFV 432s on issue to armoured infantry battalions by other versions of Warrior or equivalent vehicles such as mortar carrier, ambulance, command vehicle etc.

(3) Another 4 Milan (or LF ATGW) firing posts are held by the section that is only activated in time of deployment for war.

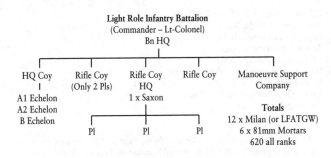

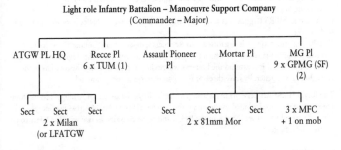

Notes:

(1) TUM is the abbreviation for Truck-Utility-Medium

(2) Air Assault Bns have an HMG Pl with 6 x .50 Calibre Machine guns mounted on TUM.

THE ROYAL REGIMENT OF ARTILLERY (RA)

Background

The Royal Regiment of Artillery (RA) provides the battlefield fire support and air defence for the British Army in the field. Its various regiments are equipped for conventional fire support using field guns, for area and point air defence using air defence missiles and for specialised artillery locating tasks.

The RA remains one of the larger organisations in the British Army with 15 Regiments included in its regular Order of Battle. Current personnel figures suggest a total of approximately 1,000 officers and 6,500 soldiers.

During late 2005 the RA had the following structure in both the UK and Germany.

	UK	Germany
Field Regiments (AS 90 SP Guns)	2	3
Field Regiments (Light Gun)		2(1) –
Depth Fire Regiments (MLRS)	1(2)	–
Air Defence Regiments (Rapier)	1	–
Air Defence Regiment (HVM)	1	1
Surveillance & Target Acquisition Regiment	1	–
Phoenix UAV Regiment	1	–
Training Regiment (School Assets Regt)	1	–
The Kings Troop (Ceremonial)	1	–

Note:
(1) Of these two Regiments one is a Commando Regiment (29 Cdo Regt) and the other is an Air Assault Regiment(7 PARA RHA). A third Regiment (40 Regiment) is in the process of converting to the Light Gun. Either of these Regiments can be called upon to provide Manoeuvre Support Artillery to reaction forces.
(2) A second MLRS Regiment is now a TA Regt with 12 Launch vehicles in peace uprateable to 18 in war.
(3) Although the artillery is organised into Regiments, much of the 'Gunner's' loyalty is directed towards the battery in which they serve. The guns represent the Regimental Colours of the Artillery and it is around the batterys where the guns are held that history has gathered. A Regiment will generally have three or four gun batterys under command.

The Royal Horse Artillery (RHA) is also part of the Royal Regiment of Artillery and its three regiments have been included in the totals above. There is considerable cross posting of officers and soldiers from the RA to the RHA, and some consider service with the RHA to be a career advancement.

Future Army Structure
Under the terms of the Future Army Structure (FAS) the following changes will take place.

a. One AS90 Regiment (40 Regt RA) will re-role as a Light Gun Regiment in support of 19 Light Brigade.

b. The Gun Groups of three AS90 batteries will be cut.

c. An additional UAV battery, a rocket battery and a STA battery will be established. Providing direct support for the activities of the Field Army will be a new surveillance and target acquisition (STA) battery equipped with the MAMBA (Ericsson ARTHUR) weapon locating radar to be formed by redeploying personnel from a former ground air defence regiment (22 Regiment RA). Other personnel from 22 Regiment are to be used to form an additional unmanned aerial vehicle (UAV) battery, while the remaining third will be re-allocated to allow the formation of a multiple rocket launcher battery.

d. There will be an overall reduction in Ground Based Air Defence but the Rapier capability will be owned and operated by the RA.

e. Tactical Groups for Formation Reconnaissance regiments and the 4th Light Role Battalion in 16 Air Assault Brigade will be established, and there will be enhancements to the current Aviation Tactical Group to provide better support for the attack helicopter regiments.

f. The FAS documentation also noted the investment being made in HUMINT for fire-support purposes. For this role the Honourable Artillery Company (HAC – a reserve regiment)is devoted to surveillance and target (STA) acquisition patrolling. The HAC provides a number of battery level patrol groupings.

Artillery training is carried out at the Royal School of Artillery at Larkhill in Wiltshire. After initial training officers and gunners will be posted to RA units worldwide, but soldiers will return to the RSA for frequent career and employment courses. Artillery recruits spend the first period of recruit training (Common Military Syllabus) at the Army Training Regiment – Lichfield.

The Royal Artillery provides the modern British armoured formation with a protective covering. The air defence covers the immediate airspace above and around the formation, with the field artillery reaching out to approximately 30 km in front and across the flanks of the formation. An armoured formation that moves out of this protective covering is open to immediate destruction by an intelligent enemy.

Divisional Artillery Group (DAG)

An armoured or mechanised division has it own artillery under command. This artillery usually consists of three Close Support Regiments, with a number of units detached from the Corps Artillery and could include TA reinforcements. In war the composition of the DAG will vary according to the task.

The following is a diagram of the artillery support available to a UK division. Expect each brigade in the division to have one Close Support Regiment with AS90 under command.

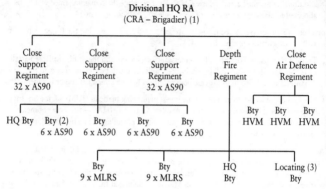

Notes:

(1) This is a diagram of the artillery support which may typically be available to an Armd Div deployed with the ARRC. Expect each brigade in the division to have one Close Support Regiment with AS 90. The Staff of an armoured or mechanised division includes a Brigadier of Artillery known as the Commander Royal Artillery (CRA). The CRA acts as the artillery advisor to the Divisional Commander, and would probably assign one of his Close Support Regiments to support each of the Brigades in the division. Artillery regiments are commanded by a Lieutenant Colonel and a battery is commanded by a Major.

(2) The number of batteries and guns per battery in an AS 90 Close Support Regiment has changed post SDR 1999 to four batteries of six guns per battery in the UK Regiments, and three batteries of six guns in the Regiments stationed in Germany.

(3) Expect the Locating Battery to have a unmanned air vehicle (UAV) troop, a Cobra radar troop and a meteorological troop.

At the beginning of 2006 Regiments of the Royal Artillery were as follows:

Field Army

1 Regiment RHA	155 mm AS 90
3 Regiment RHA	155 mm AS 90
4 Regiment RA	155 mm AS 90
5 Regiment RA	STA & Special Ops (1)
7 Parachute Regiment RHA	105 mm Lt Gun
12 Regiment RA	HVM
14 Regiment RA	All School Equipments
16 Regiment RA	Rapier
19 Regiment RA	AS 90
26 Regiment RA	155 mm AS 90
29 Commando Regiment RA	105 mm Light Gun (2)

47 Regiment RA	HVM	
32 Regiment RA	UAVs	
39 Regiment RA	MLRS	
40 Regiment RA	Light Gun	
The King's Troop RHA	13-Pounders (Ceremonial)	

Notes:

(1) STA – Surveillance and target acquisition.

(2) The Regimental HQ of 29 Commando Regiment with one battery is at Plymouth. The other two batterys are at Arbroath and Poole. Those at Poole provide the amphibious warfare Naval Gunfire Support Officers (NGSFO).

TA Artillery Regiments (early 2006)

HAC	London	STA and Special Ops
100 Regt RA (V)	Luton	Light Gun
101 Regt RA (V)	Newcastle	MLRS (12 in peace)
103 Regt RA (V)	Liverpool	Light Gun
104 Regt RA (V)	Newport	HVM
105 Regt RA (V)	Edinburgh	HVM
106 Regt RA (V)	London	HVM

Under the Future Army Structure plans the TA Artillery will comprise the following:

> 1 x OP Regiment
> 1 x STA/MLRS Regiment
> 1 x Ground Based Air Defence (HVM) Regiment
> 3 x Close Support Regiments
> 1 x UAV/General Support Regiment

ARMY AIR CORPS

Battlefield helicopters have played a major role in UK military operations since the 1960s. The AAC battlefield helicopter fleet has accumulated a vast amount of operational experience in recent years, and is arguably a more capable force than that possessed by any other European nation.

The flexibility of battlefield helicopters was demonstrated in 2003 during Operation TELIC in Iraq. Here 3 Regiment, Army Air Corps, with two Pumas from the Support Helicopter Force attached, was deployed forward as a combined-arms battlegroup, initially within 16 Air Assault Brigade and later in conjunction with 7 Armoured Brigade. The 3 Regiment battlegroup had responsibility for an area that extended over 6,000 square kilometres, and provided a versatile combat arm during the warfighting phase. In the immediate aftermath of hostilities, helicopters proved to be the most efficient means of covering the vast operational area allocated to British forces, and also in distributing humanitarian aid to isolated villages.

Force structure

The Army obtains its aviation support from Army Air Corps (AAC), which is an organisation with six separate regiments and a number of independent squadrons. The AAC also provides support for Northern Ireland on a mixed resident and roulement basis and the two squadrons concerned are sometimes referred to as the seventh AAC Regiment, although the units would disperse on mobilisation and have no regimental title.

AAC manpower is believed to number some 1,980 personnel of all ranks. Unlike the all-officer Navy and Air Force helicopter pilot establishments, almost two-thirds of AAC aircrew are non-commissioned officers. The AAC is supported by REME and RLC personnel numbering some 2,600 all ranks. Total AAC-related manpower is believed to be about 5,000 personnel of all ranks.

With certain exceptions, during peace, all battlefield helicopters come under the Joint Helicopter Command (JHC). Under strategic planning guidelines released by the MoD in 2004, the core operational formation of the AAC will remain the Air Assault Brigade – currently 16 Air Assault Brigade.

The introduction into AAC service of the WAH-64D Apache Longbow attack helicopter between 2004 and 2007 is transforming AAC doctrine, organisation, and order of battle. The British Army designation of the type is Apache AH Mk1. As of early 2006, the first Apache AH Mk1 aircraft were coming into service with front line squadrons. The decision has been taken to concentrate the Apache AH Mk 1 into three Attack Regiments.

The AAC is to equip these three Aviation Attack Regiments with a total of 48 x Apache AH Mk 1 attack helicopters. Pilot training on Apache is well under way, and AAC and RAF Support Helicopter Squadrons are being forged into a new Air Manoeuvre Arm within 16 Air Assault Brigade which includes two Battalions of the Parachute Regt. The three newly equipped Attack Regiments will be 9 Regt at Dishforth in Yorkshire, and 3 and 4 Regiments at Wattisham in Suffolk – with a full operating capability expected by June 2007.

Each attack regiment will have 2 x attack squadrons equipped with 8 x Apache AH Mk1 attack helicopters and 1 x support squadron equipped with 8 x Lynx. The Gazelle Helicopter has already started to be phased out by several units as the Apache AH Mk 1 is being introduced. The capability gap left will be filled by introducing the Battlefield Light Utility Helicopter (BLUH) in this capacity. Several Gazelle Helicopters will, however, continue to be retained for specialist tasks as required. The Lynx Helicopter will also be phased out as the Apache AH Mk 1 will replace it in its attack helicopter role. Ultimately, however, the Lynx will be replaced by the BLUH (which may be Lynx-based, according to indications in 2006).

The current (early 2006) AAC Regimental and Squadron locations are shown below. The Attack Regiments equipping with Apache AH Mk 1s are forming, and it is not at present clear whether the new regiments will retain existing squadron numbers.

Army Air Corps force structure and helicopters (early 2006)

Regiment	Squadron	Location	Helicopter/aircraft	Fleet
1 Regiment	652,661	Germany	Lynx, Gazelle	16
3 Attack Regiment	653,662 & 663	Wattisham	Apache, Lynx (forming)	24

4 Attack Regiment	654,659 & 669	Wattisham	Apache, Lynx (forming)	24
5 Regiment	655,665	Aldergrove	Lynx, Gazelle, Islander	43
9 Attack Regiment	656,664,672	Dishforth	Apache, Lynx	24
2 Regiment (Training)	670, 671,673	Middle Wallop	Apache, Lynx, Gazelle	36
Independent units				
Joint Special Forces				
Aviation Wing	657	Odiham	Lynx	12
Development & Trials	667	Middle Wallop	Lynx	6
Initial Training	660	Shawbury	Squirrel HT 1	12
7 Regiment (TA)	658, 666	Netheravon	Gazelle	12

Flights include 3 (TA) Flight (Leuchars), 6 (TA) Flight (Shawbury)

7 Flight (Brunei), 8 Flight (Herford, 12 Flight (Germany), 25 Flight (Belize), 29 BATUS Flight – Canada

The AAC Centre at Middle Wallop in Hampshire acts as a focal point for all Army Aviation, and it is here that the majority of corps training is carried out. Although the AAC operates some fixed-wing aircraft for training and liaison flying, the main effort goes into providing helicopter support for the land forces. About 200 AAC helicopters are believed to be in operational service in early 2006.

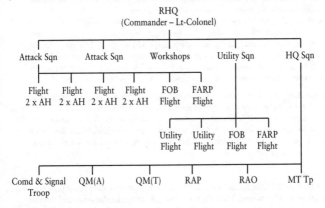

Totals: 8 x LUH (Light Utility Helicopters)
16 x AH (Attack Helicopters)

Notes:
FOB – Forward Operating Base; FARP – Forward Area Rearm/Refuel Point; RAP – Regimental Aid Post; RAO – Regimental Admin Officer; QM (A) – Quartermaster Admin; QM (T) – Quartermaster Technical

Background

The engineer support for the Army is provided by the Corps of Royal Engineers (RE). Known as Sappers, the Royal Engineers are one of the Army's six combat arms, and are trained as fighting soldiers as well as specialist combat engineers. The Corps of Royal Engineers performs highly specialised combat and non-combat, and is active all over the world in conflict and peacetime. The Corps has no battle honours, its motto *'ubique'* (everywhere), signifies that it has taken part in every battle fought by the British Army in all parts of the world.

Role

The Royal Engineers provide specialist support to the combat formations and engineer detachments can be found at all levels from the Combat Team/Company Group upwards. Combat Engineer tasks are amongst the following:

- **Defence:** Construction of field defences; laying anti-tank mines; improvement and construction of obstacles.
- **Attack:** Obstacle crossing; demolition of enemy defences (bunkers etc); mine clearance; bridge or ferry construction.
- **Advance:** Building or strengthening roads and bridges; removal of booby traps; mine clearance; airfield construction; supply of water; survey.
- **Withdrawal:** Demolition – of airfields, roads and bridges, fuel, ammunition and food dumps, railway tracks and rolling stock, industrial plant and facilities such as power stations; route clearance; laying anti-tank mines; booby trapping likely enemy future positions and items that might be attractive to the enemy. Often amongst the first soldiers into battle, and still involved in dangerous tasks such as mine clearance in the former Yugoslavia, the Sappers can turn their hands to almost any engineering task.

Recent military operations have once again highlighted the importance of combat engineers. Tasks for which engineer support was requested stretched the resources of the Corps to its limit and the first priority in almost any operational call for support is for engineers. Tracks have to be improved, roads must be built, water and power provided, mines lifted and where necessary accommodation constructed. All of these are engineer tasks that soak up large amounts of manpower.

Force structure

As of January 2006, the RE had a regular Army establishment of some 9,460 personnel and a strength of 8,780 personnel. These figures are for UK trained regular army, and therefore exclude Gurkhas, Full Time Reserve Service Personnel, and mobilised reservists. The figures also exclude those with the rank of Colonel and above who are held against staff strength and requirement. This large corps comprises 15 regular regiments (including two training regiments) and five TA regiments – presently organised as follows:

Royal Engineers: Regular Army units and locations during early 2006

Unit	Location	Country	Notes
21 Engineer Regt	Osnabruck	Germany	4 Armoured Brigade
22 Engineer Regt	Perham Down	UK	1 Mechanised Brigade
23 Engineer Regt	Woodbridge	UK	16 Air Assault Brigade
25 Engineer Regt	Antrim	UK	Supports Headquarters Northern Ireland
26 Engineer Regt	Ludgersall	Germany	3 Division
28 Engineer Regt	Hameln	Germany	Amphibious Engineers, 1 Armoured Division
32 Engineer Regt	Hohne	Germany	7 Armoured Brigade
33 Engineer Regt	Wimbish	UK	EOD
35 Engineer Regt	Paderborn	Germany	20 Armoured Brigade
36 Engineer Regt	Maidstone	UK	3 Division
38 Engineer Regt	Ripon	UK	19 Light Brigade, 16 Air Assault Brigade
39 Engineer Regt	Waterbeach	UK	RAF Support
42 Engineer Regt	Hermitage	UK	Geographic survey

The former Gurkha Engineer Regiment QGE (Queen's Gurkha Engineers) now forms part of 36 Engineer Regiment, comprising 50 Headquarters Squadron, two wheeled field squadrons (20 Field Squadron and 69 Gurkha Field Squadron) and an engineer logistic squadron (70 Gurkha Field Support Squadron).

There are also a number of independent engineer squadrons/units in the UK, as shown in the next table:

Royal Engineers: Specialist units and locations during early 2006

Unit	Location	Country	Notes
12 (Air Support) Engineer Brigade	Waterbeach	UK	Air support
29 (Corps Support) Engineer Brigade	Aldershot	UK	Corps support
59 Independent Commando Squadron	Barnstaple	UK	Commando
62 Cyprus Support Squadron	Cyprus	Cyprus	Cyprus
Military Works Force, Queen's Gurkha Engineers	Nottingham	UK	Gurkhas
Works Group RE (Airfields)	Wallingford	UK	Airfields
Engineer Resources	Bicester	UK	Logistics
Engineer Training Advisory Team (ETAT)	Sennelager	Germany	Training
Geographic Engineer Group	Hermitage	UK	Geographic survey
Band of the Corps of Royal Engineers	Chatham	UK	Band

Territorial Army Royal Engineer regiments and independent units are shown below:

Royal Engineers: Territorial Army units and locations in 2006

Unit	Location	Country
71 Engineer Regiment (V)	Fife	UK
73 Engineer Regiment (V)	Nottingham	UK
75 Engineer Regiment (V)	Manchester	UK
Royal Monmouthshire RE (Militia)	Monmouth	UK
101 Engineer Regiment (V) EOD	Catford	UK
131 Independent Commando Sqn (V)	London	UK
135 Independent Commando Sqn (V)	Ewell	UK
HQ RE Territorial Army	AldershotUK	
Central Volunteer HQ RE	Minley	UK
Military Works Force	Minley	UK

Contingents of Royal Engineers (including Volunteer Reservists) are likely to be deployed in all combat zones, including most recently Afghanistan, Iraq, Balkans, Democratic Republic of Congo, Georgia, Liberia and Sierra Leone.

Future Army Structure (FAS)

Under the late 2004 FAS proposals the following enhancements to the Royal Engineers will be implemented:

a. A new Commando Engineer Regiment (24 Commando Engineer Regiment) will be established.
b. An Air Support RHQ and associated HQ and Support Squadron will be established by the re-roling of 25 Engineer Regiment's RHQ and HQ and Support Squadron following Northern Ireland Normalisation.
c. An additional EOD squadron will be formed.
d. Two additional Close Support (CS) squadrons will be generated in order to provide support to all battlegroups within the armoured and mechanised brigades.
e. The resources cells in Field Support Squadrons will be decaderised.
f. The geographic capability will be enhanced.
g. Counter mobility support will be established within the specialist brigades.
h. Engineer reconnaissance will be embedded into formation reconnaissance regiments.
i. The Military Work Force will be enhanced and 535 Specialist Team Royal Engineers transferred from Northern Ireland on following normalisation.

Engineer Organisations

The smallest engineer unit is the field troop which is usually commanded by a Lieutenant and consists of approximately 44 men. In an armoured division a field troop can be expected to have up to four sections and each section is mounted in an APC. Engineer Regiments in the UK may have only three sections and may be mounted in wheeled vehicles such as Land Rovers and 4-Ton Trucks. An engineer troop will carry equipment, stores and explosives to enable it to carry out its immediate battlefield tasks.

Armoured Divisional Engineer Regiment (1)

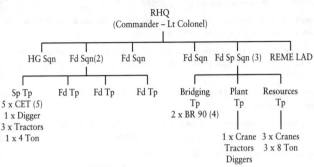

Strength: Approx 650–750 All Ranks

1) This Regiment would send most of its soldiers to man the engineer detachments that provide support for a Division's battlegroups

(2) Field Squadron (a Field Squadron will have approximately 68 vehicles and some 200 men)

(3) Field Support Squadron

(4) Or Medium Girder Bridge

(5) Combat Engineer Tractor

This whole organisation is highly mobile and built around the AFV 432 and Spartan series of vehicles. In addition to the Regimental REME LAD, each squadron has its own REME section of approximately 12 – 15 men.

THE ROYAL CORPS OF SIGNALS

The Royal Corps of Signals

The Royal Corps of Signals (R Signals) is the combat arm that provides the communications throughout the command system of the Army. Individual battlegroups are responsible for their own internal communications, but in general terms, all communications from Brigade level and above are the responsibility of the Royal Signals.

Information is the lifeblood of any military formation in battle and it is the responsibility of the Royal Signals to ensure the speedy and accurate passage of information that enables commanders to make informed and timely decisions, and to ensure that those decisions are passed to the fighting troops in contact with the enemy. The rapid, accurate and secure employment of command, control and communications systems maximises the effect of the military force available and consequently the Royal Signals act as an extremely significant 'Force Multiplier'. The Corps motto is 'First In Last Out'.

Royal Signals Missions

Royal Signals units have the following principal missions:

Communications Engineering: Communications units design, build and dismantle the tactical communications networks at division and brigade levels.

Communications Operations: Communications units operate the tactical communications networks at division and brigade levels, and also battalion and battalion group level in the case of a detached formation.

In conventional divisional and brigade level operations, battalions will typically be responsible for their own communications.

Communications Management: Communications units are responsible for the management of the whole communications nexus at division and brigade level.

These missions will need to be performed in all phases of battle:

Offensive: In the offensive: setting up command posts, setting up area communications networks and setting up wire networks to connect battalions to brigades and elsewhere as far as possible. Can set up air portable communications systems shortly after a foothold is secured on air base.

Advance: In the advance: continuing to keep forward and area communications running and providing logistics and maintenance needs for company and brigade forces as appropriate. Running wire forwards as far as possible with the advance, Setting up alternate Brigade HQs. Relocating and maintaining relay and retransmission points and ensuring communications to rear and flanks remain open.

Defensive: In the defence: re-enforcing command posts and relay points. Increasing the complexity and robustness of wire networks. Providing alternate and redundant communications for all users.

Withdrawal: In the withdrawal: Preventing communications assets falling into enemy hands, setting up alternate command posts on the line of withdrawal, running wire networks backwards to rear. Keeping nodes open and supplying logistics and maintenance support as required.

Non-Combat missions: Communications perform non-combat roles during peacetime, including national peacetime contingencies and multilateral peace support operations in foreign countries.

Force structure

As of January 2006, the Royal Signals had a regular Army establishment of some 8,440 personnel and a strength of 8,640 personnel. The Corps has eleven Regular Army regiments (including one training regiment), and 11 Territorial Army regiments, each generally consisting of between three and up to six Squadrons with between 600 and 1,000 personnel.

Royal Signals personnel are found wherever the Army is deployed including every UK and NATO headquarters in the world. The Headquarters of the Corps is at the Royal School of Signals (RSS) located at Blandford in Dorset.

Royal Signals units based in the United Kingdom provide command and control communications for forces that have operational roles both in the UK itself, including Northern Ireland, and overseas including mainland Western Europe and further afield wherever the Army finds itself. There are a number of Royal Signals units permanently based in Germany, Holland and Belgium from where they provide the necessary command and control communications and Electronic Warfare (EW) support for both the British Army and other NATO forces based in Europe. Royal Signals personnel are also based in Cyprus, the Falkland Islands, Belize and Gibraltar. Regular Army Royal Signals units are shown in the following table:

Royal Signals: Regular Army units during early 2006

Unit	Location	Notes
1 Sig Bde	Germany	Supports Allied Rapid Reaction Corps (ARRC)
2 (NC) Sig Bde	Corsham HQ	Mainly TA, national communications during contingencies
11 Sig Bde	Donnington HQ	1,000 Regular and 2,500 TA personnel, communications for JRRF
3(UK)Div HQ & Sig Regt	Bulford	Divisional command and control communications
2 Sig Regt	York	With 11 Signal Bde, currently equipping with Cormorant system
10 Sig Regt	Forming	To form part of 2 Sig Bde
14 Sig Regt (EW)	Brawdy	Electronic Warfare
15 Sig Regt	N.Ireland	Command & Control communications
21 Sig Regt (Air Sp)	JHF	Communications for the RAF Support Helicopter Force and AAC Apache
30 Sig Regt	Bramcote	Strategic satellite communications to Land & Joint Task Forces
22 Sig Regt	Forming	Falcon communications
1(UK)AD and Sig Regt	Germany	Communications for 1st (UK) Armd Div HQ and Bdes
7 (ARRC) Sig Regt	Germany	Part of 1 Sig Bde, supports Allied Rapid Reaction Corps (ARRC)
16 Sig Regt	Germany	Part of 1 Sig Bde, supports Allied Rapid Reaction Corps (ARRC)
11 Signal Regt	Blandford	Training Regt, responsible for Phase 2 and 3 signals training
Queens Gurkha Signals	Various	Support 2 Gurkha Inf Bns, 2 and 30 Sig Regts, and others

209 Sig Sqn	Catterick	Independent Sqn, supporting 19 Light Brigade HQ
213 Sig Sqn	Lisburn	Independent Sqn, supporting 39 Infantry Brigade HQ
215 Sig Sqn	Tidworth	Independent Sqn, supporting 1 Mechanised Bde within 3 Div
216 Sig Sqn	Colchester	Independent Sqn, supporting 16 Air Assault Bde HQ
218 Sig Sqn	Londonderry	Independent Sqn, supporting 8 Inf Bde HQ
228 Sig Sqn	Bulford	Independent Sqn, supporting 12 Mech Bde HQ
238 Sig Sqn	London	Independent Sqn, supports London Military District
242 Sig Sqn	Edinburgh	Independent Sqn, supports Army in Scotland & Northern England
261 Sig Sqn	Aldershot	Independent Sqn, supports 101 Logistics Bde HQ
264 Sig Sqn	Hereford	Independent Sqn, supports SAS
200 Sig Sqn	Germany	Independent Sqn, supporting 20 Armd Brigade HQ
204 Sig Sqn	Germany	Independent Sqn, supporting 4 Armd Brigade HQ
207 Sig Sqn	Germany	Independent Sqn, supporting 7 Armd Brigade HQ
262 Sig Sqn	Germany	Independent Sqn, supporting 102 Logistics Brigade HQ
628 Sig Tp	Netherlands	Independent Tp, supports AFNORTH HQ
CCU & JSSU	Cyprus	Cyprus Communications Unit and Joint Service Signal Unit
JCU (FI)	Falklands	Joint Communications Unit (Falkland Islands)

TA Units

Major Royal Signals Territorial Army (TA)units are shown in the next table.

Royal Signals : Territorial Army units during early 2006

Unit	Location
2 (NC) Sig Bde	Corsham HQ
11 Sig Bde	Donnington HQ
31 Sig Regt (V)	London
32 Sig Regt	Scotland
33 Sig Regt (V)	Lancashire & Cheshire
34 Sig Regt (V)	Yorkshire, Durham & Northumberland
35 Sig Regt (V)	South Midlands
36 Sig Regt (V)	East Anglia and Essex
37 Sig Regt (V)	Wales, Midlands, Lancashire

Unit	Location
Unit	*Location*
38 Sig Regt (V)	Yorkshire, Notts, Derbyshire, Leicester
39 Sig Regt (V)	Somerset, Gloucester, Home Counties, Oxon
40 Sig Regt (V)	Ireland
32 Sig Regt (V)	
Central Volunteer Headquarters Royal Signals (CVHQ)	London
63 Sig Sqn (V)	Independent Sqn, supports TA SAS units
81 Sig Sqn (V)	Part of CVHQ
97 Sig Sqn (V)	Independent Sqn (38 Sig Regt)
98 Sig Sqn (V)	Independent Sqn (11 Sig Bde)

Future Army Structure (FAS)

Under the FAS proposals the Regular Units of the Royal Signals will be enhanced as follows:

a. A new Signal Regiment (22 Signal Regiment) will be established, equipped initially with Ptarmigan and then Falcon.
b. Deployable unit structures (operational Divisional Signal Regiments and Brigade Signal Squadrons) will be made more robust.

Enhancements will be made to strategic communications.

The Royal Signals TA will be structured as follows:

a. There will be three Ptarmigan regiments based within 11 Signal Brigade, providing a composite Ptarmigan Regiment to the Allied Rapid Reaction Corps.
b. Within 2 (NC) Signals Brigade, a total of eight signals regiments (including 36 and 40 Signal Regiments) and four sub-units will provide NC (National Communications) units in support of the Home Defence MACA (Military Aid to the Civil Authority). In addition these units will provide bespoke support to other government departments.
c. 63 Signals Squadron (SAS) will continue to support Director Special Forces.
d. An Air Support Signal Troop will be provided for Joint Headquarters.
e. Royal Signals TA will continue to provide individual reinforcements to the Regular regiments attributed to LSDI.

Training

All Royal Signals officers undergo officer training at RMA Sandhurst (44 weeks) before taking the Royal Signals Troop Commanders' Course at the Royal School of Signals at Blandford Camp. Royal Signals officers are expected to have or to obtain university degree-level engineering qualifications.

Recruit training for other ranks involves two phases:

♦ Phase 1 – Soldier training (11 to 21 weeks: apprentices 6 months)
♦ Phase 2 – Trade training (7 – 50 weeks)

Every Royal Signals soldier, whether from the Army Training Regiment, the Army Technical Foundation College Arborfield, or the Army Apprentices College Arborfield, carries out trade training at the Royal School of Signals at Blandford Camp. The length of the course depends on the trade chosen, varying from seven weeks up to 50 weeks. All trades will carry out a common module of Basic Signalling Skills and a computer literacy module before specialising. Special Operators attend an introductory course of two weeks at the Royal School of Signals before completing their training at the Defence Special Signal School in Chicksands.

11 Signal Regiment is responsible for the special to arm training for both officers and other ranks. The Royal School of Signals at Blandford Camp conducts approximately 144 different types of courses and numbers over 714 courses run per year. There are in excess of 5,250 students completing courses throughout the year with about 1,070 here at any one time. These figures equate to approximately some 470,000 Man Training Days a year.

Organisation

We would expect the organisation of a Signal Regiment supporting an armoured division to be as follows:

Armoured Divisional Signal Regiment Organisation

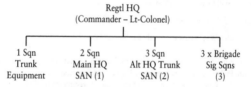

Notes: (1) SAN – Secondary Access Node (2) A Divisional HQ will have two HQs to allow for movement and possible destruction. The main HQ will be set up for approx 24 hrs with the alternative HQ (Alt HQ) set up 20-30 km away on the proposed line of march of the division. When the Main HQ closes to move to a new location, the Alt HQ becomes the Main HQ for another 24-hour period. (3) Expect a Brigade Sig Sqn to have a Radio Troop and a SAN Troop.

THE ROYAL LOGISTIC CORPS (RLC)

The RLC is the youngest Corps in the Army and was formed in April 1993 as a result of the recommendations of the MoD's Logistic Support Review. The RLC results from the amalgamation of the Royal Corps of Transport (RCT), the Royal Army Ordnance Corps (RAOC), the Army Catering Corps (ACC), the Royal Pioneer Corps (RPC) and elements of the Royal Engineers (RE). In January 2006 the RLC had a regular Army establishment of some 15,700 personnel and a strength of 15,860.

Role

The RLC has very broad responsibilities throughout the Army that include the movement of personnel throughout the world, the Army's air dispatch service, maritime and rail transport, operational re-supply, and explosive ordnance disposal which includes the hazardous bomb disposal duties in Iraq, Afghanistan and the mainland UK, the operation of numerous very large vehicle and stores depots both in the UK and overseas, the training and provision of cooks to virtually all units in the Army, the provision of pioneer labour and the Army's postal and courier service.

Force Structure

There are 22 Regular RLC Regiments (20 operational and two training regiments) and under the terms of the Future Army Structure the RLC TA will probably be structured around 15 regiments plus the Catering Support Regiment RLC (V).

The principal field elements of the RLC are the Close Support and the General Support Regiments whose primary role is to supply the fighting units with ammunition, fuel and rations (Combat Supplies).

A division has an integral Close Support Regiment which is responsible for manning and operating the supply chain to Brigades and Divisional units.

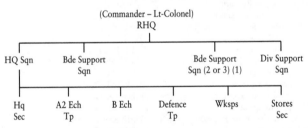

Close Support Regiment (RLC)

Notes:
(1) A regiment could have two or three Brigade Support Squadrons depending upon the size of the Division being supported.
(2) Some of these Regiments may have a Postal and Courier Squadron

The General Support Regiment's role is primarily to supply ammunition to the Royal Artillery using DROPS vehicles and to provide Tank Transporters that move armoured vehicles more rapidly and economically than moving them on their own tracks.

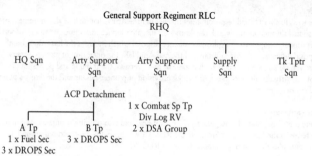

General Support Regiment RLC
RHQ

- HQ Sqn
- Arty Support Sqn
  - ACP Detachment
    - A Tp
      - 1 x Fuel Sec
      - 3 x DROPS Sec
    - B Tp
      - 3 x DROPS Sec
- Arty Support Sqn
  - 1 x Combat Sp Tp
  - Div Log RV
  - 2 x DSA Group
- Supply Sqn
- Tk Tptr Sqn

Both types of Regiment have large sections holding stores both on wheels and on the ground. A Division will typically require about 1,000 tons of Combat Supplies a day but demand can easily exceed that amount in high intensity operations.

RLC Regular Regiments

1 General Support Regiment	1 (GS) REGT
2 Close Support Regiment	2 (CS) REGT
3 Close Support Regiment	3 (CS) REGT
4 General Support Regiment	4 (GS) REGT
5 Territorial Army Training Regiment	5 (TRG) REGT
6 Support Regiment	6 (SP) REGT
7 Transport Regiment	7 (TPT) REGT
8 Artillery Support Regiment	8 (ARTY SP) REGT
9 Supply Regiment	9 (SUP) REGT
10 Transport Regiment	10 (TPT) REGT
11 Explosive Ordnance Disposal Regiment	11 (EOD) REGT
12 Supply Regiment	12 (SUP) REGT
13 Air Assault Support Regiment	13 (AIR ASSLT) REGT
14 Supply Regiment	14 (SUP) REGT
17 Port and Maritime Regiment	17 (PORT) REGT
21 Logistic Support Regiment	21 (LOG SP) REGT
23 Pioneer Regiment	23 (PNR) REGT
24 Regiment	24 REGT
27 Transport Regiment	27 (TPT) REGT
29 Regiment	29 REGT
89 Postal and Courier Regiment	89 (PC) REGT
Queen's Own Gurkha Logistic Regiment	QGLR

THE ROYAL ELECTRICAL & MECHANICAL ENGINEERS (REME)

Equipment Support remains separate from the other logistic pillar of Service Support and consequently the REME has retained not only its own identity but expanded its responsibilities. Equipment Support encompasses equipment management, engineering support, supply management, provisioning for vehicle and technical spares and financial management responsibilities for in-service equipment. In January 2006 the REME had a regular Army establishment of some 9,680 personnel and a strength of 9,730.

Role

The aim of the REME is "To keep operationally fit equipment in the hands of the troops" and in the current financial environment it is important that this is carried out at the minimum possible cost. The equipment that REME is responsible for ranges from small arms and trucks to helicopters and main battle tanks. All field force units have some integral REME support (1st line support) which will vary, depending on the size of the unit and the equipment held, from a few attached tradesmen up to a large Regimental Workshop of over 200 men. In war REME is responsible for the recovery and repair of battle damaged and unserviceable equipment.

The development of highly technical weapon systems and other equipment has meant that REME has had to balance engineering and tactical considerations. On the one hand the increased scope for forward repair of equipment reduces the time out of action, but on the other hand engineering stability is required for the repair of complex systems.

Force Structure

Seven REME Equipment Support Battalions have been established. Six of these battalions provide second line support for the British contribution to the ACE Rapid Reaction Corps (ARRC) and formations in the UK. Three battalions are based in the UK and three battalions are based in Germany to support 1(UK) Armoured Division. An Equipment Support Aviation Battalion in the UK supports the Army Air Corps units assigned to the Joint Helicopter Command.

There are currently four TA REME Equipment Support Battalions but under the Future Army Structure proposals, each armoured and mechanised brigade will be supported by a REME Battalion.

The Close Support Company will normally deploy a number of FRG's (Forward Repair Groups) and MRGs (Medium Repair Groups) in support of brigades. The company is mobile with armoured repair and recovery vehicles able to operate in the forward areas, carrying out forward repair of key nominated equipment often by the exchange of major assemblies. It is also capable of carrying out field repairs on priority equipment including telecommunications equipment and the repair of damage sustained by critical battle winning equipments.

The role of the General Support Company is to support the Close Support Companies and Divisional Troops. Tasks include the regeneration of fit power packs for use in forward repair and the repair of equipment backloaded from Close Support Companies. The General Support Company will normally be located to the rear of the divisional area in order to maximise productivity and minimise vulnerability.

ARMY MEDICAL SERVICES

Royal Army Medical Corps (RAMC)

In peace, the personnel of the RAMC are based at the various medical installations throughout the world or in field force units and they are responsible for the health of the Army.

In January 2006 the RAMC had a regular Army establishment of some 3,270 personnel and a strength of 2,910 (950 x officers and 1,860 other ranks).

Role

The primary role of the Corps is the maintenance of health and the prevention of disease. On operations, the RAMC is responsible for the care of the sick and wounded, with the subsequent evacuation of the wounded to hospitals in the rear areas. Each Brigade has a medical squadron which is a regular unit that operates in direct support of the battlegroups. These units are either armoured, airmobile or parachute trained. In addition, each division has two TA field ambulance units that provide medical support for the divisional troops and can act as manoeuvre units for the forward brigades when required.

Force Structure

All medical squadrons have medical sections that consist of a medical officer and eight Combat Medical Technicians. These sub-units are located with the battlegroup or units being supported and they provide the necessary first line medical support. In addition, the field ambulance provides a dressing station where casualties are treated and may be resuscitated or stabilised before transfer to a field hospital. These units have the necessary integral ambulance support, both armoured and wheeled to transfer casualties from the first to second line medical units.

Field hospitals may be regular or TA and all are 200 bed facilities with a maximum of eight surgical teams capable of carrying out life-saving operations on some of the most difficult surgical cases. Since 1990, most regular medical units have been deployed on operations either in Iraq, Afghanistan or the former Yugoslavia.

Casualty Evacuation (CASEVAC) is by ambulance either armoured or wheeled and driven by RLC personnel or by helicopter when such aircraft are available. A Chinook helicopter is capable of carrying 44 stretcher cases and a Puma can carry six stretcher cases and six sitting cases.

During early 2006 the Regular element of the RAMC was capable of providing 8 x major units (5 x Medical Regiments and 3 x Hospitals). The TA provides up to 15 x Hospitals and Field Ambulances.

The Queen Alexandra's Royal Army Nursing Corps (QARANC)

On 1 April 1992 the QARANC became an all-nursing and totally professionally qualified Corps. Its male and female, officer and other rank personnel, provide the necessary qualified nursing support at all levels and covers a wide variety of nursing specialities. QARANC personnel can be found anywhere in the world where Army Medical services are required. During early 2006 the QARANC strength was approximately 840 all ranks.

Royal Army Dental Corps (RADC)

The RADC fulfils the essential role of maintaining the dental health of the Army in peace and war, both at home and overseas. Qualified dentists and oral surgeons, hygienists, technicians and support ancillaries work in a wide variety of military units – from static and mobile dental clinics to field medical units, military hospitals and dental laboratories. During early 2006 the RADC strength was approximately 370 all ranks (approximately 110 officers).

THE ADJUTANT GENERAL'S CORPS (AGC)

The Adjutant General's Corps was formed on 1 April 1992 and its sole task is the management of the Army's most precious resource, its soldiers. The Corps absorbed the functions of six existing smaller corps; the Royal Military Police, the Royal Army Pay Corps, the Royal Army Educational Corps, the Royal Army Chaplain's Department, the Army Legal Corps and the Military Provost Staff Corps.

The Corps is organised into four branches, Staff and Personnel Support (SPS), Provost (PRP), Educational and Training Services (ETS) and Army Legal Services (ALS). During early 2006 the AGC consisted of over 6,800 officers and soldiers as follows:

Personnel Totals – Adjutant General's Corps	Strength
Adjutant General's Corps (Provost Branch)	2,010
Adjutant Generals Corps (Staff and Personnel Support Branch)	4,440
Adjutant Generals Corps (Educational and Training Services Branch)	340
Adjutant Generals Corps Royal (Army Legal Service)	100
	6,890

The Role of the Provost Branch

The Provost Branch was formed from the formerly independent Corps of Royal Military Police (RMP) and the Military Provost Staff Corps (MPSC). Although they are no longer independent they are still known as the AGC (PRO) and AGC (MPS) thus forming the two parts of the Provost Branch.

Royal Military Police

To provide the police support the Army requires, the RMP has the following functions:

♦ Providing operational support to units in the field
♦ Preventing crime
♦ Enforcement of the law within the community and assistance with the maintenance of discipline
♦ Providing a 24 hour response service of assistance, advice and information.

Operational support includes advising commanders and the staff who produce the operational movement plans. RMP traffic posts are deployed along the main operational movement routes and provide a constant flow of traffic information regarding the progress of front line troops and the logistical resupply. RMP units with a vehicle to man ratio of 1:3 are also a valuable force for the security of rear areas. In addition, there is a highly trained RMP close protection group that specialises in the protection of high risk VIPs.

The RMP provides the day to day police support for both the army in the UK and dependents and MoD civilians overseas. RMP units are trained and equipped to deal with the most serious crimes. The Special Investigation Branch (SIB) operates in a similar fashion to the civilian CID.

The Military Provost Staff

AGC(MPS) staff recruited from within the Army are carefully selected for the leadership, management and training skills necessary to motivate the predominantly young offenders with whom they work. The majority of AGC(MPS) personnel are located in the Military Corrective Training Centre (MCTC) at Colchester where offenders sentenced by military courts are confined.

The Role of SPS Branch

The role of SPS Branch is to ensure the efficient and smooth delivery of Personnel Administration to the Army. This includes support to individual officers and soldiers in units by processing pay and Service documentation, first line provision of financial, welfare, education and resettlement guidance to individuals and the provision of clerical skills and information management to ensure the smooth day to day running of the unit or department.

AGC (SPS) officers are employed throughout the Army, in direct support of units as Regimental Administrative Officers or AGC Detachment Commanders. They hold Commander AGC(SPS) and SO2 AGC(SPS) posts in district/Divisional and Brigade HQs and fill posts at the Adjutant General's Information Centre (AGIC) and general staff appointments throughout the Army headquarters locations.

AGC(SPS) soldiers are employed as military clerks in direct support of units within the AGC Field Detachments, in fixed centre pay offices, in headquarters to provide staff support and in miscellaneous posts such as embassy clerks, as management accountants or in AGIC as programmer analysts.

Currently, about 66% of AGC(SPS) soldiers are based in UK, 23% in Germany and 11% elsewhere. The majority, currently 70% serving with field force units, with the remaining 30% in base and training units or HQs, such as the MoD.

Members of AGC(SPS) are first trained as soldiers and then specialise as Military Clerks. AGC(SPS) officers complete the same military training as their counterparts in other Arms and Services, starting at the Royal Military Academy, Sandhurst. They are required to attend all promotion courses such as the Junior Command and Staff Course, and to pass the standard career exams prior to promotion to the rank of Major.

The Role of the ETS Branch

The AGC(ETS) Branch has the responsibility for improving the efficiency, effectiveness and morale of the Army by providing support to operations and the developmental education, training, support and resettlement services that the Army requires to carry out its task. ETS personnel provide assistance at almost all levels of command but their most visible task is the manning of Army Education Centres wherever the Army is stationed. At these centres officers and soldiers receive the educational support necessary for them to achieve both civilian and military qualifications.

The Role of the ALS Branch

The AGC(ALS) Branch advises on all aspects of service and civilian law that may affect every level of the Army from General to Private soldiers. Members of the branch are usually qualified as solicitors or barristers. In addition to the AGC personnel attached to major units throughout the Army the Corps is directly responsible for the following:

SMALLER CORPS

THE INTELLIGENCE CORPS (Int Corps) – The Int Corps deals with operational intelligence, counter-intelligence and security (Personnel strength in January 2006 was 1,440).

THE ROYAL ARMY VETERINARY CORPS (RAVC) – The RAVC looks after the many animals that the Army has on strength. Veterinary tasks in today's army are mainly directed towards guard or search dogs and horses for ceremonial duties (Personnel strength in January 2006 was 190).

THE ARMY PHYSICAL TRAINING CORPS (APTC) – Consists mainly of SNCOs who are responsible for unit fitness. The majority of major units have a representative from this corps on their strength (Personnel strength in January 2006 was 440).

SMALL ARMS SCHOOL CORPS (SASC) – A small corps with the responsibility of training instructors in all aspects of weapon handling (Personnel strength in January 2006 was 150).

THE GENERAL SERVICE CORPS (GSC) – A holding unit for specialists. Personnel from this corps are generally members of the reserve army.

The Royal Gibraltar Regiment

Gibraltar also has its own single battalion of the Royal Gibraltar Regiment comprising one regular and two volunteer companies.

THE REGULAR ARMY RESERVE

Types of Reservist

Members of the Army Reserve fall into two main components:

♦ Retired regular reserve
♦ Volunteer reserve

Strength of the Reserve Forces at 1 April 2005 was as follows:

Component Category	Total	
Regular Reserve	Army Reserve	31,420
	Individuals liable to recall	102,760
Volunteer Reserve	Territorial Army	32,480
	OTC	4,770
Total Reserve Strength	Regular Reserve + Volunteer Reserve	177,430

Retired regular reserve

The Regular reserve is comprised of people who have a mobilisation obligation by virtue of their former service in the regular army. For the most part, these reservists constitute a standby rather than ready reserve, and are rarely mobilised except in times of national emergency or incipient war. Some 420 retired regular reservists were called-up for Iraq operations in 2003.

The Regular Reserve consists of Individual Reservists (IR), who have varying obligations in respect of training and mobilisation, depending on factors such as length of regular service, age and sex. Categories of Individual Reservists are as follows:

♦ Officer Reserve – with a compulsory training obligation of four to six years after leaving regular or reserve service
♦ Regular Reserve – non-commissioned officers and other ranks who have a compulsory training obligation of up to six years after leaving regular service
♦ Long-term Reserve – men (but not women) who have completed their Regular Reserve obligation, who serve in this capacity until the age of 45 and who have no training obligation
♦ Military pensioners – ex-regular personnel who have completed pensionable service, who have a legal liability for recall up to the age of 60 (55 is the maximum age in general practice), and who have no training obligation

Many ex-regulars join the Volunteer Reserve Forces after leaving regular service – giving them a dual Reserve status.

Volunteer Reserve

The Volunteer reserve consists mainly of people who have joined the Territorial Army directly from the civilian community. These personnel form the main part of the active, ready reserve for the British Army, train regularly, and are paid at the same rates as the regular forces on a pro-rata basis.

Most TA volunteers commit to a minimum of some 40 days training a year, comprising one drill night in a week, one week-end in a month and 14 days annual training. Some reservists exceed these minima.

The Reserve Forces Act 1996 provided for other categories of reservists, such as:

♦ Full-Time Reserve Service (FTRS) – reservists who wish to serve full-time with regulars for a predetermined period in a specific posting
♦ Additional Duties Commitment – part-time service for a specified period in a particular post.

The Act also provided two new categories of service, including:

♦ Sponsored Reserves, being contractor staff who have agreed to join the Reserves and have a liability to be called up when required to continue their civilian work on operations alongside the Service personnel who depend upon them. Some 1,500 sponsored reservists have served in Iraq.

Territorial Army units are widely dispersed across the country – much more so than the Regular Forces, and in many areas they are the visible face of the Armed Forces. They help to keep society informed about the Armed Forces, and of the importance of defence to the nation, and have an active role supporting the Cadet organisations. They provide a means by which the community as a whole can contribute to Britain's security.

Territorial Army Restructuring 2006

Plans to make the Territorial Army (TA) more capable and relevant to future operations were announced by Armed Forces Minister Adam Ingram in March 2006.

These changes form part of a broader Army restructuring, under the Future Army Structure (FAS) initiative, which should allow the Army to deploy more rapidly though the creation of new medium-sized fighting units. The new structure requires an Army in which Regular and Reserve elements are more closely linked than ever before.

The proposed changes will give the TA:

♦ Enhanced training opportunities – TA units will work more closely with their Regular counterparts making it easier for TA soldiers to integrate when they are mobilised
♦ Over 1600 more Engineers, 400 more 'Yeomanry' (Royal Armoured Corps), 400 more Army Air Corps and more Intelligence Corps and other supporting services
♦ Fewer infantry (910), signallers (120), logisticians (220) and volunteer Army Medical Corps (1600), however it is expected most will change role and very few will need or want to leave

- Increased support for TA recruits, with more full-time staff responsible for administration, welfare, training and employer support.

These changes should result in the formation of five new regiments and there will be no change in the overall size of the TA, nor to its budget.

The TA infantry will be reorganised to form 14 TA infantry battalions as an integral part of the Future Infantry Structure. TA battalions will now be named after the regular Regiments of which they will form a part, rather than after the regions in which they are based.

Three TA centres (out of around 350) will revert to Cadet centres, but any displaced personnel will be offered the chance of transferring to other units. The changes will take place over a number of years.

TA units will work more closely with their Regular counterparts. Each TA unit will be affiliated with two Regular units; a primary affiliation with a unit that it is expected to join on operations, and a secondary affiliation with a unit with whom it will work for routine training. Training with Regular counterparts will make it easier for TA soldiers to integrate when they are mobilised.

The new TA Regiments to be formed are:

- 1 x Army Air Corps regiment to support the Apache Attack Helicopter regiments in the regular army
- 1 x Engineer Regiment in the North East
- 1 x Military Intelligence battalion, also in the North East
- 1 x Transport Regiment, in the South West
- 1 x Supply Regiment, based in Stoke on Trent

The establishment size of the TA will remain at around 42,000 personnel. The current TA establishment size is 41,914 with TA Manning at around 82 per cent.

The detail regarding the future TA structure is given in the table below:

Current Structure	Personnel	Future Structure	Personnel
Royal Armoured Corps			
4 x Yeomanry Regts	1319	4 x Yeomanry Regts	1750
Royal Artillery			
1 x OP Regt	3014	1 x OP Regt	2507
1 x MLRS Regt		1 x STA/MLRS Regt	
3 x GBAD Regts		1 x GBAD Regts	
2 x Close Support Regts		3 x Close Support Regts	
		1 x UAV/GS Regt	
Royal Engineers			
2 x Close Support Regts	3084	1 x Close Support Regts	4678
2 x Airfield Support Regts		2 x Airfield Support Regts	
1 x EOD Regt		1 x EOD Regt	
1 x Geographic Squadron		1 x Geographic Squadron	
1 x Commando Squadron		1 x Commando Squadron	

Current Structure	Personnel	Future Structure	Personnel
1 x Amphibious Troop		1 x Amphibious Troop	
1 x Military Works Force		2 x General Support Regts	
		1 x Independent CS Squadron	
		1 x Infrastructure Support Gp	

Royal Signals

3 x PTARMIGAN Regts	5387	3 x PTARMIGAN Regts	
6 x National Comms Regts		8 x National Comms Regts	
2 x EUROMUX Regts		5 x Sqns	
7 x Sqns			

Infantry

15 x Battalions	7540	14 x Battalions	6687

Army Air Corps

1 x LUH Regt	156	1 x LUH Regt	550
		1 x AH Support Regt	

Royal Logistic Corps

5 x Transport Regts	6824	9 x Transport Regts	6602
2 x Logistic Support Regts		2 x Supply Regts	
1 x Support Regt		1 x Pioneer Regt	
1 x Pioneer Regt		1 x Port Regt	
1 x Port Regt		1 x Movement Control Regt	
2 x Movement Control Regts		1 x Postal Regt	
2 x Postal Regts		1 x Catering Support Regt	
1 x Catering Support Regt			

Royal Army Medical Corps

1 x Ambulance Regt	6884	3 x General Support Med Regts	5268
11 x Field Hospitals		11 x Field Hospitals	
1 x Medical Evacuation Regt		1 x Medical Evacuation Regt	
4 x Field Ambulances		5 x Medical Sqns	
5 x Medical Sqns			

Royal Electrical & Mechanical Engineers

4 x Battalions	1635	4 x Battalions	1557

Intelligence Corps

1 x Battalion	508	2 x Battalions	704

Royal Military Police

4 x Companies	379	4 x Companies	618

Abbreviations: OP – Observation Post; MLRS – Multi Launch Rocket System; GBAD – Ground Based Air Defence; STA – Surveillance and Target Acquisition Regiment; UAV – Unmanned Air Vehicle; GS – General Support; CS – Close Support; LUH – Light Utility Helicopter; AH – Apache Helicopter; Tpt – Transport; Med – Medical.

The TA Order of Battle in late 2005 (before restructuring) was as follows:

Territorial Army units, as identified in late 2005

Unit location	HQ Location	Company/Squadron/Battery
Infantry		
Tyne Tees Regt	Durham	Scarborough; Middlesborough; Bishop Auckland; Newcastle; Ashington.
King's and Cheshire Regt	Warrington	Liverpool; Warrington; Manchester; Crewe.
51st Highland Regiment	Perth	Dundee; Peterhead; Inverness; Dunbarton; Stirling.
52nd Lowland Regiment	Glasgow	Edinburgh; Ayr; Glasgow; Galashiels.
East and West Riding Regt	Pontefract	Huddersfield; Barnsley; Hull; York; Wakefield.
East of England Regiment	Bury St Edmunds	Norwich; Lincoln; Leicester; Mansfield; Chelmsford.
London Regiment	Battersea	Westminster; Edgeware; Balham; Camberwell; Mayfair; West Ham.
3rd (Volunteer) Battalion, Princess of Wales's Royal Regt	Canterbury	Farnham; Brighton; Canterbury.
Royal Rifle Volunteers	Reading	Oxford; Reading; Portsmouth; Milton Keynes.
Rifle Volunteers	Exeter	Gloucester; Taunton; Dorchester; Truro; Exeter.
West Midlands Regiment	Wolverhampton	Birmingham; Kidderminster; Burton; Stoke; Shrewsbury.
Royal Welsh Regiment	Cardiff	Wrexham; Swansea; Cardiff; Colwyn Bay.
Lancastrian & Cumbrian Volunteers	Preston	Barrow in Furness; Blackburn; Workington; Preston.
Royal Irish Rangers	Portadown	Newtonards; Newtonabbey.
4th (Volunteer) Battalion, The Parachute Regiment	Pudsey	London; Pudsey; Glasgow.
Royal Armoured Corps		
Royal Yeomanry	London	Swindon; Leicester; Croydon; Nottingham; London.
Royal Wessex Yeomanry	Bovington	Bovington; Salisbury; Cirencester; Barnstable.
Royal Mercian & Lancastrian Yeomanry	Telford	Dudley; Telford; Chester; Wigan.
Queen's Own Yeomanry	Newcastle	York; Ayr; Belfast; Cupar; Newcastle.

Royal Artillery

Honourable Artillery Company	London	5 all based in the City of London.
100 Regiment	Luton	Luton; Bristol; Nottingham.
101 Regiment	Gateshead	Blyth; Newcastle; South Shields.
103 Regiment	St Helens	Liverpool; Manchester; Bolton.
104 Regiment	Newport	Wolverhampton; Newport; Worcester.
105 Regiment	Edinburgh	Newtownards; Glasgow; Arbroath.
106 Regiment	London	Bury St Edmunds; London; Leeds: Southampton.
Central Volunteers HQ RA	London	

Royal Engineers

Royal Monmouthshire RE (Militia)	Monmouth	Cwmbran; Swansea; Warley.
71 Regiment	Leuchars	Paisley; Newcastle.
73 Regiment	Nottingham	Sheffield; Nottingham; Chesterfield; St Hellier(Jersey).
75 Regiment	Failsworth	Birkenhead; Stoke on Trent; Walsall.
101 Regiment	London	London; Rochester; Tunbridge Wells.
131 Independent Commando Squadron	London	
135 Topographical Squadron	Ewell	
412 Amphibious Engineer Troop	Hameln	
Central Volunteer HQ RE	Camberley.	

Royal Signals

31 Signal Regiment	London	Coulsdon; Eastbourne; London.
32 Signal Regiment	Glasgow	Aberdeen; East Kilbride; Edinburgh.
33 Signal Regiment	Huyton	Manchester; Liverpool; Runcorn.
34 Signal Regiment	Middlesborough	Leeds; Darlington; Middlesborough.
35 Signal Regment	Coventry	Birmingham; Newcastle-Under-Lyme; Rugby; Shrewsbury.
36 Signal Regiment	Ilford	Grays; Colchester; Cambridge.
37 Signal Regiment	Redditch	Cardiff; Stratford-Upon-Avon; Manchester; Coventry.
38 Signal Regiment	Sheffield	Derby; Sheffield; Nottingham.
39 Signal Regiment	Bristol	Uxbridge; Banbury; Gloucester.
40 Signal Regiment	Belfast	Belfast; Limavady; Bangor.
71 Signal Regiment	London	Lincolns Inn; Bexleyheath; Chelmsford.
1 Signal Squadron	Bletchley.	
2 Signal Squadron	Dundee.	
5 Communications Company	Chicksands.	

63 Signal Squadron (SAS)		
81 Sig Sqn (V)	London	
97 (BRITFOR) Signal Sqn	Balkans	
98 Sig Sqn (V)	Donington	

Royal Logistic Corps

150 (Northumbria) Transport Regt	Hull	Hull; Tynemouth; Leeds; Doncaster.
151 Logistic Support Regiment	Croydon	Romford; Sutton; Barnet; Southall.
156 Transport Regiment	Liverpool	Liverpool; Birkenhead; Salford; Bootle.
157 Logistic Support Regiment	Cardiff	Cardiff; Telford; Swansea; Carmarthen; West Bromwich.
158 Transport Regiment	Peterborough	Peterborough; Kempston; Ipswich; Loughborough.
Scottish Transport Regiment	Dunfermline	Dunfermline; Glasgow; Edinburgh; Glenrothes; Irvine.
168 Pioneer Regiment	Grantham	Grantham; Cramlington; Coulby Newham.
CVHQ and HR RLC TA	Grantham.	

Royal Electrical & Mechanical Engineers

101 Battalion REME	Queensferry	Prestatyn; Coventry; Clifton; Grangemouth.
102 Battalion REME	Newton Aycliffe	Newton Aycliffe; Rotherham; Scunthorpe; Newcastle upon Tyne.
103 Battalion REME	Crawley	Portsmouth; Redhill; Ashford.
104 Battalion REME	Bordon	Northampton.
HQ REME TA	Bordon	

Army Medical Services

201 Field Hospital	Newcastle	Newton Aycliffe; Stockton-on-Tees; Newcastle upon Tyne.
202 Field Hospital	Birmingham	Birmingham; Stoke on Trent; Oxford; Shrewsbury.
203 Field Hospital	Cardiff	Cardiff; Swansea; Abergavenny.
204 Field Hospital	Belfast	Belfast; Ballymena; Newtownards; Armagh.
205 Field Hospital	Glasgow	Glasgow; Aberdeen; Dundee; Edinburgh.
207 Field Hospital	Manchester	Stockport; Blackburn; Bury.
208 Field Hospital	Liverpool	Liverpool; Ellesmere; Lancaster.
212 Field Hospital	Sheffield	Sheffield; Bradford; Nottingham; Leeds.
243 Field Hospital	Keynsham	Keynsham; Exeter; Plymouth; Portsmouth.

256 Field Hospital	London	Walworth; Hammersmith; Kingston; Bow.
306 Specialist Field Hospital	York	
253 Field Ambulance	Belfast	
254 Field Ambulance	Cambridge	
152 Ambulance Regiment	Belfast	Londonderry; Belfast; Bridgend.
C (144) Parachute Medical Squadron	London	
B (220) Medical Squadron	Maidstone	
B (250) Medical Squadron	Hull	
B (225) Medical Squadron	Dundee	
C (251) Medical Squadron	Sunderland	
C (222) Medical Squadron	Leicester	
HQ Army Medical Service TA	York	

Adjutant General's Corps

4 Regiment, Royal Military Police	Aldershot	West Bromwich; Brixton.
5 Regiment, Royal Military Police	Livingston	Livingston; Stockton-on-Tees.
CVHQ AGC	Worthy Down	

Intelligence Corps

3 Military Intelligence Bn (V)	London	London; Edinburgh; York; Keynsham; Birmingham.

Special Air Service

21 Regiment SAS

23 Regiment SAS

Army Air Corps

7 Regiment AAC	Netheravon
CVHQ AAC:	Netheravon

Officer Training Corps

Territorial Army: Officer Training Corps Units

Aberdeen University Officer Training Corps

Birmingham University Officer Training Corps

Bristol University Officer Training Corps

Cambridge University Officer Training Corps

East Midlands University Officer Training Corps

City of Edinburgh University Officer Training Corps

Exeter University Officer Training Corps

Glasgow and Strathclyde Universities Officer Training Corps

Leeds University Officer Training Corps

Liverpool University Officer Training Corps

London University Officer Training Corps

Manchester and Salford University Officer Training Corps

Northumbrian University Officer Training Corps

Oxford University Officer Training Corps

Queens University Officer Training Corps

Sheffield University Officer Training Corps
Southampton University Officer Training Corps
Tayforth University Officer Training Corps
University of Wales Officer Training Corps

MAJOR ARMY EQUIPMENT

Challenger 2

385 Challenger 2 available for service. Crew 4; Length Gun Forward 11.75 m; Height 3.04 m; Width 4.2 m with applique armour; Ground Clearance 0.51 m; Combat Weight 66.5 tonnes– MLC 76; Main Armament 1 x 120 mm L30 CHARM Gun; Ammunition Carried max 49 rounds stowed – APFSDS, HESH and Smoke; Secondary Armament Co-axial 7.62 mm Chain Gun; Loaders pintle mounted 7.62 mm GPMG; Ammunition Carried 4000 rounds 7.62 mm; Engine CV12 12 cylinder – Auxiliary Power Unit 4 – stroke diesel; Gearbox TN54 epicyclic – 6 forward gears and 2 reverse; Road Speed 59 kph; Cross-Country Speed 40 kph; Fuel Capacity 1,592 litres usable internal plus 2 x 175 litre external fuel drums.

Challenger 2 is manufactured by Vickers Defence Systems and production was undertaken at their factories in Newcastle-Upon-Tyne and Leeds. At 1999 prices Challenger 2 is believed to cost £4 million per vehicle.

Although the hull and automotive parts of the Challenger 2 are based upon that of its predecessor Challenger 1, the new tank incorporates over 150 improvements which have achieved substantially increased reliability and ease of maintenance. The Challenger 2 turret is, however, of a totally new design. The vehicle has a crew of four – commander, gunner, loader/signaller and driver and is equipped with a 120 mm rifled Royal Ordnance L30 gun firing all current tank ammunition natures plus the new depleted uranium (DU) round with a stick charge propellant system.

The design of the turret incorporates several of the significant features that Vickers had developed for its Mk 7 MBT (a Vickers turret on a Leopard 2 chassis). The central feature is an entirely new fire control system based on the Ballistic Control System developed by Computing Devices Company (Canada) for the US Army's M1A1 MBT. This second generation computer incorporates dual 32-bit processors with a MIL STD1553B databus and has sufficient growth potential to accept Battlefield Information Control System (BICS) functions and navigation aids (a GPS satnav system). The armour is an uprated version of Challenger 1's Chobham armour.

The first production models of the Challenger 2 were taken into service during mid 1994. Production of the UK's Challenger 2 contract was completed in 2001.

The only export order so far is an Omani order for 38 x Challenger which includes 2 x Driver Training Vehicles and 4 x Challenger Armoured Repair and Recovery Vehicles.

Challenger Repair and Recovery Vehicle (CRARV)

(81 available for service In Service) Crew 3; Length 9.59 m; Operating Width 3.62 m; Height 3.005 m; Ground Clearance 0.5 m; Combat Weight 62,000 kg; Max Road Speed 59 kph; Cross Country Speed 35 kph; Fording 1.07 m; Trench Crossing 2.3 m; Crane – Max Lift 6,500 kg at 4.9 m reach; Engine Perkins CV12 TCA 1200 26.1 V-12 direct injection 4-stroke diesel.

Between 1988 and 1990 the British Army ordered 81 Challenger CRARV in two batches and the contract was completed with the last vehicles brought into service during 1993. A 'Type 58' tank Challenger 2 Regiment has 5 x CRARRV, one with each sabre squadron and one with the REME Light Aid Detachment (LAD).

The vehicle has a crew of three plus additional space in a separate compartment for another two REME fitters. The vehicle is fitted with two winches (main and auxiliary) plus an Atlas hydraulically operated crane capable of lifting a complete Challenger 2 powerpack. The front dozer blade can be used as a stabiliser blade for the crane or as a simple earth anchor.

<u>MCV – 80 Fv 510 (WARRIOR)</u>

MCV – 80 Fv 510 (Warrior)

(780 available – possibly 660 in service). Weight loaded 24,500 kg: length 6.34 m: Height to turret top 2.78 m: Width 3.0 m: Ground Clearance 0.5 m: Max Road Speed 75 kph: Road Range 500 km: Engine Rolls Royce CV8 diesel: Horsepower 550 hp: Crew 2 (carries 8 infantry soldiers): Armament L21 30 mm Rarden Cannon: Coaxial EX-34 7.62 mm Hughes Helicopter Chain Gun: Smoke Dischargers Royal Ordnance Visual and Infra Red Screening Smoke (VIRSS).

Warrior is an armoured infantry fighting vehicle (AIFV) that replaced the AFV 432 in the armoured infantry battalions. The original buy of Warrior was reduced to 789 units with the majority of vehicles in service by late 1995. Warrior is in service with three armoured infantry battalions in the UK and six armoured infantry battalions in Germany.

Warrior armed with the 30 mm Rarden cannon gives the crew a good chance of destroying enemy APC's at ranges of up to 1,500 m and the vehicle carries a crew of three and seven dismounted infantry. The vehicle is NBC proof, and a full range of night vision equipment is included as standard.

The vehicle has seen successful operational service in the Gulf (1991), with British troops serving in the Balkans and more recently in Iraq. The vehicle has proven protection against mines, and there is dramatic BBC TV footage of a Warrior running over a Serbian anti-tank mine in Bosnia with little or no serious damage to the vehicle or crew .

159

The hull and mechanical components of Warrior are exceptional and few other vehicles in the world can match it for reliability and performance. The Warrior armament fire control system and electronics require upgrading if the vehicle is to remain in service to 2025 as intended.

A Warrior Mid-Life Improvement Programme is due to be implemented between 2007 and 2012. This should provide a new power pack, vehtronics enhancement, a digital fire control system (FCS)and a modern medium calibre cannon system. This extension of capability for Warrior will provide the necessary lead time for the introduction of future advanced capability systems vehicles to replace both Challenger 2 and Warrior.

The future digitisation programme in-service date (ISD) has slid to around 2017. Current thinking suggests that the British Army may replace existing rifle platoon Warrior with the improved Warrior 2000. This would release existing Warrior to be refitted to fulfil roles currently carried out by ageing and obsolescent FV 432s. This plan would create a new Battalion Assault Support Vehicle (BASV) which can carry Manoeuvre Support elements, principally 81 mm mortars, at the same pace as the Warrior fighting vehicles.

Numbers in UK service are believed to include 482 x Warrior Basic; 59 x Warrior RA; 126 x Warrior Rec and Rep. The Kuwait MoD has signed a contract for the purchase of 230 Warrior vehicles some of which are Recce vehicles armed with a 90 mm Cockerill gun.

AT – 105 Saxon

(605 in service of which 482 are baseline vehicles) Weight 10,670 kg: Length 5.16 m: Width 2.48 m: Height 2.63 m: Ground Clearance (axles) 0.33 m: Max Road Speed 96 kph: Max Road Range 510 km: Fuel Capacity 160 litres: Fording 1.12 m: Gradient 60 degrees: Engine Bedford 600 6-cylinder diesel developing 164 bhp at 2,800 rpm: Armour proof against 7.62 rounds fired at point blank range: Crew 2 + 10 max.

The Saxon was manufactured by GKN Defence and the first units for the British Army were delivered in late 1983. The vehicle, which can be best described as a battlefield taxi is designed around truck parts and does not require the extensive maintenance of track and running gear normally associated with APC/AIFVs.

As a vehicle capable of protecting infantry from shell splinters and machine gun fire in Europe during the Cold War years Saxon was a useful addition to the formerly larger Army. It does not, however, have the speed and agility which the lessons of recent mobile combat suggest will be necessary for infantry to survive in the assault in the future. The vehicle is fitted with a 7.62 mm Machine Gun for LLAD.

Each vehicle cost over £100,000 at 1984 prices and they are on issue to mechanised infantry battalions assigned to 3 (UK) Division.

The Army holds a number of Saxon IS (Patrol) vehicles for service in counter insurgency operations. The IS equipped vehicle has a Cummins BT 5.1 engine instead of the Bedford 6-cylinder installed on the APC version, and other enhancements for internal security operations such as roof-mounted searchlights, improved armour, a barricade removal device and an anti-wire device.

Saxon Patrol comes in two versions, troop carrier and ambulance. The troop carrier carries 10 men and the ambulance two stretcher cases. Industry sources suggest that this latest contract was for 137 vehicles at a cost of some £20 million resulting in a unit cost per vehicle of approximately £145,000.

Saxon is in service with the following overseas customers: Bahrain – 10: Brunei – 24: Hong Kong – 6: Malaysia – 40: Oman – 15.

Milan 2

Missile – Max Range 2,000 m; Mix Range 25 m; Length 918 mm; Weight 6.73 kg; Diameter 125 mm; Wing Span 267 mm; Rate of Fire 3-4 rpm; Warhead – Weight 2.70 kg; Diameter 115 mm; Explosive Content 1.79 kg; Firing Post– Weight 16.4 kg; Length 900 mm; Height 650 mm; Width 420 mm; Armour Penetration 352 mm; Time of Flight to Max Range 12.5 secs; Missile Speed 720 kph; Guidance Semi-Automatic command to line of sight by means of wires:

Milan 2 is a second generation anti-tank weapon, the result of a joint development project between France and West Germany with British Milan launchers and missiles built under licence in the UK by British Aerospace Dynamics. We believe that the cost of a Milan missile is currently in the region of £12,000 and that to date the UK MoD has purchased over 50,000 missiles.

Milan 2 comes in two main portable components which are the launcher and the missile, it then being a simple matter to clip both items together and prepare the system for use. On firing, the operator has only to keep his aiming mark on the target and the SACLOS guidance system will do the rest.

Milan was the first of a series of infantry anti-tank weapons that started to challenge the supremacy of the main battle tank on the battlefield. During fighting in Chad in 1987 it appears that 12 Chadian Milan posts mounted on Toyota Light Trucks were able to account for over 60 Libyan T-55's and T-62's. Reports from other conflicts suggest similar results.

Milan is on issue throughout the British Army and an armoured infantry battalion could be expected to be equipped with up to 12 firing posts and 120 missiles.

LF ATGW

Max Range 2,500 m: Length 1.08 m; Guidance – automatic self guidance; Total weight 21 kg.

The LF ATGW, based on the US Javelin system, is a more sophisticated guided weapon with a range of some 2,500 m. LF ATGW will equip Light Forces, Mechanised and Armoured Infantry, and Formation Reconnaissance units.

A production contract was signed in early 2003 worth over £300 million. Industry sources suggest that up to 5,000 missiles and 300 firing posts have been ordered. First deliveries to the UK have been made and the system will replace Milan.

The US Army and Marine Corps have been using Javelin for some years and the system is either in service, or has been selected by Australia, Ireland, Jordan, Lithuania, New Zealand and Taiwan. The US has used Javelin in both Iraq and Afghanistan.

Although Javelin has been developed mainly to engage armoured fighting vehicles, the system can also be used to neutralise bunkers, buildings, and low-flying helicopters. Javelin's top-attack tandem warhead is claimed to defeat all known armour systems.

In UK service Javelin will have a number of modifications including an enhanced command launch unit (CLU) with a wider field of view, and the ability to recognise targets at longer ranges.

First UK Javelin deliveries will go to rapid-reaction units such as 16 Air Assault Brigade and 3 Commando Brigade Royal Marines. It will then be issued to infantry units in the armoured, mechanised and light roles.

Over 7,000 Javelin launchers have been manufactured since 1995.

5.56 mm Individual Weapon (IW) (SA 80 and SA 80A2)
Effective Range 400 m: Muzzle Velocity 940 m/s: Rate of Fire from 610-775 rpm: Weight 4.98 kg (with 30 round magazine): Length Overall 785 mm: Barrel Length 518 mm: Trigger Pull 3.12-4.5 kg:

Designed to fire the standard NATO 5.56 mm x 45 mm round the SA 80 was fitted with an X4 telescopic (SUSAT) sight as standard. The total buy for SA 80 was for 332,092 weapons. Issues of the weapon are believed to have been made as follows:

Royal Navy	7,864
Royal Marines	8,350
Royal Air Force	42,221
MoD Police	1,878
Army	271,779

At 1991/92 prices the total cost of the SA80 Contract was in the order of £384.16 million. By late 1994 some 10,000 SA 80 Night Sights and 3rd Generation Image Intensifier Tubes for use with SA80 had been delivered.

The SA 80 had a mixed press, and following some severe criticism of the weapons mechanical reliability the improved SA 80A2 was introduced into service during late 2001.

SA 80A2: Some thirteen changes were made to weapon's breech block, gas regulation, firing-pin, cartridge extractor, recoil springs, cylinder and gas plug, hammer, magazine and barrel. Since modification the weapon has been extensively trialled.

Mean time before failure (MTBF) figures from the firing trials for stoppages, following rounds fired are as follows:

	SA 80A2	LSW
UK (temperate)	31,500	16,000
Brunei (hot/wet)	31,500	9,600
Kuwait (hot/dry)	7,875	8,728
Alaska (cold/dry)	31,500	43,200

The first SA 80A2 were in operational service during early 2002 and these weapons were in service across the army by late 2004. The cost of the programme was £92 million and some 200,000 weapons should have been modified by the time the programme ends in May 2006.

During late 2001 the British Army Combat Shooting Team took part in the Australian Army's skill at arms meeting in Brisbane using the new SA 80A2. Teams from eight nations took part in the competition and the British Army team won. The team's SA 80s fired 21,000 rounds in nine days without a stoppage.

5.56 mm Light Support Weapon (LSW)

Range 1,000 m; Muzzle Velocity 970 m/s; Length 900 mm; Barrel Length 646 mm; Weight Loaded with 30 round magazine 6.58 kg; Rate of Fire from to 610-775 rpm.

The LSW has been developed to replace the GPMG in the light role and about 80% of the parts are interchangeable with the 5.56 IW (SA 80). A great advantage for the infantryman is the ability of both weapons to take the same magazines. A rifle section will have two, four-man fire teams and each fire team one LSW.

Like the SA 80 the LSW is currently experiencing some difficulty in firing 5.56 ammunition supplied by other NATO countries. This problem is under review.

An Image Intensifier night sight, the CWS, has been produced for LSW which gives excellent night vision out to 400 m.

5.56mm Minimi Light Machine Gun

Effective range 800 m; Calibre 5.56 mm; Weight 7.1 kg; Length 914 mm; Feed 100-round disintegrating belt; Cyclic rate of fire 700 to 1000 rounds per minute.

FN Herstal's Minimi belt fed 5.56 mm Light Machinegun (LMG), is entering service on a scale of one per four-man fire team. The Minimi has been used operationally by British troops in Afghanistan and Iraq and the UK MoD is buying 2,472 weapons. The contract which will boost the firepower within infantry sections will be complete by 2007.

The Minimi is in service with the Australian, Canadian and New Zealand armies as well as the US Armed Forces.

7.62 mm General Purpose Machine Gun (GPMG)

Range 800 (Light Role), 1,800 m (Sustained Fire Role); Muzzle Velocity 538 m/s; Length 1.23 m; Weight loaded 13.85 kg (gun + 50 rounds); Belt Fed; Rate of Fire up to 750 rpm; Rate of Fire Light Role 100 rpm; Rate of Fire Sustained Fire Role 200 rpm.

An infantry machine gun which has been in service since the early 1960s, the GPMG can be used in the light role fired from a bipod or can be fitted to a tripod for use in the sustained fire role. The gun is also found pintle mounted on many armoured vehicles. Used on a tripod the gun is effective out to 1,800 m although it is difficult to spot strike at this range because the tracer rounds in the ammunition belt burns out at 1,100 m.

Machine Gun platoons in air assault battalions remain equipped with the GPMG in the sustained fire role. GPMG performance has recently been enhanced by the issue of a Maxi Kite night image intensification sight giving excellent visibility out to 600 m.

.5 Inch Heavy Machine Gun

Effective range – up to 2000 m; Calibre 12.7 mm; Weight 38.15 kg (gun only); Length; 1,656 mm; Barrel Length 1,143 mm; Muzzle Velocity 915 m/s; Cyclic rate of fire – 485 – 635 rounds per minute.

The L1A1 12.7 mm Heavy Machine gun (HMG) is an updated version of the Browning M2 'Fifty-cal' – generally recognised as one of the best heavy machine guns ever developed. Currently, the HMG provides integral close-range support from a ground mount tripod or fitted to a Land Rover TUM using a Weapon Mount Installation Kit (WMIK) and a variety of sighting systems. The performance of the HMG has recently been enhanced with a new 'soft mount' (to limit recoil and improve accuracy) and a quick change barrel.

AS 90

178 available; Crew 5; Length 9.07 m; Width 3.3 m; Height 3.0 m overall; Ground Clearance 0.41 m; Turret Ring Diameter 2.7 m; Armour 17 mm; Calibre 155 mm; Range (39 cal) 24.7 kms (52 cal) 30 kms; Recoil Length 780 mm; Rate of Fire 3 rounds in 10 secs (burst) 6 rounds per minute (intense) 2 rounds per minute (sustained); Secondary Armament 7.62 mm MG; Traverse 6,400 mills; Elevation –89/+1.244 mills; Ammunition Carried 48 x 155 mm projectiles and charges (31 turret & 17 hull); Engine Cummins VTA903T turbo-charged V8 diesel 660hp; Max Speed 53 kph; Gradient 60%; Vertical Obstacle 0.75 m; Trench Crossing 2.8 m; Fording Depth 1.5 m; Road Range 420 kms.

AS 90 was manufactured by Vickers Shipbuilding and Engineering (VSEL) at Barrow-in-Furness. 179 Guns were delivered under a fixed price contract for £300 million. These 179 guns completely equipped six field regiments replacing the older 120 mm Abbot and 155 mm M109 in British service. At the beginning of 2005 three of these Regiments were under the command of 1(UK) Armoured Division in Germany and three under the command of 3 (UK) Div in the United Kingdom.

AS 90 is currently equipped with a 39 calibre gun which fires the NATO L15 unassisted projectile out to a range of 24.7 kms (Base Bleed ERA range is 30 kms). Funding is available for the re-barreling of 96 x AS 90 with a 52 calibre gun with ranges of 30 kms (unassisted) and 60 t0 80 kms with improved accuracy and long range ERA ammunition. The current in service date for the 52 calibre gun is 2002/3 based on a firm programme which will fit 50% of the guns by November 2002 and up to 90% of them by the following April 2003.

AS 90 has been fitted with an autonomous navigation and gunlaying system (AGLS), enabling it to work independently of external sighting references. Central to the system is an inertial dynamic reference unit (DRU) taken from the US Army's MAPS (Modular Azimuth Positioning System). The bulk of the turret electronics are housed in the Turret Control Computer (TCC) which controls the main turret functions, including gunlaying, magazine control, loading systems control, power distribution and testing.

Artillery has always been a cost-effective way of destroying or neutralising targets. When the cost of a battery of guns, (approx £20 million) is compared with the cost of a close air support aircraft, (£40 million) and the cost of training each pilot, (£4 million +) the way ahead for governments with less and less to spend on defence is clear.

227 mm MLRS

63 launchers in service – 54 operational in 3 Regiments; Crew 3; Weight loaded 24,756 kg; Weight Unloaded 19,573 kg; Length 7.167 m; Width 2.97 m; Height (stowed) 2.57 m; Height (max elevation) 5.92 m; Ground Clearance 0.43 m; Max Road Speed 64 kph; Road Range 480 km; Fuel Capacity 617 litres; Fording 1.02 m; Vertical Obstacle 0.76 m; Engine Cummings VTA-903 turbo-charged 8 cylinder diesel developing 500 bhp at 2,300 rpm; Rocket Diameter 227 mm; Rocket Length 3.93 m; M77 Bomblet Rocket Weight 302.5 kg; AT2 SCATMIN Rocket Weight 254.46 kg; M77 Bomblet Range 11.5 –32 kms; AT2 SCATMIN Rocket Range 39 kms; One round 'Fire for Effect' equals one launcher firing 12 rockets; Ammunition Carried 12 rounds (ready to fire).

The MLRS is based on the US M2 Bradley chassis and the system is self-loaded with 2 x rocket pod containers, each containing 6 x rockets. The whole loading sequence is power assisted and loading takes between 20 and 40 minutes. There is no manual procedure.

A single round 'Fire for Effect' (12 rockets) delivers 644 bomblets or 336 scatterable mines and the coverage achieved is considered sufficient to neutralise a 500 m x 500 m target or produce a minefield of a similar size. Currently the weapon system accuracy is range dependent and therefore more rounds will be required to guarantee the effect as the range to the target increases. Future smart warhead sub munitions currently under development will enable pinpoint accuracy to considerably extended ranges. Ammunition for the MLRS is carried on the DROPS vehicle which is a Medium Mobility Load Carrier. Each DROPS vehicle with a trailer can carry 8 x Rocket Pod Containers and there are 15 x DROPS vehicles supporting the 9 x M270 Launcher vehicles within each MLRS battery.

The handling of MLRS is almost a military 'art form' and is an excellent example of the dependence of modern artillery on high technology. Getting the best out of the system is more than just parking the tubes and firing in the direction of the enemy. MLRS is the final link in a chain that includes almost everything available on the modern battlefield, from high speed communications, collation of intelligence, logistics and a multitude of high technology artillery skills and drills. Unmanned aerial vehicles (UAVs)can be used to acquire targets, realtime TV and data links are used to move information from target areas to formation commanders and onward to the firing positions. Helicopters can be used to dump ammunition and in some cases to move firing platforms. The refining of this capability is an interesting and dynamic future development area in which available technologies are currently being harnessed and applied.

MLRS is deployed as independent launcher units, using 'shoot-and-scoot' techniques. A battery of nine launchers will be given a battery manoeuvre area (BMA), within which are allocated three troop manoeuvre areas (TMA). These TMAs will contain close hides, survey points and reload points. In a typical engagement, a single launcher will be given its fire mission orders using burst data transmission.

An important initial piece of information received is the 'drive on angle'; the crew will drive the launcher out of the hide (usually less than 100 m) and align it with this angle. Using the navigation equipment, its location is fed into the ballistic computer which already has the full fire mission details. The launcher is then elevated and fired and the process can take as little as a few minutes to complete.

As soon as possible after firing, the vehicle will leave the firing location and go to a reload point where it will unload the empty rocket pods and pick up full ones; this can be done in less than five minutes. It will then go to a new hide within the TMA via a survey point to check the accuracy of the navigation system (upon which the accuracy of fire is entirely dependent). The whole of this cycle is co-ordinated centrally, and details of the new hide and reload point are received as part of the fire mission orders. The complete cycle from firing to being in a new hide ready for action might take half an hour.

In a typical day, a battery could move once or twice to a new BMA but this could impose a strain upon the re-supply system unless well planned (bearing in mind the need for the ammunition to be in position before the launcher vehicle arrives in a new BMA). The frequent moves are a result of security problems inherent in MLRS's use. In addition to attack by radar-controlled counterbattery fire, its effectiveness as an interdiction weapon makes it a valuable target for enemy special forces units. Although MLRS will be hidden amongst friendly forces up to 15 km behind the FEBA, its firing signature and small crew (three) will force it to move continually to avoid an actual confrontation with enemy troops.

There are currently (early 2006) 2 x MLRS Regiments (one Regular and one TA). The Regular Regiment operates 18 launcher vehicles and the TA Regiment 12 in peace and 18 in war.

Under development is the GMLRS rocket which will have a range of over 70 km and be fitted with a 90 kg plus unitary warhead. This warhead would be insensitive munitions compliant. In addition, it would feature inertial measurement unit (IMU) guidance and be global positioning system (GPS) aided.

The US Army is currently operating 857 MLRS, the French have 58, the West Germans 154 and the Italians 21.

Starstreak HVM

(135 Fire Units on Stormer and 145 on Light Mobile Launcher) Missile Length 1.39 m; Missile Diameter 0.27 m; Missile Speed Mach 3+; Maximum Range 5.5 kms;

Short Missile Systems of Belfast were the prime contractors for the HVM (High Velocity Missile) which continues along the development path of both Blowpipe and Javelin. The system can be shoulder launched or mounted on the LML (lightweight multiple launcher) or vehicle borne on the Alvis Stormer APC. The Stormer APC has an eight round launcher and 12 reload missiles can be carried inside the vehicle.

HVM has been optimised to counter threats from fast pop-up type strikes by attack helicopters and low flying aircraft. The missile employs a system of three dart type projectiles which can make multiple hits on the target. Each of these darts has an explosive warhead. It is believed that the HVM has an SSK (single shot to kill) probability of over 95%.

12 Regiment RA stationed at Sennelager in Germany is equipped with HVM and supports 1 (UK) Division. The UK HVM Regiment is 47 Regiment RA stationed at Thorney Island. There are currently (April 2006) three TA HVM regiments (to be reduced to one under the TA restructuring programme).

12 Regiment is believed to be configured as follows:

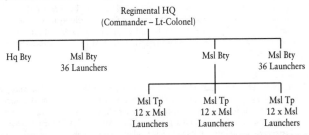

Note: The Regiment has 108 launchers divided amongst the three missile batteries. An HVM detachment of four is carried in a Stormer armoured vehicle and in each vehicle there are four personnel. Inside the vehicle there are 12 ready to use missiles with a further eight stored inside as reloads.

During mid 2001 Thales Air Defence was awarded a £66 million order for an Identification Friend-or-Foe (IFF) system for the Starstreak HVM.

In early 2005 the MoD announced the procurement of additional missiles worth about £180 million for the high velocity missile system.

Rapier (FS'C')
(57 fire units available) Guidance Semi Automatic to Line of Sight (SACLOS); Missile Diameter 13.3 cm; Missile Length 2.35 m; Rocket Solid Fuelled; Warhead High Explosive; Launch Weight 42 kg; Speed Mach 2+; Ceiling 3,000 m; Maximum Range 6,800 m; Fire Unit Height 2.13 m; Fire Unit Weight 1,227 kg; Radar Height (in action) 3.37 m; Radar Weight 1,186 kg; Optical Tracker Height 1.54 m; Optical Tracker Weight 119 kg; Generator Weight 243 kg; Generator Height 0.91 m.

The Rapier system provides area, 24 hour (through cloud), Low Level Air Defence (LLAD) over the battlefield.

Rapier Field standard C (FSC) incorporates a range of technological improvements over its predecessor including an advanced three-dimensional radar tracker acquisition system designed by Plessey. The towed system launcher mounts eight missiles (able to fire two simultaneously) which are manufactured in two warhead versions. One of these is a proximity explosive round and the other a kinetic energy round. The total cost of the Rapier FSC programme is £1,886 million.

The UK's future Rapier air defence capability will be 16 Regiment Royal Artillery (the Royal Air Force Regiment Rapier squadrons in the process of disbanding) and the capability of 16 Regiment is being enhanced by the creation of a fourth battery. The possible configuration of 16 Regiment will then be four batteries, each of two troops with four fire units per troop.

Rapier in all of its versions has now been sold to the armed forces of at least 14 nations. We believe that sales have amounted to over 25,000 missiles, 600 launchers and about 350 radars.

Future plans: The MoD plans to meet the future Ground Based Air Defence (GBAD) requirement from 2008 with 24 x Rapier fire units and 84 x high velocity missile launchers. Rapier will be deployed by the Army, with the RAF Regiment relinquishing the role. GBAD will be commanded by a new joint headquarters within the RAF command structure at RAF High Wycombe.

Lynx AH – Mark 7/9
(110 in service). Length Fuselage 12.06 m; Height 3.4 m; Rotor Diameter 12.8 m; Max Speed 330 kph; Cruising Speed 232 kph; Range 885 km; Engines 2 Rolls-Royce Gem 41; Power 2 x 850 bhp; Fuel Capacity 918 litres (internal); Weight (max take off) 4,763 kg; Crew one pilot, one air-gunner/observer; Armament 8 x TOW Anti-Tank Missiles; 2-4 7.62 mm machine guns; Passengers-able to carry 10 PAX; Combat radius approximately 100 kms with a two hour loiter.

Until the introduction of Apache, Lynx was the helicopter used by the British Army to counter the threat posed by enemy armoured formations. Armed with 8 x TOW missiles the Lynx was the mainstay of the British armed helicopter fleet. However, in addition to its role as an anti-tank helicopter, Lynx can be used for fire support using machine guns, troop lifts, casualty evacuation and many more vital battlefield tasks.

As an armed helicopter, during hostilities, we would have expected Lynx to operate on a section basis, with two or three Lynx aircraft armed with TOW directed by a Section Commander possibly flying in a Gazelle. The Section Commander would control what is in reality an airborne tank ambush and following an attack on enemy armour decide when to break contact. Having broken contact, the aircraft would return to a forward base to refuel and rearm. Working from forward bases, some of which are within 10 kms of the FEBA, it is suggested that a Lynx section could be 'turned around' in less than 15 minutes. Lynx with TOW replaced SCOUT with SS11 as the British Army's anti-tank helicopter.

We believe that there are 86 Lynx Mark 7 in British service and that there are also 23 Lynx Mark 9 (the latest version) in the inventory.

Lynx is known to be in service with France, Brazil, Argentina, The Netherlands, Qatar, Denmark, Norway, West Germany and Nigeria. The naval version carries anti-ship missiles.

Battlefield Light Utility Helicopter (BLUH)
The Battlefield Light Utility Helicopter (BLUH) will replace the capability currently provided by 45 Gazelle AH 1 and 109 Lynx Mk 7 and Mk 9. BLUH capability will include Intelligence, Surveillance, Target Acquisition and Reconnaissance (ISTAR), direction of fire, mobility support, assistance in command and control, and casualty evacuation. An option was taken in April 2002 to reduce BLUH numbers from 102 to 85.

As of early 2006, the BLUH programme focus hinges on a proposal from Westland Helicopters Ltd (WHL) – since 2004 owned by the Italian Finmeccanica Agusta helicopter company – with its Future Lynx (FLynx). Potential competitors to Flynx include the Agusta AB139, European collaborative NH90, Sikorsky UH-60M and Eurocopter EC655 helicopters. The current In-Service Date is October 2008. The BLUH programme has an estimated cost of £1.1bn for 85 helicopters.

If the Westland Flynx is selected to meet the BLUH requirement, it would signify that some of these 85 helicopters would replace Lynxes and Gazelles in the three newly forming AAC attack regiments, as well as all the Lynx AH7s and most of the Gazelles in other AAC squadrons.

Apache (AH Mk1)
(67 delivered) Gross Mission Weight 7,746 kgs (17,077 lb); Cruise Speed at 500 m – 272 kph; Maximum Range (Internal Fuel with 20 minute reserve) 462 kms; General Service Ceiling 3,505 metres (11,500 ft); Crew 2; Carries – 16 x Hellfire II missiles (range 6,000 metres approx); 76 x 2.75" CRV-7 rockets; 1,200 30mm cannon rounds; 4 x Air-to-Air Missiles; Engines 2 x Rolls Royce RTM-332.

The UK MoD ordered 67 Apache based on the US Army AH-64D manufactured by Boeing in 1995. Boeing built the first eight aircraft, and partially assembled the other 59. The UK Westland helicopter company undertook final assembly, flight testing and programme support at their Yeovil factory. Full operating capability for all three Apache Attack Regiments is expected by June 2007.

We believe that there will be 48 operational aircraft in three regiments (each of 16 aircraft). The remaining 19 aircraft will be used for trials, training and a war maintenance reserve (WMR).

The Apache can operate in all weathers, day or night, and can detect, classify and prioritise up to 256 potential targets at a time. Apart from the 'Longbow' mast-mounted fire control radar, the aircraft is equipped with a 127 x magnification TV system, 36 x magnification thermal imaging, and 18 x magnification direct view optics. The missile system incorporates Semi-Active Laser and Radio Frequency versions of the Hellfire missile, whose range is at least 6 kms. Apart from the Rolls-Royce engines, specific British Army requirements include a secure communications suite and a Helicopter Integrated Defensive Aids System (HIDAS). Programme cost is some £3 billion.

It is believed that an air-to-air weapon capability will continue to be investigated and trials of the Shorts Starstreak missile onboard an AH-64 have continued in the United States. Any longer term decision to proceed will be based on the results of these US Army trials.

The night vision system of 67 Apache AH Mk1 attack helicopters is to be upgraded in the near future. The M-TADS/PNVS, which is designated Arrowhead, will replace the existing forward-looking infra red (FLIR) and daylight television image intensifier with new sensors to provide improved target identification over longer ranges, better pilot performance and reduced life-cycle costs. Army Air Corps (AAC) aviators are said to have been keen to proceed with the upgrade, because the damp UK climate significantly degrades the effectiveness of the existing Target Acquisition and Designation Sight/Pilot Night Vision Sensor

The Apache AH Mk 1 presents a completely new capability for the AAC with significant implications for Air Manoeuvre doctrine in Land and Joint Operations. The Apache certainly gives the British Army the 'punch' necessary for operations during the next decade.

Panther Command and Liaison Vehicle (Panther MLV)

The UK MoD announced in July 2003 that the BAE Systems Land Systems (formerly Alvis) Multirole Light Vehicle (MLV) had been selected as the British Army's Future Command and Liaison Vehicle (FCLV). The first procurement contract was signed in November 2003 for an initial 401 vehicles, with an option for up to 400 more. The vehicle has been named the Panther Command and Liaison Vehicle (CLV). In June 2004, Thales Defence Optronics was selected to provide the Driver's Vision Enhancer (DVE) for the Panther CLV. Thales' DVE driver's sight is based on an uncooled thermal imager.

Panther CLV is based on a design by Iveco Defence Vehicles Division of Italy and the vehicles will be manufactured during the period 2006 to 2009. A Development and Demonstration contract covers the build and test of seven vehicles which were delivered in late 2005, with a planned in-service date of mid 2007. Acquisition cost for some 401 vehicles is £193 million spread over five years.

The current gross vehicle weight of a Panther MLV is 7.1 tonnes. The vehicle is to be air transportable, underslung beneath a Chinook helicopter or carried inside C130, C17 and A400M aircraft.

The 401 x Panther vehicles will replace in-service vehicles as follows:

CVRT Spartan	137
Truck Utility Medium (Landrover)	225
Saxon	3
FV432	31
FV436	5

Of the above, some 326 Self Defence Weapon (SDW) variant vehicles will be available. These vehicles will be armed with a 7.62 mm L7 general purpose machine gun but this could be upgraded to a 12.7 mm/cal weapon if required. These SDW vehicles will be fitted with a surveillance and target acquisition (STA) system.

Future Rapid Effect System (FRES)

The FRES Programme is the UK Ministry of Defence (MoD) forward plan to provide the British Army with a family of medium-weight, network-enabled, air-deployable armoured vehicles to meet a variety (possibly 16) battlespace roles.

The FRES requirement is for a family of fighting platforms (including a range of Ground Manoeuvre Reconnaissance roles), which only when integrated with a variety of other capabilities produces a complete system of systems. It will seek to make full use of any intelligence-gathering capabilities that are, or become, available. However, the project is still in its Assessment Phase (due for completion in November 2006) and therefore the precise nature of the interface with other capabilities is not yet determined.

Following acceptance into service it is expected that there will be three FRES-equipped brigades and this will enable the UK to deploy armoured forces more rapidly in support of national and alliance interests. The exact number of FRES type vehicles to be procured has not yet been determined but it is expected to be at least 2,000 if the current fleet of CVR(T), Saxon and FV432 series vehicles are to be replaced.

A major FRES requirement is that it should be able to be transported in a C-130 Hercules aircraft which will place severe constraints on the platform weight and eventual design. As yet there does not appear to have been a decision as to whether FRES will be tracked or wheeled. FRES vehicle groups are based around the following requirements:

Group 1 FRES utility vehicles are expected to include protected mobility, light armoured support, command-and-control, medical, equipment support and a driver-training vehicle.

Group 2 FRES vehicles will cover intelligence, surveillance, target acquisition and reconnaissance (ISTAR) and fire control. This group will include vehicles that also improve indirect fire support, direct fire support, indirect fire control, engineer reconnaissance, ground-based surveillance, scout, anti-tank guided weapon and an enhanced protected mobility vehicle.

Group 3 FRES vehicles will include the formation communications variants (Falcon) and electronic warfare versions (Soothsayer). Variants of the former are expected to include Bowman gateway and a variety of Falcon and Wasp capable platforms.

Group 4 FRES vehicles will be formation force protection and manoeuvre support and will include an armoured vehicle launched bridge, armoured vehicle engineer, armoured engineer tractor and CBRN reconnaissance and survey.

Group 5 FRES vehicles currently consists of a remotely delivered mine system to replace the current Shielder, based on a Stormer chasis.

If the FRES programme goes ahead we would expect to see the first vehicles accepted into service around 2012 with a phased approach to achieving full operational capability thereafter.

CHAPTER 4 – THE ROYAL AIR FORCE

Personnel Summary (at 1 January 2006)

Royal Air Force	Trained Requirement	Trained Strength	Total Trained & Untrained Strength
Officers	10,150	9,510	10.510
Other Ranks	38,600	38,120	39,210
Total	48,760	47,630	49,720

Plans were announced in July 2005 for the RAF personnel total to be reduced from 'around' 49,000 to 41,000 by 2008. The RAF will achieve the required reduction, through normal outflow, reduced recruitment and a targeted redundancy programme. Recruitment targets are therefore being reduced by some 4,000 posts (to around 6,000 in total) over the financial years 2006, 2007 and 2008. In addition a requirement for about 2,750 redundancies has been identified over the same period.

On 1 December 2005 there were 2,130 trained pilots in the RAF with an estimated 150 under training.

Royal Air Force Squadrons (as at early 2006)

	2006	1980
Strike/Attack Squadrons	5	14
Offensive Support Squadrons	4	5
Air Defence (Interceptor) Squadrons	3	16
Maritime Patrol Squadrons	2	4
Reconnaissance Squadrons	5	5
Airborne Early Warning Squadrons	2	1
Transport/Tanker Squadrons	8	9
Search and Rescue Squadrons	2	2
Helicopter Squadrons (2 SAR)	8	4
Surface to Air Missile Squadrons	4	8
Ground Defence Squadrons	6	5

Note. Squadron figures above include those assigned to the Joint Force Harrier and the Joint Helicopter Command – see next table.

Under Joint Force Arrangements

Joint Force Harrier.

2 x Royal Navy Harrier Squadrons; 2 x Royal Air Force (GR9/9A and GR7/7A) Squadrons.

Joint Helicopter Command.

4 x Royal Naval helicopter squadrons; 6 x Army Aviation Regiments (including 1 x Volunteer Reserve); 7 x Royal Air Force Helicopter Squadrons (including 1 x RAuxAF Helicopter Support Squadron).

RAF Squadron Listing (as at 1 May 2006)

Squadron	Aircraft	Base
1 Sqn	9 x Harrier GR9/9A	RAF Cottesmore (JFH)
	1 x Harrier T 12	
II (AC) Sqn	12 x Tornado GR4A	RAF Marham (Recce)
3 Sqn	12 x Typhoon	RAF Cottesmore (from 1 April 2006)
4 Sqn	9 x Harrier GR7/7A	RAF Cottesmore (JFH)
	1 x Harrier T10	(eventually GR9/9A and T 12)
5 Sqn	5 x Sentinel R1 (ASTOR)	RAF Waddington
6 Sqn	11 x Jaguar GR3/3A	RAF Conningsby (disbands in 2007)
	1 x Jaguar T4	
7 Sqn	5 x Chinook HC2	RAF Odiham (JHC)
	1 x Gazelle	
8 Sqn	3 x Sentry AEW1	RAF Waddington
9 Sqn	12 x Tornado GR4	RAF Marham
12 Sqn	12 x Tornado GR4	RAF Lossiemouth
13 Sqn	12 x Tornado GR4A	RAF Marham (Recce)
14 Sqn	12 x Tornado GR4	RAF Lossiemouth
18 Sqn	18 x Chinook HC2	RAF Odiham (JHC)
22 Sqn	8 x Sea King HAR3/3A	RMB Chivenor (Sqn HQ)*
23 Sqn	3 x Sentry AEW	RAF Waddington
24 Sqn	11 x Hercules C3, C4/C5	RAF Lyneham
25 Sqn	16 x Tornado F3	RAF Leeming
27 Sqn	10 x Chinook HC2	RAF Odiham (JHC)
28 Sqn	22 x Merlin HC3	RAF Benson
30 Sqn	11 x Hercules C3, C4/C5	RAF Lyneham
31 Sqn	12 x Tornado GR4	RAF Marham
32 (The Royal) Sqn		RAF Northolt
	5 x BAe 125 CC3	
	2 x BAe 146 CC2	
	3 x Augusta A 109	
33 Sqn	15 x Puma HC1	RAF Benson (JHC)
39 Sqn	4 x Canberra PR9	RAF Marham (1 PRU) (Disbanded July 2006
	1 x Canberra T4	
41 Sqn	12 x Jaguar GR3	RAF Coltishall (disbanded in March 2006)
	1 x Jaguar T4	
43 Sqn	16 x Tornado F3	RAF Leuchars
47 Sqn	11 x Hercules C3, C4/C5	RAF Lyneham
51 Sqn	3 x Nimrod R1	RAF Waddington
70 Sqn	11 x Hercules C3,C4/C5	RAF Lyneham

78 Sqn	1 x Chinook HC2	RAF Mount Pleasant (JHC)
	2 x Sea King HAR3/3A	(Falklands)
84 Sqn	4 x Griffin HAR2	RAF Akrotiri
99 Sqn	4 x C-17	RAF Brize Norton
100 Sqn	16 x Hawk T1/T1A	RAF Leeming
101 Sqn	7 x VC10 K3/K4	RAF Brize Norton
	10 x VC10C1K	
111 Sqn	16 x Tornado F3	RAF Leuchars
120 Sqn	8 x Nimrod MR2	RAF Kinloss
201 Sqn	7 x Nimrod MR2	RAF Kinloss
202 Sqn	8 x Sea King HAR3/3A	RAF Boulmer (Sqn HQ)*
216 Sqn	8 x Tristar K1/KC1/C2/C2A	RAF Brize Norton
230 Sqn	18 x Puma HC1	RAF Aldergrove (JHC)
617 Sqn	12 x Tornado GR4	RAF Lossiemouth
1312 Flight	1 x Hercules C1	RAF Mount Pleasant
	1 x VC10 K3/4	
1435 Flight	4 x Tornado F3	RAF Mount Pleasant

Notes.

(1) * Headquartered at RMB Chivenor, 22 Sqn maintains three detachments at Chivenor ('A' Flight), Wattisham ('B' Flight) and Valley ('C' Flight). 202 Sqn has detachments at Boulmer ('A' Flight and Headquarters), Lossiemouth ('D' Flight) and Leconfield ('E' Flight).

(2) JFH means that a squadron is assigned to the Joint Force Harrier and JHC means that a squadron is assigned to the Joint Helicopter Command.

(3) There are RAF flying units deployed in Cyprus, Falklands and periodically Gibraltar on national missions.

(4) RAF flying units are supporting UN/NATO operations in the area of the former Yugoslavia, Afghanistan, and Iraq.

RAF Training Units (as at 1 May 2006)

No 1 Flying Training School (1 FTS)

67 x Tucano T1	
72 (R) Sqn	RAF Linton-on-Ouse
207 (R) Sqn	RAF Linton-on-Ouse

No 3 Flying Training School (3 FTS)

11 x Jetstream T1; 9 x Dominie T1/T2 ; 8 x Tutor T1	
45 (R) Sqn	RAF Cranwell
55 (R) Sqn	RAF Cranwell

No 4 Flying Training School (4 FTS)

69 x Hawk T1/T1A	
19 (R) Sqn	RAF Valley
208 (R) Sqn	RAF Valley

Joint Elementry Flying Training School (JEFTS)

18 x Firefly M260	RAF Barkstone Heath
6 x Firefly M260A	RAF Cranwell
14 x Firefly M260	RAF Church Fenton

Defence Helicopter Flying School (DHFS)
28 x Squirrel HT1; 6 x Griffin HT1
60 (R) Sqn and Central Flying School   RAF Shawbury
Search and Rescue Training Flight (SARTF)
4 x Griffin HT1   RAF Valley
University Air Squadrons
90 x Tutor T1 Various locations
Volunteer Gliding Schools (VGS)
80 x Viking; 53 Vigilant Various locations

RAF Operational Conversion Units (as at 1 April 2006)

15 (R) Sqn	26 x Tornado GR4	RAF Lossiemouth
17 (R) Sqn	6e x Typhoon	RAF Coningsby (Typhoon OEU)
20 (R) Sqn	9 x Harrier GR7/7A/9/9A	RAF Wittering
	4 x Harrier T10/T12	
29 Sqn	12e x Typhoon	RAF Coningsby (Typhoon OCU)
42 (R) Sqn	3 x Nimrod MR2	RAF Kinloss
56 (R) Sqn	20 x Tornado F3	RAF Leuchars
203 (R) Sqn	3 x Sea King HAR3/3A	RAF St Mawgan

Note. The (R) in a squadron designation represents a training unit/reserve squadron. In the majority of cases this reserve squadron is the Operational Conversion Unit (OCU) for the particular aircraft type and the reserve squadron has a mobilisation role.

Royal Air Force Regiment

1 Sqn RAF Regt	RAF St Mawgan	Ground Defence (Honnington March 2007)
2 Sqn RAF Regt	RAF Honnington	Ground Defence with parachute capability
3 Sqn RAF Regt	RAF Aldergrove	Ground Defence
15 Sqn RAF Regt	RAF Honnington	Rapier (Disbands March 2008)
26 Sqn RAF Regt	RAF Honnington	Rapier (Disbands March 2008)
27 Sqn RAF Regt	RAF Honnington	CBRN Defence (RAF element of Joint CBRN Regiment)
34 Sqn RAF Regt	RAF Leeming	Ground Defence
51 Sqn RAF Regt	RAF Lossiemouth	Ground Defence
63 (QCS) Sqn	RAF Uxbridge	Ground Defence & Ceremonial
Rapier FSC OCU	RAF Honnington	(Joint Training and Operational Conversion Unit – disbanding)
RAF STO Centre	RAF Honnington	Tactical Survive to Operate Training Centre
No 1 RAF STO HQ	RAF Wittering	Tactical Survive to Operate HQ
No 2 RAF STO HQ	RAF Leeming	Tactical Survive to Operate HQ
No 3 RAF STO HQ	RAF Marham	Tactical Survive to Operate HQ
No 4 RAF STO HQ	RAF Honnington	Tactical Survive to Operate HQ
RAF Regt Depot	RAF Honnington	Training & Administration

RAF Miscellaneous Units

FJ&WOEU	3 x Tornado F3	RAF Coningsby
(Fast Jet and Weapons	2 x Tornado GR4	
Operational Evaluation Unit)	4 x Harrier GR7/7A and GR9/9A	
		1 x Jaguar GR3/3A
RAF Centre of Aviation Medicine	2 x Hawk T1	RAF Henlow
RAF Aerobatic Team (The Red Arrows)	10 x Hawk T1A	RAF Scampton
Station Flight	1 x Islander CC2	RAF Northolt

Royal Auxiliary Air Force

3 Sqn	RAF Henlow	Tactical Provost Wing
501 Sqn	RAF Brize Norton	Operations Support Squadron
504 Sqn	RAF Cottesmore	Operations Support Squadron
600 Sqn	RAF Northolt	Headquarters Augmentation Unit
603 Sqn	Edinburgh	Operations Support Squadron
606 Sqn	RAF Benson	Helicopter Support Squadron
609 Sqn	RAF Leeming	Operations Support Unit
612 Sqn	RAF Leuchars	Air Transportable Surgical Squadron
2503 Sqn RAF Regt	RAF Waddington	RAuxAF Regiment Field Squadron
2620 Sqn RAF Regt	RAF Marham	RAuxAF Operations Support Squadron
2622 Sqn RAF Regt	RAF Lossiemouth	RAuxAF Regiment Field Squadron
2623 Sqn RAF Regt	RAF Honnington	RAuxAF Regiment Force Protection Squadron
2624 Sqn RAF Regt	RAF Brize Norton	RAuxAF Operations Support Squadron
4624 Sqn RAF Regt	RAF Brize Norton	RAuxAF Movements Squadron
4626 Sqn	RAF Lyneham	RAuxAF Aeromed Evacuation Unit
7006 Flight	RAF High Wycombe	Intelligence Flight
7010 Flight	RAF High Wycombe	Photographic Interpretation Flight
7630 Flight	DISC Chicksands	Intelligence Flight
7644 Flight	RAF High Wycombe	Corporate Communication Squadron
Mobile Met Unit	RAF Benson	RAFVR Meteorological Services
1359 Flight	RAF Lyneham	Hercules Reserve Aircrew

BRITISH AIRLINE FLEETS

In an emergency, the UK Government has the power to enlist the assistance of the United Kingdom's civil airline and aircraft charter fleets. In total, there are over 50 registered airlines and aircraft charter companies operating over 930 fixed-wing passenger and transport aircraft and over 400 helicopters. The largest of the British-registered airlines is British Airways operating about 250 aircraft, carrying on average about 35 million passengers per year. Other major British airlines include Virgin Atlantic with 30 aircraft, Britair with 41 aircraft, the discount airline Easyjet with 112 aircraft. Bristow Helicopters – UK subsidiary of Offshore

Logistics is the largest helicopter charter operator with a fleet of some 300 helicopters. British companies employ some 10,000 trained pilots active in commercial operations in the UK.

HIGHER MANAGEMENT OF THE ROYAL AIR FORCE

The Ministry of Defence (MoD) is a Department of State, headed by the Secretary of State for Defence (SofS) who implements national defence policy and plans the expenditure of the defence budget. The MoD is the highest level of headquarters for the Armed Forces, both administrative and operational. All major issues of policy are referred to the SofS or to one of his three Ministerial colleagues.

- Minister of State for the Armed Forces
- Parliamentary Under-Secretary of State for Defence Procurement
- Parliamentary Under-Secretary of State for Veterans Affairs

Under the direction of the Defence Council (described in Chapter 1) management of the Services is the responsibility of the Service Boards, in the case of the Royal Air Force the Air Force Board is the senior management directorate.

AIR FORCE BOARD

The routine management of the Royal Air Force is the responsibility of the Air Force Board, the composition of which is as follows:

- The Secretary of State for Defence
- Minister of State for the Armed Forces
- Parliamentary Under-Secretary of State for Defence Procurement
- Parliamentary Under-Secretary of State for Veterans Affairs
- Parliamentary Under-Secretary of State for Defence
- Chief of the Air Staff
- Air Member for Personnel
- Controller of Aircraft
- Air Member for Logistics
- AOC Strike Command
- Assistant Chief of the Air Staff

Air Force Board Standing Committee (AFBSC)

Attended by senior RAF commanders, the AFBSC dictates the policy required for the Royal Air Force to function efficiently and meet the aims required by the Defence Council and government. The Chief of the Air Staff is the chairman of the Air Force Board Standing Committee.

Decisions made by the Defence Council or the Air Force Board are implemented by the air staff at various headquarters worldwide. The Chief of the Air Staff is the officer ultimately responsible for the Royal Air Force's contribution to the national defence effort. He maintains control through the AOC (Air Officer Commanding), and the staff branches of the various Royal Air Force Headquarters.

Air Marshal Sir Glenn Torpy KCB CBE DSO BSc(Eng) FRAeS RAF
Born in 1953, Air Marshal Torpy joined the Royal Air Force in 1974 after studying Aeronautical Engineering at Imperial College, London. He completed two tours flying the Jaguar in the reconnaissance role, a tour as a Qualified Weapons Instructor on the Hawk, and commanded a Tornado GR1A tactical reconnaissance squadron. Air Marshal Torpy saw active service with No 13 Squadron during the 1991 Gulf War and was awarded the Distinguished Service Order in the Gulf Honours List.

Air Marshal Sir Glenn Torphy

He graduated from the Royal Air Force Staff College in 1987, and subsequently filled a staff appointment in the Ministry of Defence before moving to be Personal Staff Offcer to the Air Officer Commanding-in-Chief Strike Command. He was the Station Commander Royal Air Force Bruggen, Germany, before graduating from the Royal College of Defence Studies in December 1997 and subsequently completing the Higher Command and Staff Course in April 1998. Air Marshal Torpy was ACOS J3 (Operations) in the PJHQ during Operation DESERT FOX and the Kosovo crisis, and spent a short time as Director Air Operations in the Ministry of Defence before taking over as Assistant Chief of the Defence Staff (Operations). He became the Air Officer Commanding No 1 Group in March 2001. During his time at No 1 Group he commanded the British Forces participating in Exercise SAIF SAREEA II and in 2003 was the UK Air Contingent Commander for Operation IRAQI FREEDOM, for which he was awarded the US Legion of Merit for his part in the coalition operation. In July 2003 he became Deputy

Commander-in-Chief Strike Command. He was appointed as Chief of Joint Operations on 26 July 2004, and was made a Knight Commander of the Bath in January 2005.

He was appointed Chief of the Air Staff on 1 May 2006.

As of May 2006 the Chief of the Air Staff maintains effective command and control of the Royal Air Force by means of three principal headquarters.

♦ HQ Strike Command
♦ HQ Personnel and Training Command
♦ Defence Logistics Organisation (via Director General Logistics Strike)

Colocation and Integration of Command Headquarters
However, during late 2005 the UK MoD announced plans for HQ Strike Command and HQ Personnel and Training Command to be collocated and integrated by 1 April 2008.

The announcement followed a study that had been conducted into the potential for increasing the effectiveness of the two headquarters based at RAF High Wycombe and RAF Innsworth (currently in May 2006) by rationalising and collocating them on a single site. The study concluded that RAF High Wycombe offered the best value for money and was operationally more effective.

In addition, the study showed that, as a result of collocation, the headquarters will require some 1,000 fewer posts (500 service, 500 civilian) than the two current organisations. However, following the moves, the new personnel strength at RAF High Wycombe will probably change from about 2,050 posts now (1,540 service and 510 civilian) to around 2,150 (1,400 service and 750 civilian) by 2008.

The target date for initial operations at the collocated headquarters is October 2006. However, in view of its role in managing the overall drawdown in RAF numbers, the Personnel Management Agency will not relocate to High Wycombe until April 2008.

It is likely that the total estimated cost of removal and transfer of staff and operations for the collocated RAF Headquarters at High Wycombe is in the region of £23 million. £6 million is for staff costs, £3 million of which is identified for staff relocation packages. Another £3 million, spread over a period of 10 years, is for additional housing cost allowance payable to civilian staff. £17 million is for operational costs.

Strike Command (as at May 2006)
From its headquarters at RAF High Wycombe, Strike Command (STC) currently controls all of the United Kingdom's front line aircraft world wide. Its assets include fighters, strike/attack, transport and maritime aircraft and helicopters. As the commander of Strike Command, the AOCinC is responsible for the day to day national peacetime operations of the Command. In war, Strike Command is an essential part of the NATO organisation and as such is a component of SACEUR European Theatre air assets.

Notes.
(1) The Air Warfare Centre was formerly known as the CTTO.
(2) Groups are normally commanded by Air Vice Marshals.
(3) Strike Command also supports operations in Afghanistan, the Balkans and the Gulf.

Reorganised in 2000 and again in 2003 and 2004, Strike Command, based on 3 Groups is about to undergo yet another reorganisation. As of December 2005, Strike Command controlled about 4,600 civilians and 31,000 servicemen and women – well over two thirds of the present strength of the Royal Air Force. The personnel and aircraft are spread through some 200 units of various sizes, the majority of which are in the United Kingdom.

AIR WARFARE CENTRE (AWC)
The Air Warfare Centre is responsible for formulating tactical doctrine and conducting operational trials. Formed from the old CTTO, DAW, EWOSE, ORB and OEUs, the AWC also maintains liaison with MoD research establishments and industry, and close contact with RAF operational commands as well as with the Royal Navy, Army and Allied air forces. The AWC HQ is collocated with the Defence Electronic Warfare Centre at RAF Waddington. The AWC is administered by HQ Strike Command, but is responsible jointly to the Assistant Chief of Air Staff, and to the Commander-in-Chief for the conduct of trials, and development of tactics for all Royal Air Force operational aircraft. Branches and locations of the AWC are as follows:

HQ	Waddington
Operational Doctrine (OD&T)	Cranwell & High Wycombe
Tactics (TD&T)	Waddington
Electronic Warfare (EWOS)	Waddington
Operational Analysis (OA)	High Wycombe, Waddington & Cranwell
Operational Testing & Evaluation (OT&E)	Boscombe Down, Coningsby, Odiham & Ash

NO 1 GROUP (MAY 2006)
No 1 Group is an Air Combat Group containing all fast jet assets including the Joint Force Harrier (JFH), formerly part of No 3 Group, and the Joint Force Air Component (JFAC) HQ, which is currently a centrally provided asset. The JFAC HQ provides the deployable Air

Command and Control required to support expeditionary warfare and links in to the other Joint Force Component HQs under PJHQ direction.

1 Group Squadron Listing (as at 1 May 2006)

1 Sqn	9 x Harrier GR9/9A	RAF Cottesmore (JFH)
	1 x Harrier T 12	
II (AC) Sqn	12 x Tornado GR4A	RAF Marham (Recce)
3 Sqn	12 x Typhoon	RAF Cottesmore (from 1 April 2006)
4 Sqn	9 x Harrier GR7/7A	RAF Cottesmore (JFH)
	1 x Harrier T10	(eventually GR9/9A and T 12)
6 Sqn	11 x Jaguar GR3/3A	RAF Conningsby (disbands in 2007)
	1 x Jaguar T4	
9 Sqn	12 x Tornado GR4	RAF Marham
12 Sqn	12 x Tornado GR4	RAF Lossiemouth
13 Sqn	12 x Tornado GR4A	RAF Marham (Recce)
14 Sqn	12 x Tornado GR4	RAF Lossimouth
15 (R) Sqn	26 x Tornado GR4	RAF Lossiemouth
17 (R) Sqn	6e x Typhoon RAF	RAF Conningsby (Typhoon OEU)
20 (R) Sqn	9 x Harrier GR7/7A/9/9A	RAF Wittering
	4 x Harrier T10/T12	
25 Sqn	16 x Tornado F3	RAF Leeming
29 Sqn	8e x Typhoon	RAF Conningsby (Typhoon OCU)
31 Sqn	12 x Tornado GR4	RAF Marham
39 Sqn	4 x Canberra PR9	RAF Marham (1 PRU)
	1 x Canberra T4	
43 Sqn	16 x Tornado F3	RAF Leuchars
56 (R) Sqn	20 x Tornado F3	RAF Leuchars
100 Sqn	16 x Hawk T1/T1A	RAF Leeming
111 Sqn	16 x Tornado F3	RAF Leuchars
617 Sqn	12 x Tornado GR4	RAF Lossiemouth

No 2 Group (May 2006)

No 2 Group is the Air Combat Support Group containing all Air Transport/Air-to-Air Refuelling assets, the Force Protection assets, and the Air Combat Service Support Units (ACSSU) which include deployable supporting elements covering engineering, armament, communications, supply, movements, medical, administrative and catering.

2 Group Squadron Listing (as at 1 May 2006)

24 Sqn	11 x Hercules C3, C4/C5	RAF Lyneham
30 Sqn	11 x Hercules C3, C4/C5	RAF Lyneham
47 Sqn	11 x Hercules C3, C4/C5	RAF Lyneham
99 Sqn	4 x C-17	RAF Brize Norton
101 Sqn	7 x VC10 K3/K4	RAF Brize Norton
	10 x VC10C1K	
216 Sqn	8 x Tristar K1/KC1/C2/C2A	RAF Brize Norton

70 Sqn	11 x Hercules C1/C3,C4/C5	RAF Lyneham
32 (The Royal) Sqn		RAF Northolt
	5 x BAe 125 CC3	
	2 x BAe 146 CC2	
	3 x Augusta A 109	

2 Group also supports the Defence CBRN School at Winterbourne Gunner, the RAF Regiment and various UK Air Combat Service and Support Units

No 3 Group (May 2006)

No 3 Group is the Battle Management Group containing Surveillance, Target Acquisition and Reconnaissance (ISTAR), Air Surveillance and Control System (ASACS), Maritime and SAR assets.

During March 2006 the RAF announced the closure of No 3 Group. Group units will be reassigned to No 1 Group and No 2 Group during 2006 and 2007.

3 Group Squadron Listing (as at 1 May 2006)

5 Sqn	5 x Sentinel R1 (ASTOR)	RAF Waddington
8 Sqn	3 x Sentry AEW1	RAF Waddington
22 Sqn	8 x Sea King HAR3/3A	RMB Chivenor (Sqn HQ)*
23 Sqn	3 x Sentry AEW	RAF Waddington
42 (R) Sqn	3 x Nimrod MR2	RAF Kinloss (Nimrod OCU)
51 Sqn	3 x Nimrod R1	RAF Waddington
120 Sqn	8 x Nimrod MR2	RAF Kinloss
201 Sqn	7 x Nimrod MR2	RAF Kinloss
202 Sqn	8 x Sea King HAR3/3A	RAF Boulmer (Sqn HQ)*
203 (R) Sqn	3 x Sea King HAR3//3A	RAF St Mawgan
SARTF	4 x Griffin HT1	RAF Valley

Note. * Headquartered at RMB Chivenor, 22 Sqn maintains three detachments at Chivenor ('A' Flight), Wattisham ('B' Flight) and Valley ('C' Flight). 202 Sqn has detachments at Boulmer ('A' Flight and Headquarters), Lossiemouth ('D' Flight) and Leconfield ('E' Flight).

3 Group is also responsible for RAF Bentley Priory, RAF Fylingdales and RAF Neatishead and the majority of ASACS units.

Joint Helicopter Command (JHC)

The UK armed forces' Joint Helicopter Command (JHC) became operational on 1 April 2000. During early 2006 the JHC had about 420 aircraft under command.

Royal Air Force

34 x Chinook HC2/2a
33 x Puma HC1
22 x Merlin HC3
4 x Griffin HAR2
2 x Sea King HAR3

Royal Navy
33 x Sea King HC4
6 x Lynx Mk7
8 x Gazelle Mk1

Army
110 x Lynx
105 x Gazelle
67 x Apache Mk1
6 x Bell 212
6 x Islander

The RAF Contribution to the JHC is as follows:

RAF JHC Squadrons (May 2006)

7 Sqn	5 x Chinook HC2	RAF Odiham
	1 x Gazelle	
18 Sqn	18 x Chinook HC2	RAF Odiham
27 Sqn	10 x Chinook HC2	RAF Odiham
28 Sqn	22 x Merlin HC3	RAF Benson
33 Sqn	15 x Puma HC1	RAF Benson
78 Sqn	1 x Chinook HC2	RAF Mount Pleasant
	2 x Sea King HAR3	(Falklands)
84 Sqn	4 x Griffin HAR2	RAF Akrotiri
230 Sqn	18 x Puma HC1	RAF Aldergrove

JHC Personnel Totals (mid 2005)

JHC Command Group

Army	1,101
Royal Air Force	253
Royal Navy	820

Joint Helicopter Force (Northern Ireland)

Army	411
Royal Air Force	358
Royal Navy	2

RAF Benson

Army	0
Royal Air Force	1,412
Royal Navy	0

RAF Odiham

Army	174
Royal Air Force	1,573
Royal Navy	0

16 Air Assault Brigade

Army	7,490
Royal Air Force	76
Royal Navy	3
Totals	**13,673**

UK AIR SURVEILLANCE AND CONTROL SYSTEM (ASACS)

One of Strike Command's main responsibilities is the UK Air Surveillance and Control System (ASACS). AOC Strike Command is tasked with providing early warning of air attack against the UK air defence region; to provide fighter and missile defences and the associated ground control system; fighter co-ordination with Royal Naval ships operating in adjacent waters and to maintain the integrity of UK air space in war.

ASACS is comprised of a number of individual static and mobile units that provide the minute-to-minute information on air activity required to defend the UK and NATO partners. Manned by officers of Fighter Control under the Operations Support Branch with the support of airmen Aerospace Systems Operators, ASACS is a computer-based system which gathers and disseminates information on all aircraft flying in and around the UK Air Defence Region. The information within is used by the Air Defence Commander when deciding whether to investigate or perhaps even destroy an aircraft flying in an area without permission. Information comes from the RAF's ground-based radars and from the air defence systems of neighbouring NATO partners. ASACS can also receive information via digital data-links from other ground, air or sea-based units including No 1 Air Control Centre, which is part of the UK's Rapid Reaction Force.

A new digital data-linked Control and Reporting Centre (CRC) was opened at RAF Scampton in January 2006. The CRC at Scampton, together with a similar installation at RAF Boulmer, (operational since July 2004) replaces obsolete equipment with an up to date digital capability. These two CRCs should provide state of the art air defence cover until a definitive, fully integrated NATO air defence system comes on line from around 2012.

Each CRC has geographical areas of responsibility and within their own areas, the CRCs receive and process information provided round-the-clock by military and civilian radars. In addition to this radar data, the CRCs also exchange information using digital data-links with neighbouring NATO partners, AEW aircraft and ships.

The second ASACS function is the control of air defence aircraft. Fighter Controllers provide the tactical control required for Air Defence aircraft to police the UK's airspace in peace and war, and they are also involved in the peacetime training of the RAF Air Defence assets. Fighter Controllers also provide support to Ground Attack forces when undertaking training with their Air Defence counterparts.

The CRCs are supported by a number of Reporting Posts (RPs) across the UK. In addition to those found at the CRCs, the locations of the RPs reflect the locations of the main RAF Air Defence radars that feed information into the UK ASACS. In addition to the radars, units have varying capabilities for the exchange of data-link information. The RPs are found at RAF Benbecula in the Hebrides, RAF Staxton Wold near Scarborough and RP Portreath, which is a satellite of RAF St Mawgan on the north coast of Cornwall.

The future location of some ASACS units, especially those currently at RAF Scampton, RAF Kirton-in-Lindsey and RAF Boulmer is under review and we would expect an announcement regarding future intentions towards the end of 2006/early 2007.

ASACS – Mobile Elements
No 1 Air Control Centre (1 ACC) provides the RAF with a mobile command and control capability able to deploy within the UK or anywhere in the world at short notice. The unit has recently been transformed into a fully capable Tactical Air Command and Control System (TACCS) following delivery of state of the art communications and data-link equipment to supplement the two new mobile radars recently delivered into its inventory. No 1 ACC is based at RAF Boulmer when in the UK.

Sentry AEW
The Sentry AEW1 makes a large contribution to ASACS using digital datalinks. The Sentry can deploy rapidly in response to crisis or conflict to provide the Air Defence Commander with information on potential aggressors. The roles within the Mission Crew of the Sentry mirror those within the UK ASACS CRCs, the posts being filled again with Fighter Controllers and Aerospace Systems Operators.

United Kingdom Combined Air Operations Centre
The nerve centre of ASACS is the United Kingdom Combined Air Operations Centre (UKCAOC) at Headquarters Strike Command at RAF High Wycombe. The UKCAOC is responsible for the overall coordination of the Air Defence, Ground Attack and Maritime Air elements of the RAF together with the air forces and navies of our NATO partners. ASACS information is monitored and controlled 24 hours a day. Within the UKCAOC, control and reporting centres are linked with other elements of the NATO Air Defence Ground Environment (NADGE) and with the Ballistic Missile Early Warning Systems (BMEWS) station at RAF Fylingdales in North Yorkshire. The latter is networked with the US operated BMEWS at Thule (Greenland) and Clear (Alaska). By extending high-level radar cover some 3,000 miles across Eastern Europe, Fylingdales would give advance warning of intermediate range ballistic missiles launched against the UK and Western Europe, and of inter-continental ballistic missiles against the North American continent. Fylingdales also tracks satellites and space debris.

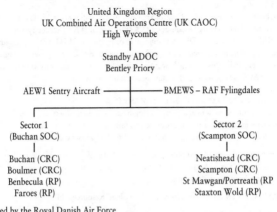

United Kingdom Region
UK Combined Air Operations Centre (UK CAOC)
High Wycombe
|
Standby ADOC
Bentley Priory

AEW1 Sentry Aircraft ——————— BMEWS – RAF Fylingdales

Sector 1
(Buchan SOC)
|
Buchan (CRC)
Boulmer (CRC)
Benbecula (RP)
Faroes (RP)

Sector 2
(Scampton SOC)
|
Neatishead (CRC)
Scampton (CRC)
St Mawgan/Portreath (RP)
Staxton Wold (RP)

* Operated by the Royal Danish Air Force
RAF Saxa Vord (RP) closed on 1 March 2006.

Key. SOC – Sector Operations Centre
      CRC – Control and Reporting Centre
      RP – Reporting Post

In the Falkland Islands there are Reporting Posts at Mount Kent, Mount Alice and Byron Heights.

From late 2003 the majority of UK ASACS units are under the command of 3 Group.

I-UKADGE (Improved-UK Air Defence Ground Environment) is the communications system upon which the air defences depend for their operational effectiveness. The system is fully automated and integrated with the NATO Air Defence Ground Environment (NADGE), which includes sites stretching from Northern Norway to Eastern Turkey, and the Portuguese Air Command and Control System (POACCS). These systems integrate the various sites which are equipped with modern radars, data processing and display systems and are linked by modern digital communications. Computerised data exchange and information from a number of sources such as radars, ships and aircraft is moved around the system on a number of routes to minimise the disruptive effects of enemy action. ICCS (Integrated Command and Control System) provides to the commanders and air defence staff the information gathered in the system and UNITER brings together all the nodes on a digital network.

JTIDS (Joint Tactical Information Distribution/Display System) is a secure tactical datalink network to enable the UK armed forces to participate in Allied operations. JTIDS is now in service throughout the UK armed Forces. The RAF is believed to operate some 60 terminals and the majority of these equip 2 x Tornado F3 squadrons and the AEW1 Sentry aircraft.

BACCS

The Backbone Air Command & Control System (BACCS) will replace ASACS as a component of the North Atlantic Treaty Organisation (NATO) Integrated Air Defence System (NATINADS) around 2009. The programme will be based on NATO ACCS requirements with additional UK requirements being nationally funded. BACCS will provide computer-based static capability covering early warning, air policing and operational training using the existing ASACS radar sensors and communications infrastructure.

RAF Personnel & Training Command (RAF PTC)

HQ PTC controls all personnel aspects ranging from conditions of service, recruiting, training, education, manning, career management, resettlement and pensions. The headquarters also deals with all policy matters relating to medical, dental, legal and chaplaincy.

The Command employs 14,000 people, including 3,000 civilians, at more than 30 locations. It is responsible for over 500 training aircraft of which about 150 are gliders. Headquarters staff number some 1,400 service personnel.

The HQ PTC budget for 2005-2006 was £911 million (Resource DEL).

In general terms the command has the responsibility for: Personnel and Career Management; Flying and Ground Training; Recruiting and Selection; Manning and Manpower Planning; UASs and Air Cadets; Personnel Management of RAF Reserves; Medical, Dental and Nursing Services; Legal and Chaplaincy Service; Bands; Provost and Personnel Security Services; Ceremonials; Service Funds and Community Support; Dress Policy and RAF News.

HQ PTC has a configuration similar to the following.

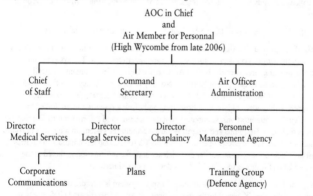

The RAF Training Group Defence Agency forms an integral part of RAF PTC. The Agency comprises nine RAF stations UK-wide with additional minor units elsewhere.

PTC Flying Training Units

RAF Training Units (as at 1 May 2006)

No 1 Flying Training School (1 FTS)
       67 x Tucano T1

72 (R) Sqn	RAF Linton-on-Ouse
207 (R) Sqn	RAF Linton-on-Ouse

No 3 Flying Training School (3 FTS)
       11 x Jetstream T1; 9 x Dominie T1/T2 ; 8 x Tutor T1

45 (R) Sqn	RAF Cranwell
55 (R) Sqn	RAF Cranwell

No 4 Flying Training School (4 FTS)
       69 x Hawk T1/T1A

19 (R) Sqn	RAF Valley
208 (R) Sqn	RAF Valley

Joint Elementry Flying Training School (JEFTS)

18 x Firefly M260	RAF Barkstone Heath
6 x Firefly M260A	RAF Cranwell
14 x Firefly M260	RAF Church Fenton

Defence Helicopter Flying School (DHFS)
       28 x Squirrel HT1; 6 x Griffin HT1

60 (R) Sqn and Central Flying School	RAF Shawbury

Search and Rescue Training Flight (SARTF)

4 x Griffin HT1	RAF Valley

University Air Squadrons

90 x Tutor T1	Various locations

Volunteer Gliding Schools (VGS)

80 x Viking;	53 Vigilant Various locations

RAF Operational Conversion Units (as at 1 April 2006)

15 (R) Sqn	26 x Tornado GR4	RAF Lossiemouth
20 (R) Sqn	9 x Harrier GR7/7A/9/9A	RAF Wittering
	4 x Harrier T10/T12	
29 Sqn	12e x Typhoon	RAF Conningsby (Typhoon OCU)
42 (R) Sqn	3 x Nimrod MR2	RAF Kinloss
56 (R) Sqn	20 x Tornado F3	RAF Leuchars
203 (R) Sqn	3 x Sea King HAR3/3A	RAF St Mawgan

Note. The (R) in a squadron designation represents a training unit/reserve squadron. In the majority of cases this reserve squadron is the Operational Conversion Unit (OCU) for the particular aircraft type and the reserve squadron has a mobilisation role.

The organisation of an OCU is obviously tailored to fit the size of the aircraft fleet being supported. As an example, we believe that No 29 Reserve Sqn (Tornado F3 OCU) is organised along the following lines.

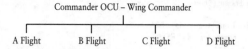

Commander OCU – Wing Commander

| A Flight | B Flight | C Flight | D Flight |

A and B Flights generally provide flying training with about 15-18 x staff crews and about 12 x student crews. C Flight is a standards flight – training instructors, and D Flight provides simulators and a dome air combat trainer.

RAF Communications

In July 2004 the MoD announced the creation of an RAF Communications Hub. As a result communications units would move to RAF Leeming (North Yorkshire).

This means that communications personnel would move from RAF Sealand (Expeditionary Radar and Airfield Squadron – ERAS) to RAF Leeming by April 2006. Communications personnel from RAF Brize Norton (Tactical Communications Wing) and RAF High Wycombe would move to RAF Leeming in 2007.

As of May 2006, major RAF Signals (communications) units are as shown below.

Unit	Location
2 SU	RAF Bampton Castle
9 SU	RAF Boddingtons
81 SU	RAF Bampton Castle
303 SU	Falkland Islands
591 SU	RAF Digby
1001 SU	RAF Oakhanger (SATCOMS)
Tactical Communications Wing	RAF Brize Norton

RAF signals communications fall into three categories. First, there is a large complex of HF transmitter and receiver facilities in the UK, including communications centres with automatic message routing equipment. Operations include those on behalf of Strike Command, the Military Air Traffic Organisation, NATO, and the Meteorological Office.

Second, the RAF Signals Staff operate message relay centres, both automatic and manual and also manages the RAF's General Purpose Telephone network. RAF command operating procedures are monitored on all networks to ensure high standards are achieved and maintained. To reduce risk of compromise, all RAF communications facilities designed to carry classified information are checked for communications electrical security by Command Staff. For the use of the all the armed forces, the MoD has procured a fixed telecommunications network called Boxer under a Private Finance Initiative (PFI) contract, which will save the increasing expense of renting lines from the private sector.

Third, the main operation of the Skynet Satellite Communications System, which offers overseas formations telegraphed, data and speech communications, is controlled by RAF Command. RAF Oakhanger is the focal point of military satellite communications in the UK. Two satellite communications (Satcom) units are based at Oakhanger, No 1001 Signals Unit and a NATO Satellite Ground Terminal. From 1998, 3 x Skynet 4 Stage 2 replaced the existing Skynet satellites when they reached the end of their operational life, and entered service late in 1998. In addition, a management service for the NATO 4 series of satellites is provided. From 2008, Skynet 5 is expected to enter service and provide the next generation of flexible and survivable satellite communications services for military use, and will replace the Skynet 4 constellation at the end of its predicted life.

Robust military satellite communications services are essential to support inter and intra-theatre information exchange requirements and ensure that deployed and mobile forces are not constrained by the need to remain within the range of terrestrial communications.

AOC Signals has a large engineering design staff of engineers, technicians and draughtsmen. Manufacturing resources include a general mechanical engineering and calibration capacity, plus a facility for the systems design, development and installation of certain airborne signals role equipment.

RAF Logistics

Since the MoD-wide reorganisation of 2000, logistics support for all three Services is the responsibility of Defence Logistics Organisation (DLO). Two DLO Directorates are responsible for logistic provision to the RAF.

♦ DG Log (Strike) – 1, 2 & 3 Groups
♦ DG Log (Supply Chain) - Commodities Group and Munitions Group

At the MoD, the officer who is ultimately responsible for logistics is the Air Member for Logistics who is one of the 11 Air Force Board Members.

For Strike Command, the Chief of Staff Support (COS Support) is the senior Logistics commander and the principal two star officer (Air Vice Marshal) who interfaces directly with the DLO. COS Support has a place on the Strike Command Management Board.

The RAF's logistics hub has moved from RAF Wyton and was established at RAF Wittering in April 2006. Prior to this 85 (Expeditionary Logistics) Wing (ELW), (including 2 Mechanical Transport Squadron, Mobile Catering Support Unit (MCSU), elements of the Force Development Squadron (FDS) and the Wing Command Group) moved to RAF Wittering from RAF Stafford in September 2005. RAF Stafford is due for closure in December 2007.

RAF Procurement

Like logistics, UK procurement is managed on a tri-service basis by the Defence Procurement Agency (DPA). The DPA was launched on 1 April 1999 as an Executive Agency of the Ministry of Defence (MoD), replacing the MoD Procurement Executive. The core role of the DPA is the procurement of military equipment to meet the operational requirements of the armed forces. RAF operational requirements are formulated and managed by Integrated Project Teams (IPT). RAF personnel are seconded to the DPA for the duration of their appointments – usually two to three years.

OVERSEAS BASES

Strike Command has responsibility for all RAF bases overseas.

RAF Akrotiri, Cyprus

The RAF use the airfield at Akrotiri as a staging post for transport aircraft, and as a temporary operating base for aircraft carrying out Armament Practice Camps. Akrotiri is the permanent base of 84 Squadron who perform Search and Rescue duties as well as a support role for the UN peacekeeping forces on the island. In addition, a detachment of the RAF Regiment is stationed at Akrotiri to assist with airfield defence.

RAF Ascension Island

Situated in the middle of the Atlantic Ocean, and over 700 miles from its nearest neighbour, Ascension Island was used extensively as a staging base during the Falklands War. This is still the major role for the Station, which it performs for both the RAF and the USAF.

RAFU Goose Bay, Canada

A team of RAF personnel is stationed at Goose Bay in Labrador to support RAF fast jet aircraft carrying out low level flying training over Labrador. The fast jets are usually accompanied by VC-10s, Tristars or Hercules aircraft, providing AAR or transport support.

RAF Gibraltar

Although aircraft are no longer stationed at RAF Gibraltar, Hercules and Nimrod and Tornado aircraft make regular visits.

Mount Pleasant, Falkland Islands

Mount Pleasant was opened in 1984 to establish a fighter and transport presence in the Islands following the Falklands War. Currently based at Mount Pleasant are No 1435 Flight with 4 x Tornado F3s, No 1312 Flight, with 1 x VC10 tanker and 1 x Hercules C1, as well as No 78 Squadron with 1 x Chinook and 2 x Griffin. Ground units include Signals Units and a Rapier surface to air missile detachment.

Mobile Air Movement Squadron (MAMS)

During operations and exercises, aircraft often visit overseas airfields where no regular RAF ground handling organisation exists. For this purpose, Strike Command has a Mobile Air Movement Squadron (MAMS) at RAF Lyneham, which provides teams who are expert in all aspects of loading and unloading aircraft.

RAF STATION ORGANISATION

An indication of the manner in which an RAF Station might be organised is as follows:

This example is an RAF Station with 3 x Tornado GR4 flying squadrons – each with 12 x aircraft. The 36 aircraft will have cost at least £780 million (at 1980s prices) in total purchase costs, and the combined running costs for the operation of these three squadrons will be in the region of some £120 million pounds per annum.

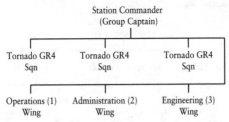

Station Commander
(Group Captain)

Tornado GR4 Sqn   Tornado GR4 Sqn   Tornado GR4 Sqn

Operations (1) Wing   Administration (2) Wing   Engineering (3) Wing

Notes. (1) Ops Wing; (2) Admin Wing; (3) Eng Wing; (4) Expect the commanders of the Tornado Sqns to be Wing Commanders aged between 34-40; Ops, Admin and Eng Wings will almost certainly be commanded by Wing Commanders from their respective branch specialities – these Wing Commanders will probably be a little older than the commanders of the flying squadrons.

Flying Squadron Organisation

Sqn Commander
(Wing Commander)

Flight Commander
(Sqn Leader)
6 x Tornado GR4

Flight Commander
(Sqn Leader)
6 x Tornado GR4

Department Leaders (1)

Note. Generally 1 x Tornado GR4 will be held in reserve (IUR)

Note. (1) These departmental leaders have responsibility for weapons, airframes, propulsion, electronics, flight guidance and control systems, communications, automatic navigation and attack controls and report to the squadron commander.

193

Administration Wing Organisation

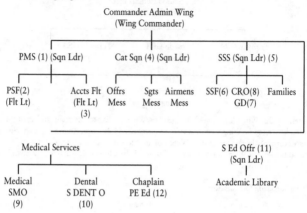

Notes. (1) Personnel Management Squadron; (2) Personal Services Flight; (3) Accounts Flight; (4) Catering Sqn; (5) Station Services Sqn; (6) Station Services Flight; (7) General Duties Flight; (8) Community Relations Officer (9) Senior Medical Officer; (10) Senior Dental Officer; (11) Senior Education Officer; (12) Physical Education.

Operations Wing Organisation

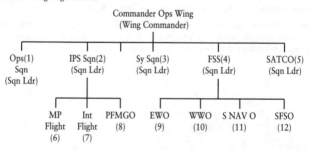

Notes. (1) Operations Sqn; (2) Intelligence & Planning Sqn; (3) Security Sqn – includes RAF Police & Station Defence Personnel; (4) Flying Support Sqn; (5) Senior Air Traffic Control Officer; (6) Mission Plans Flight; (7) Intelligence Flight; (8) Pre-flight Message Generation Officer; (9) Electronic Warfare Officer; (10) Wing Weapon Officer; (11) Senior Navigation Officer; (12) Station Safety Officer.

Engineering Wing

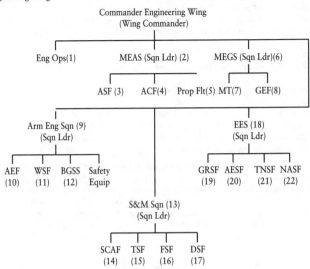

Notes. (1) Engineering Ops; (2) Mechanical Engineering Aircraft Sqn; (3) Aircraft Servicing Flight; (4) Aircraft Components Flight; (5) Propulsion Flight; (6) Mechanical Engineering Ground Squadron; (7) Mechanical Transport; (8) General Engineering Flight; (9) Armament Engineering Sqn; (10) Armament Engineering Flight; (11) Weapon Storage Flight; (12) Bomb Group Supply Section; (13) Supply & Movements Sqn; (14) Supply Control & Accounts Flight; (15) Technical Supply Flight; (16) Forward Supply Flight; (17) Domestic Supply Flight; (18) Electrical Engineering Squadron; (19) Ground Radio Servicing Flight; (20) Avionics Electrical Systems Flight; (21) Tornado Navigation Systems Flight; (22) Navigation and Attack Systems Flight.

RAF AIRCRAFT

As of April 2006 there were approximately 775 fixed wing aircraft of 22 various types in RAF service (including those not in front line service).

- ◆ Current major re-equipment programmes are:
- ◆ Joint Strike Fighter to replace current Harrier GR7
- ◆ Future Air Combat System to replace Tornado GR4
- ◆ Future Strategic Tanker Aircraft (FSTA) to replace VC10 and Tristar
- ◆ Typhoon to replace Jaguar and Tornado F3 (in progress)
- ◆ Hawk 128 Advanced Jet Trainer to replace Hawk T1/T1A

- A400M to replace the Hercules C1/C3 fleet
- Nimrod MRA4 to replace Nimrod MR2
- Brimstone anti-armour weapon to equip Tornado GR4 and Harrier
- Beyond Visual Range Air-to-Air Missile (BVRAAM – Meteor) to equip Typhoon

TORNADO GR-4

In 2006, the latest strike variant of the Tornado – the GR4 – is in service with:

9 Squadron	12 x Tornado GR4	Marham
12 Squadron	12 x Tornado GR4	Lossiemouth
14 Squadron	12 x Tornado GR4	Lossiemouth
31 Squadron	12 x Tornado GR4	Marham
617 Squadron	12 x Tornado GR4	Lossiemouth
15 (Reserve) Squadron	26 x Tornado GR4	Lossiemouth

Crew 2; Wingspan (open) 13.9 m; Wingspan (swept) 8.6 m; Height 5.9 m; Length 16.7 m; Max Weapon Load 18,000 lb/8,180 kg; Max Take Off Weight 27,900 kg; Max Speed Mach 2.2 (1,452 mph/2,333 kph); Max Ferry Range approx 3,900 km; Required Runway Length approx 900 m. Engines 2 x Turbo-Union RB 199-34R Mk103 Turbofans; Armament 1 x 27 mm Mauser Cannon, 3 x weapon points under fuselage, 4 x weapon points under wings; AIM-9L Sidewinder AAM; ALARM; JP233; BL755 CBU; Paveway II, III, EPR (IV); Brimstone; Storm Shadow CASOM.

The Tornado Multi-Role Combat aircraft (MRCA) has been the RAF's principal strike weapon system over the past two decades. Designed in the Cold War to penetrate Soviet air defence at low level, the Tornado is nuclear-capable. Since the withdrawal from service of the WE177 nuclear bomb in 1998, the Tornado strike capability has been restricted to conventional weapons. The Tornado MRCA was jointly developed by the UK, West Germany and Italy under a collaborative agreement and manufactured by a consortium of companies formed under the name of Panavia. The Tornado GR-1 was the most numerous and important aircraft in the RAF inventory, and the GR-1 operated in the strike/attack and reconnaissance roles. The first prototype flew in 1974 and the first RAF Squadron equipped with the GR-1 became operational in 1982.

During the 1990 Gulf War, Tornado GR1s were amongst the first aircraft in action from 17 January 1991. During the war, the Tornado GR1 force flew 1,500 operational sorties divided almost equally between offensive counter air targets such as airfields and air defence sites, and interdiction targets such as bridges. The RAF deployed 48 x GR1 in the area during hostilities. A total of six GR1s were lost in action, five of which were involved in low-or medium- level attacks with 1,000 pound bombs and one that was flying a low-level JP233 mission. The final three weeks of the air war saw the Tornado GR1 force concentrating almost exclusively on day and night precision attacks dropping LGBs from medium altitude.

There are plans to maintain the Tornado GR4 in service until 2018. 142 x Tornado GR-1s have been upgraded to GR4 standard under the Tornado Mid-Life Update (MLU) programme costing some £943m. Deliveries began in 1998 and were scheduled for completion by the end of 2003. Compared to the GR1, the GR4 has a Forward-Looking Infra-Red (FLIR), a wide angle Head-Up Display (HUD), improved cockpit displays, Night-Vision Goggle (NVG) compatibility, new avionics and weapons systems, updated computer software, and Global Positioning System (GPS). The upgrade also re-arms the Tornado with the Storm Shadow stand-off missile, Brimstone advanced anti-armour weapon, and the Paveway EPW LGB. New sensors include the RAPTOR and Vicon reconnaissance pods and an improved Thermal Imaging Airborne Laser Designator (TIALD) targeting pod. A separate programme covered an integrated Defensive Aids Suite consisting of the radar warning receiver, Sky Shadow radar jamming pod and BOZ-107 chaff and flare dispenser. The standard Tornado GR4 can also fulfil tactical reconnaissance tasks when equipped with an external camera pod.

During the Iraq War of 2003 (Operation Telic), GR4s from all five active Tornado squadrons were deployed. One Tornado was lost to friendly fire. The Storm Shadow air-launched cruise missile was fired operationally for the first time from a Tornado GR4 during conflict.

Expect a Tornado GR4 squadron to have 15 established crews.

RAF Tornado GR4 aircraft are due to be phased out of service in 2015.

Tornado GR4A
In service with:

II (AC) Squadron	12 x Tornado GR4A	Marham
13 Squadron	12 x Tornado GR4A	Marham

The Tornado GR4A is used as a combat reconnaissance aircraft – also upgraded under the GR1 series MLU – and has no cannons mounted in the forward fuselage. Replacing these are an internally-mounted Sideways Looking Infra-Red system and a Linescan infra-red surveillance system.

TORNADO F3
In service with:

25 Squadron	16 x Tornado F3	Leeming
43 Squadron	16 x Tornado F3	Leuchars
111 Squadron	16 x Tornado F3	Leuchars
1435 Flight	4 x Tornado F3	Mount Pleasant
56 (Reserve) Squadron	20 x Tornado F3	Leuchars

Crew 2; Wingspan (open) 13.9 m; Wingspan (swept) 8.6 m; Height 5.9 m; Length 18.7 m; Max Weapon Load 8,500 kg; Max Take Off Weight 27,900 kg; Max Speed Mach 2.2 (1,452 mph/2,333 kph); Engines 2 x Turbo-Union RB 199-34R-Mk104 Turbofans; Intercept Radius

1,850 km (subsonic) or 550 km (supersonic); Radar Foxhunter Air Intercept radar known as the A124; Armament 1 x 27mm Mauser Cannon; AAM 4 x Sky Flash; AMRAAM; 4 x AIM-9L Sidewinder, ASRAAM; ALARM.

The Air Defence Variant (ADV) of the Tornado from which the F3 was developed flew for the first time in October 1979. The aircraft has a long-range, autonomous capability that enables operations to be conducted some 350 nm away from bases in bad weather, in an ECM environment and operating against multiple targets at high or low level, which can be engaged at distances in excess of 20 nm. With tanker support, the Tornado F3 Combat Air Patrol (CAP) time is increased from 2 hrs and 30 mins to a loiter time of several hours. The Tornado F3 was originally armed with 4 x semi-recessed Sky Flash, 4 x Sidewinder AIM-9L missiles, and a single Mauser 27 mm cannon and had about 80% commonality with the Tornado GR1. The main difference between the Tornado GR and the F3 is the extended fuselage, longer range air intercept Foxhunter Radar (replacing the terrain-following/ground mapping radar of the Tornado GR1) and the armament. Extension of the fuselage provides additional space for avionics and an extra 900 litres of fuel. RAF Tornado F3s are equipped with the Joint Tactical Information Distribution System (JTIDS). Operating in conjunction with Sentry AEW1 airborne early warning aircraft and other allied fighters, the system gives a real-time picture of the air battle, including information obtained by other sensors in other fighters or airborne early warning (AEW) aircraft.

RAF Tornado F3s were sent to the Gulf in August 1990 and by the end of hostilities on the 28 February 1991, 18 x F3 aircraft had flown some 2,500 sorties during their deployment including 700 sorties during the period of hostilities. Tornado F-3s from all four active UK squadrons were deployed during the 2003 Iraq War (Op Telic).

Under the recent £140 million Tornado F3 Capability Sustainment Programme (CSP), 100 F-3s were upgraded to incorporate the Raytheon AIM-120 Advanced Medium-Range Air-to-Air Missile (AMRAAM), and the Matra BAe Dynamics Advanced Short- Range Air-to-Air Missile (ASRAAM). For the Iraq War, F-3s were also modified to carry the ALARM anti-radiation missile. The F3 will almost certainly stay in service until 2007-2010. Its replacement is the Eurofighter Typhoon. Expect a Tornado F3 Squadron to have between 16 and 20 established crews.

Tornado in World Service
(Original Procurement Figures)

	GR1/IDS	F2/F3/ADV	ECR/GR1A/Recce
UK	199	170	26
Germany	302	–	36
Italy	70	24 (leased from UK)	–
Saudi Arabia	96	24	–

EUROFIGHTER TYPHOON

In service with:

3 Sqn	12 x Typhoon	RAF Cottesmore (from 1 April 2006)
17 (R) Sqn	6e x Typhoon	RAF Conningsby (Typhoon OEU)
29 Sqn	12e x Typhoon	RAF Conningsby (Typhoon OCU)

Crew 1; Length 15.96 m; Height 5.23 m; Wingspan 10.95 m; Max Speed 1,321mph/2,125 kph; Empty Weight 22,000 lb/9,999 kg; Max Take-Off Weight 46,305 lb/21,000 kg; Engine 2 x Eurojet EJ200 turbofans; Ferry Range 5,382 km (3,310 miles) with 4 x drop tanks; Armament 1 x 27mm (first RAF batch only); Air Interdiction. 2 x Storm Shadow, 2 x ALARM, 4 x AMRAAM, 2 x ASRAAM, 2 x 1,500 litre fuel tank, 1 x 1,000 litre fuel tank; Close Air Support. 18 x Brimstone, 4 x AMRAAM, 2 x ASRAAM, 1 x 1,000 litre fuel tank. SEAD. 6 x ALARM, 4 x AMRAAM, 2 x ASRAAM, 1 x 1,000 litre fuel tank; Maritime Attack. 4 x Penguin, 4 x AMRAAM, 2 x ASRAAM, 2 x 1,500 litre fuel tank, 1 x 1,000 litre fuel tank; also Sidewinder AAM; Meteor BVRAAM; Paveway II,III, EPR (IV) LGB; JDAM or other PGB.

The first production aircraft flew in 2003, and delivery of the first aircraft started during early 2004. The Typhoon is to replace the Tornado F3 and then the Jaguar. It is planned that the Typhoon front-line will comprise seven squadrons, of which four will be primarily air defence, two swing-role, and one offensive support covering a full range of combat air operations. Initial deliveries will be to the Typhoon hub at RAF Coningsby. Subsequent aircraft will go to Tornado F3 squadrons at Leeming and Leuchars before Jaguar squadrons are re-equipped.

The Typhoon (formerly EFA – European Fighter Aircraft) is a single seat, STOL capable aircraft optimised for air superiority/air defence and ground attack roles. Germany, Italy and Spain are UK partners in the most costly European collaboration programme to date. The air forces of the four countries have ordered a total of 620 Eurofighters (UK 232, Germany 180, Italy 121, and Spain 87). The UK will receive its aircraft in 3 x Tranches. Tranche 1 – 55 aircraft (mainly air defence aircraft with some multi-role towards the end of the tranche).

Tranche 2 – 89 aircraft.

Tranche 3 – 88 aircraft (Final decision on production and numbers not required before 2007).

The original estimated procurement cost of the RAF Typhoons was some £16.7bn, including research and development costs – making it the most expensive weapon system yet produced for the UK armed forces. The latest unit cost estimate is £64.8 million across Tranche 1 and Tranche 2 aircraft.

Typhoon is a fifth-generation combat aircraft with fully digital, integrated aircraft, avionics and weapon systems. Typhoon is designed to perform at least five air missions. Air Superiority, Air Interdiction, Suppression of Enemy Air Defence (SEAD), Close Air Support

(CAS) and Maritime Attack. It may in time be modified to fulfil naval aircraft carrier roles, and a navalised version of Typhoon may be the longer term answer to the Joint Strike Fighter programme if difficulties with the United States cannot be resolved.

The aircraft is designed to carry 6 x medium-range and 2 x short-range air-to-air missiles. The aircraft has 13 x store stations and an internal gun fitted on the starboard side. A range of air-to-ground weapons can be carried, including the new Storm Shadow CASOM, Brimstone anti-armour weapon, and the future Precision Guided Bomb (PGB). No modifications will be necessary to carry 'smart' weapons and three stations can carry external fuel pods. The Captor radar is a collaboration European design. Other sensors include the Infra-Red Search and Track (IRST) system. The Defensive Aids Sub-System (DASS) equipment is carried in 2 x wing pods that are an integral part of the wing. The datalink is provided by the Multiple Image Data System (MIDS). The aircraft will be able to operate from a 500 metre strip.

There has been much discussion regarding the quality and performance of this aircraft. During an exchange in the House of Lords on 13 January 2006 the Parliamentary Under-Secretary of State Lord Bach commented " I must refer to the senior United States Air Force General who, fresh from an exhilarating first flight in Typhoon and, naturally, quite excited, was heard to say "This is the best fast jet in the world".

JAGUAR GR3 AND T4

In service with:

6 Squadron	11 x Jaguar GR3	Conningsby
	1 x Jaguar T4	

Note. 41 Sqn with 12 x Jaguar GR3 (RAF Coltishall) disbanded on 31 March 2006.

Crew (GR3/3A) 1 (T4) 2; Length (GR 3/3A) 16.83 m; Wingspan 8.69 m; Height 4.89 m; All Up Operational Weight approx 11,000 kg; Max Weapons Load 10,000 lb/4,500 kg; Max Speed 1,056 mph/1,690 k/ph; Weapons Engines 2 x Rolls-Royce Turbomeca Adour Mk 106s; Armament 2 x 30 mm Aden Cannon, (T4)1 x 30 mm Aden Cannon; 2 x Sidewinder AAM; JP233; CBU-87; Paveway II, III; BL 755; CRV-7 rockets.

Produced to meet a joint Anglo-French requirement in 1965 for a dual-role advanced/operational trainer and tactical support aircraft, the Jaguar has been transformed into a potent fighter-bomber. The RAF originally intended to use the aircraft purely as an advanced trainer, but this was later changed to the offensive support role on cost grounds. The first RAF aircraft took to the air in October 1969, and each air force placed orders for 200 aircraft – the RAF opting for 165 single-seat and 35 two-seat aircraft and at its peak the Jaguar equipped eight front-line squadrons in the UK and Germany.

Of the remaining RAF Jaguar fleet, aircraft have recently undergone a major upgrade programme and been designated as the Jaguar GR3 (T4 for the 2-seat variant). The Adour 104 engine has been changed for the more powerful Adour 106 under a £61m contract. The upgrade also included improved avionics. Global Positioning System (GPS) and Terrain Referenced Navigation (TRN) integrated into the Inertial Navigator (IN) internal and external Night Vision Goggles (NVG) compatible lighting, helmet- mounted sight and ASRAAM capability, and new Head-Up Display (HUD) and Head- Down Displays (HDD). Also incorporated are a Thermal Imaging and Laser Designator series 400 capability integrated with Map and Symbol Generator graphics, a new Jaguar Mission Planner system, provision for the Vicon 18-601 Electro-Optic reconnaissance pod, provision for a Jaguar Replacement Reconnaissance Pod, and a Paveway III and EPR Laser Guided Munitions capability. Expect a Jaguar GR3 Squadron to have 16 established crews.

Based on current plans the Jaguar fleet will be withdrawn from Royal Air Force service by 2009.

HARRIER

The RAF's Harriers are in service with:

1 Squadron	9 x Harrier GR9/9A	Cottesmore
	1 x Harrier T12	
4 Squadron	13 x Harrier GR7	Cottesmore
	1 x Harrier T10	
	(eventually GR9/9A and T 12)	
20 (Reserve Squadron)	9 x Harrier GR7/7A/9/9A	Wittering
	6 x Harrier T10/T12	

Note. All of these aircraft are now part of the Joint Force Harrier (JFH) organisation. JFH comprises 2 x Royal Navy (Fleet Air Arm) Harrier Squadrons (800 Sqn and 801 Sqn) and 2 x RAF Harrier Squadrons.

Crew (GR7, GR7A, GR9, GR9A) 1; (T Mark 10, T12) 2; Length (GR7, GR7A,GR9) 14.1 m; Length (T10, T12) 17 m; Wingspan (normal) 9.2 m; Height (GR7) 3.45 m; Height (T10) 4.17 m; Max Speed 1,065 k/ph (661 mph) at sea level; All Up Operational Weight approx 13,494 kg; Engine (GR7, GR9, T10, T12) 1 x Rolls-Royce Pegasus Mk 105 (GR7A, GR9A) 1 x Rolls-Royce Pegasus Mk 107; Ferry Range 5,382 km (3,310 miles) with 4 x drop tanks; Armament on seven available wing stations. 2 x 30 mm Aden guns, 4 x wing weapon pylons and 1 x under-fuselage weapon pylon, conventional or cluster bombs; 2 x Sidewinder AIM-9L AAM, ASRAAM; up to 16 x Mk 82 or six Mk 83 bombs; 4 x Maverick air-to-ground anti-armour missiles, Paveway II and III laser-guided bombs; Brimstone anti-armour missiles, CRV-7 rocket pods; 2 x Storm Shadow CASOM.

The RAF will standardise on the Harrier GR9/9A in a move announced by the MoD in 2002, UK MoD officials said the type rationalisation was in preparation for the introduction of the Future Joint Combat Aircraft and the Future Aircraft Carrier in 2012.

The MoD explained that the optimum development of the JFH is to support only one Harrier type to its end of service life, the "more capable GR 9".

The JFH received its first upgraded Harrier GR9 from BAE Systems' Warton facility in November 2005. Under the terms of a £500 million programme the avionics of some 60 x Harrier GR 7/7A will be upgraded to GR9 standard and 11 x Harrier T 10 will be upgraded to T 12 standard.

The GR9 programme will incorporate a major upgrade to the aircraft's avionics and weapons systems and enable the aircraft to carry a variety of current and future weapons. These include Maverick air-surface missiles, Brimstone anti-armour missiles and AIM-9L Sidewinder air-to-air missiles for self-defence. A new, stronger composite rear fuselage will also be fitted. These aircraft will become Harrier GR9s, whilst those with the uprated engines and weapons systems will be Harrier GR9As. The programme also includes an upgrade of the two-seater T10 aircraft to the equivalent GR9 standard known as the Harrier T12.

The Harrier GR9 is the latest of the Harrier 'Jump Jets' originating from the 1960s. Capable of taking off and landing vertically, the Harrier is not tied to airfields with long concrete runways but, if necessary can be dispersed to sites in the field close to the forward edge of the battle area.

All three in-service RAF Harrier squadrons were deployed for the 2003 Iraq War in Operation Telic. And to date (April 2006) Harriers have been deployed in Afghanistan in support of ISAF (International Security Assistance Force) since September 2004. Aircraft operate from Kandahar airfield.

Expect a Harrier GR9 Squadron to have 15 established crews.

Joint Strike Fighter/Joint Combat Aircraft
Current plans under the UK Joint Combat Aircraft programme are for the Joint Strike Fighter (JSF) to replace the Harrier. The estimated in-service date is 2012 to coincide with the first of the new UK aircraft carriers (CVF) entering service.

The US DoD placed a contract for the Lockheed Martin F-35 in October 2001. The JSF/FJCA programme is driven by the US requirement for up to 3,000 aircraft. BAe Systems and Rolls-Royce form the principal partners of Lockheed Martin, along with the US company Northrop Grumman and General Electric. Other international parties to the programme include Italy, Netherlands, Turkey, Canada, Denmark and Norway. The UK is to select either the Short Take Off Vertical Landing (STOVL) or Carrier Variant (CV) version of JSF, or possibly both. The likely date for a production contract is 2006. The joint RAF/RN requirement for the JSF is 150 aircraft with first deliveries in 2010 to meet an in-service date of 2012. The projected UK procurement cost is approximately £4.3bn including £2bn for R&D and £2.3bn for production. By 2015 the only offensive aircraft in the RAF inventory should be the Typhoon and the JSF.

Once in service we would expect the JSF to be capable of undertaking air interdiction operations making low or medium-level attacks using precision-guided, freefall or retarded bombs. Close air support missions against targets in the forward edge of the battle area and fleet air defence patrols in the area of vessels that require protection from enemy air attack.

RAF Lossiemouth will be home for the new Joint Combat Aircraft.

Unmanned Combat Air Vehicles

In July 2005 Adam Ingram (Minister of State – Armed Forces), stated that the MoD is pursuing a twin track strategy to explore the conceptual thinking and underlying technology for unmanned combat air vehicles (UCAVs) The former involves participation in the US Joint Unmanned Combat Air System Programme concept work. The latter is focused on ensuring the UK is able to make intelligent choices with respect to UCAV design, technology development and manufacture, and is intended to enhance the UK's industrial position to undertake either an indigenous or collaborative programme should a firm military requirement for UCAVs emerge in the future.

In addition, the UK MoD is considering a proposal from Thales UK as preferred bidder for a tactical unmanned air vehicles (UAV) system manufactured in the UK to meet the Watchkeeper requirement for an intelligence, surveillance, target acquisition and reconnaissance capability.

SENTRY AEW1

In service with:

8 Squadron	3 x Sentry AEW1	Waddington
23 Squadron	3 x Sentry AEW1	Waddington

Crew; 5 x Flight Crew and 12/13 x Mission Crew; Length 46.61m; Wingspan 44.42 m; Height 12.73 m; All Up Operational Weight 147,400 kg; Max Speed 853 k/ph (530 mph); Patrol Endurance 6 hrs (can be enhanced by AAR); (Ferry Range 3,200 km; Engines 4 x CFM-56-2A-3; Armament provision for self-defence air-to-air missiles.

Deliveries of the Sentry AEW1 commenced in March 1991 and delivery of all seven airframes was complete in early 1992. These seven aircraft are of the same type as the 18 delivered to the multinational NATO early warning force between 1982/1985. Powered by four CFM 56-2A-3 engines, the Sentry is designed to cruise at 29,000 feet whilst detecting air and surface contacts with its AN/APY-2 surveillance radar. Information is then transmitted back to interceptor aircraft and ground air-and-ship-based units using a wide variety of digital datalinks. All are equipped with the Joint Tactical Information Distribution System (JTIDS) and a 665,360 word memory secure communication system. Between 1998–2000, RAF Sentry aircraft were upgraded under the Radar System Improvement Programme (RSIP) costing some £120 million. New Global Positioning System navigation equipment was also installed. Most recently, Sentry AEW1 aircraft were deployed in support of Operation Telic during the 2003 Iraq War, and for Operation Oracle in support of ISAF in Afghanistan from 2002.

NIMROD

In service with:

120 Squadron	8 x Nimrod MR2	Kinloss
201 Squadron	7 x Nimrod MR2	Kinloss
42 (Reserve) Squadron	3 x Nimrod MR2	Kinloss

Note. This group of units is known as the Kinloss Air Wing. We are reasonably certain that there are approximately 18 aircraft in this group at any one time. Aircraft are shown as being allocated to squadrons for ease of accounting – real numbers may change almost daily.

51 Squadron	3 x Nimrod R1	Waddington

Nimrod MR2. Crew 13; Length 38.63 m; Span 35 m; Height 9.08 m; Max Speed 575mph/926 km; Max All Up Weight 87,090 kg; Endurance 10-12 hrs; Operating range 3,800 miles, 6,080 km; Ferry Range 9,265 km; ; Engines 4 x Rolls Royce Spey RB 168-20 Mark 250 Turbofans; Armament. Sidewinder AIM-9, Harpoon, 9 x Mark 46 or Stingray Torpedoes, bombs.

Nimrod is a development of the basic Comet No 4C airframe that dates from the late 1940's. Both the current variants are descended from the original Nimrod MR Mark 1 version (first flight May 1967) upgraded during the 1980s. The first is the MR Mark 2P, which has been developed for long-range maritime patrol. The Nimrod MR2 carries out three main roles; Anti-Submarine Warfare (ASW), Anti-Surface Unit Warfare (ASUW) and Search and Rescue (SAR). Its long ferry range enables the crew to monitor maritime areas far to the north of Iceland and up to 4,000 km out into the Western Atlantic. With AAR (Air-to-Air Refuelling), its range and endurance is greatly extended. The MR 2 is a very lethal submarine killer carrying the most up to date sensors and data processing equipment linked to the weapon systems. In addition to weapons and sonar-buoys, a searchlight mounted in the starboard wing pod can be used for search and rescue (SAR) operations. Crew members comprise 2 x Pilots and a flight engineer operate the flight deck, 2 x Navigators, an Air Electronics Officer (AEO), the sonar-buoy sensor team of 3 x Air Electronic Operators and 4 x Air Electronic Operators to manage a wide range of avionics and weapon systems .

The second version is the R Mark 1, an aircraft specially fitted out for the gathering of electronic intelligence and only three are known to be in service. This is a highly secret aircraft that has been in RAF service since 1971 and about which little is known except that it has been spotted on patrol over the Baltic Sea. The Nimrod R1s are externally distinguishable from the maritime reconnaissance version by the absence of the magnetic anomaly detection tail booms and a distinctive pod on the leading edge of the port wing. In-flight refuelling probes were added in 1982.

Under a £2.2 billion contract in July 1996, the Nimrod upgrade programme involved 21 Nimrod MR2 aircraft to Maritime Reconnaissance Attack 4 (MRA4) standard, together with training and integrated logistics support packages. The programme would involve the total replacement of the aircraft's systems and over 80% of its airframe, resulting in the RAF receiving back practically a new aircraft. There has been a substantial programme cost escalation (estimated programme cost £3.8bn by 2005) and considerable slippage. Numbers of MR4 to be procured have reduced from 21 to 12 as a result of cost escalation. The consequence of the Nimrod MRA4 in-service date slip is that the Nimrod MR2 will remain in service until at least mid-2010. The operational impact of the slippage will be partly mitigated by existing measures to introduce upgrades to some Nimrod MR2 systems, notably Replacement Acoustic Processors (RAP), navigation systems, datalinks and other communications to address inter-operability issues.

Nimrod MRA4 will have a reach extending to some 6,000 miles, compared to the current MR2 capability of some 3,800 miles. Rolls BR710 engines replace RR Spey engines. Other capability improvements over MR2 include increased time on station, a major improvement in overall sensor performance and weapon carrying capability. The new digital, integrated mission system features the Searchwater 2000 radar, UYS503/AQS970 sonar, DASS 2000 ECM, and EL/L8300UK ESM. The crew complement has reduced by 25%.

Weapons will include torpedoes (Tigerfish), AGM-84 Harpoon anti-ship missiles (range 50 nautical miles) or AIM-9 Sidewinder air-to-air missiles for defence against hostile aircraft.

Nimrod MRA4 aircraft will be based at RAF Kinloss.

ASTOR
In service with:

| 5 Sqn | 5 x Sentinel R1 (ASTOR) | RAF Waddington |

Crew 2 with 3 mission systems operators; Length 30.3 m; Height 7.57 m; Wingspan 28.6 m; Empty Weight 22,817 kg; Max Take-Off Weight 43,094 kg; Range 6,500 nm/12,000 km; Endurance 14 plus hours; Operating altitude 15,000 m; Engines 2 x RR BR710; Systems ASARS-2 radar derivative; narrowband datalink subsystem (NDLS), wideband data link based on Common Data Link (CDL); Defensive Aids Subsystem (DASS) developed for the Nimrod MRA4, including missile warning system, radar warning receiver, towed radar decoy and chaff and flare dispensers.

The Airborne Stand-off Radar (ASTOR) is a new British capability for operations over and around the battlefield. It is to form the UK equivalent to the US E-8 Joint Surveillance Target Attack Radar System (JSTARS). ASTOR is to provide a long range all weather theatre surveillance and target acquisition system capable of detecting moving, fixed and static targets. It is designed to meet a joint Army and RAF requirement. The production contract was signed in December 1999 for the supply of 5 x air-platforms, 8 x ground stations, and contractor logistic support. The principal elements of ASTOR are the Bombardier Global Express aircraft and the Raytheon ASARS-2 side looking airborne radar used on the U-2. The radar operates at high altitude and in all weathers to provide high resolution. ASARS-2 has been reported to provide images of the battlefield at ranges of 160 km, at altitudes up to 47,000 feet. High speed data-links transfer the data from aircraft to ground stations in near real-time. The system has directional and broadcast data links which are interoperable with existing US U-2Rs, JSTARS and command and control networks.

Full operational capability should be achieved by 2008. The main ASTOR operating centre will be based at RAF Waddington in the UK. The projected procurement cost is just over £1bn.

HAWK
In service with:

100 Squadron	16 x Hawk T1/1A	Leeming (target towing)
No 4 Flying Training School (4 FTS)	69 x Hawk T1/1A	Valley – 19 (R) and 208 (R) Sqns
Red Arrows	10 x Hawk T1A	Scampton

Crew 2; Span 9.39 m; Length 11.96 m; Height 3.99 m; Weight Empty 3,647 kg; Max Take Off Weight 8,569 kg; Max Speed 622 mph/1,000 kph at sea level; Combat Radius 556 km (345 miles); Engine 1 x Rolls Royce/Turbomeca Adour Mk 151 turbofan; Armament. (Hawk T1) 1 x 30 mm Aden cannon pack and up to 5,600 lb (2,540 kg) of under-wing stores for rockets, bombs and missiles, (Hawk T1A) – in addition has inboard pylons for Sidewinder AIM-9 AAM.

The Hawk first flew in 1974, and entered RAF service two years later both as an advanced flying trainer and a weapons training aircraft. It has an economical Adour engine – an un-reheated version of the same turbofan powering the Jaguar. Hawks are used to teach operational tactics such as air-to-air and air-to-ground firing, air combat and low-level operating procedures to pilots destined for the 'fast-jet' squadrons. As a weapons trainer, the Hawk is armed with an Aden cannon carried beneath the fuselage, and rocket pods or practice bombs can be fitted to under-wing pylons. To fulfil its mobilisation role as a fighter aircraft, the Hawk carries a 30 mm Aden cannon and two Sidewinder air-to-air missiles, and is designated T1A (89 delivered to the RAF). The Hawk is a strong and rugged aircraft designed to cut training and maintenance costs. The aircraft has a long fatigue life to ensure a service career throughout the 1990s and beyond.

During January 1998, the MoD announced plans to extend the fatigue life of the Hawk T1/1A in RAF service. Up to 80 Hawks were involved in a 'return-to-works' (RTW) programme that saw their centre and rear fuselage sections being replaced with new production units from the Hawk Series 60 production line. This programme will extend the Hawk's service life to 2010.

The Hawk has been widely exported as a trainer and single-pilot fighter ground attack aircraft – in numerical terms, by far the most successful British export programme since the Hawker Hunter. By early 2005, over 800 Hawks had been exported or ordered, including 189 for the US Navy under licence arrangements, in addition to the 176 delivered to the RAF.

The numbers of fast jet pilots who successfully completed advanced training in each of the last five years is as follows:

Financial Year	Number of trained pilots
2000–2001	48
2001–2002	55
2002–2003	67
2003–2004	50
2004–2005	48

Hawk 128

In July 2003 the Hawk 128 was selected as the new Advanced Jet Trainer (AJT) for the RAF and Royal Navy fast-jet aircrew training. Aircrew trained on the Hawk 128 will move onto operational service with Harrier, Tornado, Typhoon and the future Joint Combat Aircraft. Hawk 128 will be able to provide pilots in training with the all-digital, fly-by-wire experience necessary for pilots flying the latest generation of fast jets.

The initial contract is for 20 Hawk 128s with an option for a further 24 aircraft. If all 44 aircraft are purchased the total contract value will be in the region of £3.5 billion (including 20 years through life support). We would expect an in-service date of around 2010-2011.

TUCANO

In service with:

No 1 Flying Training School (1 FTS)	67 x Tucano T1	RAF Linton-on-Ouse (includes RAF Topcliffe)

Crew 2; Length 9.86 m; Height 3.40 m; Span 11.28 m; Max Speed 507 kph/315 mph; Service Ceiling 8,750 m; Range 1,916 kms; Engine 1,100shp Garrett TPE-331 turboprop.

Originally designed by the Brazilian aerospace company Embraer, the Tucano was selected in 1985 to replace the Jet Provost as the RAF basic trainer. The development and production contract was awarded to Shorts of Belfast under licence. The first squadron aircraft was delivered in June 1988. Student training on the aircraft started at RAF Church Fenton in December 1989. The RAF version of the Tucano, designated the Tucano T1, has been modified in many ways from the basic Embraer 312. A Garrett TPE 331 engine is fitted in place of the original PT6 and represents a 50% power increase. Fatigue life has been extended from 8,000 to 12,000 hours by fitting strengthened wings and landing gear, a ventral air brake has been added, plus a new canopy which is bird strike resistant up to 270 knots. The original RAF purchase was for 126 x Tucano. Two training sorties can be completed before the aircraft requires refuelling.

C-130 Hercules
In service with:

24 Squadron	11 x Hercules C3/C4/C5	Lyneham
30 Squadron	11 x Hercules C3/C4/C5	Lyneham
47 Squadron	11 x Hercules C3/C4/C5	Lyneham
70 Squadron	11 x Hercules C3/C4/C5	Lyneham

The LTW (Lyneham Transport Wing) appears to have a total of 44 aircraft. The squadron totals are given as a guide to what we believe are the average aircraft figures per squadron at any one time.

Hercules C3
Crew 5/6; Capacity 92 troops or 64 paratroops or 74 medical litters; Max freight capacity 43,399 lb/19,685 kg; Length C1 29.79 m C3 34.69 m; Span 40.41 m; Height 11.66 m; Weight Empty 34,287 kg; Max All-up Weight 45,093 kg; Max speed 374 mph/602 kph; Service Ceiling 13,075 m; Engines 4 x Allison T-56A-15 turboprops.

The C-130 Hercules is the workhorse of the RAF transport fleet. Over the years it has proved to be a versatile and rugged aircraft, primarily intended for tactical operations including troop carrying, parachuting, supply dropping and aeromedical duties. The Hercules can operate from short unprepared airstrips, but also possesses the endurance to mount long range strategic lifts if required. The aircraft is a derivative of the C-130E used by the United States Air Force, but is fitted with British Avionic equipment, a roller-conveyor system for heavy air-drops and with more powerful engines. The crew of five includes, pilot, co-pilot, navigator, air engineer and air loadmaster.

As a troop carrier, the Hercules can carry 92 fully armed men, while for airborne operations 64 paratroops can be dispatched in two simultaneous 'sticks' through the fuselage side doors. Alternatively, 40 paratroops can jump from the rear loading ramp. As an air ambulance the aircraft can accommodate 74 stretchers. Freight loads that can be parachuted from the aircraft include. 16 x 1 ton containers or 4 x 8,000 pound platforms or 2 x 16,000 pound platforms or 1 x platform of 30,000 pounds plus. Amongst the many combinations of military loads that can be carried in an air-landed operation are 3 x Ferret scout cars plus 30 passengers or 2 x Land Rovers and 30 passengers or 2 x Gazelle helicopters.

Of the original 66 C1 aircraft, some 31 have been given a fuselage stretch producing the Mark C3. The C3 'stretched version' provides an additional 37% more cargo space. Refuelling probes have been fitted above the cockpit of both variants and some have received radar warning pods under the wing tips. One aircraft, designated Mark W2, is a special weather version and is located at the DRA Farnborough.

Hercules C-130J C4/C5

The RAF has replaced some of its Hercules C1/C3 aircraft with second-generation C-130Js on a one-for-one basis. Twenty-five Hercules C4 and C5 aircraft were ordered in December 94, and the first entered service in 2000 – two years behind schedule. Deliveries were completed by 2003 at a total cost of just over £1bn. The C4 is the same size as the older Hercules C3 which features a fuselage lengthened by 4.57 m (15ft 0 in) than the original C1. The Hercules C5 is the new equivalent of the shorter model. With a flight deck crew of two plus one loadmaster, the C-130J can carry up to 128 infantry, 92 paratroops, 8 NATO standard pallets or 24 CDS bundles. The Hercules C4/C5s have new Allison turboprop engines, R391 6-bladed composite propellers and a Full Authority Digital Engine Control (FADEC). This propulsion system increases take-off thrust by 29% and is 15% more efficient. Consequently, there is no longer a requirement for the external tanks to be fitted. An entirely revised 'glass' flight deck with head-up displays (HUD) and four multi-function displays (MFD) replacing many of the dials of the original aircraft. These displays are compatible with night-vision goggles (NVG).

Average number of flying hours per aircraft July – December 2005

	July	August	September	October	November	December
C-130	103	99	88	84	96	114

C-17 Globemaster

In service with:

99 Squadron	4 x C-17A	Brize Norton

Crew of 2 pilots and 1 loadmaster. Capacity Maximum of 154 troops. Normal load of 102 fully-equipped troops, up to 172,200 lb (78,108 kg) on up to 18 standard freight pallets or 48 litters in the medevac role; Wingspan 50.29 m; Length overall 53.04 m; Height overall 16.8 m; Loadable width 5.5 m; Cruising speed 648 kph (403 mph); Range (max payload) 4,444 km (2,400 miles); Engines 4 x Pratt and Whitney F117 turbofans.

The C-17 meets an RAF requirement for a interim strategic airlift capability pending the introduction of Future Transport Aircraft (A400). The decision to lease four C-17 aircraft for some £771m from Boeing was taken in 2000, and the aircraft entered service in 2001. The lease is for a period of seven years, with the option of extending for up to a further two years. The C-17 fleet is capable of the deployment of 1,400 tonnes of freight over 3,200 miles in a seven day period. The aircraft is able to carry one Challenger 2 MBT, or a range of smaller armoured vehicles, or up to three WAH-64 Apache aircraft at one time. Over 150 troops can be carried. Inflight refuelling increases the aircraft range.

No 99 Sqn has some 158 flight crew and ground staff.

Average number of flying hours per aircraft July – December 2005

	July	August	September	October	November	December
C-17	239	244	177	221	178	236

A400M (Previously Future Large Aircraft – FLA)

The MoD committed to 25 x Airbus A400M in 2000 to meet the Future Transport Aircraft (FTA) requirement for an air lift capability to replace the remaining Hercules C-130K C1/C3 fleet. The A400 is a collaborative programme involving eight European nations (Germany, France, Turkey, Spain, Portugal, Belgium, Luxembourg and United Kingdom), procuring a total of 180 aircraft. The expected UK cost is some £2.4 billion for 25 aircraft. The projected in-service date has slipped from 2007 to 2010.

The A400M should provide tactical and strategic mobility to all three Services. The capabilities required of the A400M include the ability to operate from well established airfields and semi-prepared rough landing areas in extreme climates and all weather by day and night; to carry a variety of vehicles and other equipment, freight, and troops over extended ranges; to be capable of air dropping paratroops and equipment; and to be capable of being unloaded with the minimum of ground handling equipment. The A400M should also meet a requirement for an airlift capability to move large single items such as attack helicopters and some Royal Engineers' equipment.

Airbus Military SL of Madrid, a subsidiary of Airbus Industrie, is responsible for management of the whole of the A400M programme. Companies involved in the programme are; BAE Systems (UK), EADS (Germany, France and Spain), Flabel (Belgium) and Tusas Aerospace Industries (Turkey). Final assembly will almost certainly take place in Spain. In May 2003, the European consortium engine TP400-D6 was selected for the A400M military transport aircraft over the rival Pratt & Whitney proposal.

The most commonly quoted argument in favour of the A400M over the C-130J is that this aircraft could carry a 25 ton payload over a distance of 4,000 km. Thus, it is argued that a fleet of 40 x A400M could carry a UK Brigade to the Gulf within 11.5 days, as opposed to the 28.5 days required to make a similar deployment with 40 x C-130s. To operate a fleet of 40 x A400M would of course require aircraft from elsewhere in Europe. In any event, we believe that the RAF will probably retain its C-17s, and will operate a mixed transport fleet comprising the C-130J, A-400 and C-17.

The first aircraft is scheduled to fly in early 2008 with deliveries between 2009 and 2025. Some reports regarding the A400M refer to the Future Transport Aircraft (FTA).

Air-to-Air Refuelling Aircraft

The RAF Air-to-Air Refuelling fleet mainly comprises 17 x VC10 K3 and K4 aircraft flown by No 101 Squadron based at RAF Brize Norton. These are supported by 8 x Tristar K1/KC1/C2/C2A (216 Sqn, Brize Norton) aircraft used for both transport and AAR. The RAF AAR capability is the most specialised in NATO, and has been extensively deployed in recent allied coalition operations in Afghanistan, and Iraq.

TRISTAR
In service with:

216 Squadron	8 x Tristar K1/KC1/C2/C2A	RAF Brize Norton

Passengers Up to 265; Length 50.09 m; Span 50.17 m; Max Speed 545mph/872 km/h at 30,000 ft; Engines 3 x Rolls-Royce RB211-524B4 turbofans.

The RAF operates a number of Tristar aircraft in the transport role from RAF Brize Norton. Three versions of the Tristar aircraft, the K1, KC2 and C2/C2A are in RAF service.

The K1 aircraft is a dedicated tanker with a single fuelling point.

The KC1 version has a dual role as a transport aircraft and a tanker. Provided with a side door it can carry 160 passengers and over 40 tons of freight out to a range of 5,700 miles and when used as a tanker, the aircraft can carry up to 136 tons of fuel.

Both tanker versions are capable of receiving fuel in-flight.

C2 and C2A aircraft retain the basic Tristar configuration of 265 seats (260 for passengers) with underfloor baggage space and can carry up to 16 tons of freight. All versions are capable of operating in the casualty evacuation role.

During operations in Afghanistan Tristar aircraft have been extremely valuable in providing air-to-air refuelling for US Navy aircraft. The boom refuelling system on US Air Force (KC-135) tankers is not compatible with US Navy aircraft but the RAF's drogue system is.

Earlier in this decade there were 9 x Tristar in service – 2 x K1, 4 x KC1, 2 x C2 and 1 x C2A. Tristar will be replaced towards the end of the decade by the Future Strategic Tanker Aircraft (FSTA).

Average number of flying hours per aircraft July – December 2005

	July	August	September	October	November	December
Tristar	196	137	155	155	118	102

VC 10
In service with:

101 Squadron	7 x VC10 K3/K4	RAF Brize Norton
	10 x VC10 C1K	

Crew 4; Capacity Passengers 150 or 78 medical litters; Length 48.36 m; Height 12.04 m; Span 44.55 m; Max Speed 425 mph; Range 7,596 kms;   All-up operational weight 146,513 kgs; Engines 4 x Rolls Royce Conway turbofans.

The VC-10 is a fast transport aircraft which entered service in 1966 and for many years was the backbone of Strike Command's long-range capability, providing flexibility and speed of deployment for British Forces. The aircraft is operated in two versions the C1K (passenger, freight and refuelling) and the K3/K4 (refuelling).

C1K. This multi-purpose aircraft can be operated in the troop transport, freight and aeromedical roles in addition to maintaining scheduled air services. The VC-10 carries a flight deck crew of four – captain, co-pilot, navigator and engineer – and has a flight deck seat for a supernumerary crew member. Normal cabin staff are two air loadmasters and two air stewards.

On scheduled services up to 150 passengers are carried. Under the floor of the aircraft are two large holds which can carry up to 8.5 tons of freight. If necessary, the aircraft can be converted for use as a freighter or an air ambulance when 78 stretcher cases can be carried. Refueling pods are carried under the wings and the C1K can replenish its own fuel tanks or those of other aircraft.

K3 and K4. These aircraft are used mainly for refuelling. The K3 can carry 78 tons of fuel incorporating a fuselage fuel tank. The K4 can carry 68 tons of fuel.

Average number of flying hours per aircraft July – December 2005

	July	August	September	October	November	December
VC-10	102	114	116	122	119	72

FUTURE STRATEGIC TANKER AIRCRAFT

The Future Strategic Tanker Aircraft (FSTA) is planned to replace the air-to-air refuelling (AAR) and some elements of air transport (AT) capability currently provided by the RAF's fleet of VC10 and TriStar aircraft. AAR is a key military capability that provides force multiplication and operational range enhancement for front line aircraft across a range of defence roles and military tasks. The projected in-service date is toward the end of this decade and the projected life cycle cost of the programme under Public Finance Initiative (PFI) arrangements is some £13.1bn. As of April 2006 the project is in its assessment phase and as such, it does not have a formally approved development programme or a firm date for introduction to service.

In 2004 the Air Tanker Consortium comprised of Rolls-Royce, EADS, Cobham and Thales were confirmed as bidder most likely to offer a value for money solution. It is believed that Air Tanker are proposing the A330-200 aircraft as the FSTA platform. Some analysts predict an FSTA fleet of about 10 aircraft.

CHINOOK HC2/HC2A

In service with:

7 Squadron	5 x Chinook HC2	Odiham
18 Squadron	18 x Chinook HC2	Odiham
27 Squadron	10 x Chinook HC2	Odiham
78 Squadron	1 x Chinook HC2	Mount Pleasant

All the above aircraft are under the control of the Joint Helicopter Command (JHC).

Crew 3/4; Fuselage Length 15.54 m; Width 3.78 m; Height 5.68 m; Weight (empty) 10,814 kg; Internal Payload 8,164 kg; Rotor Diameter 18.29 m; Cruising Speed 158 mph/270 kph;

Service Ceiling 4,270 m; Mission Radius (with internal and external load of 20,000 kgs including fuel and crew) 55 kms; Rear Loading Ramp Height 1.98 m; Rear Loading Ramp Width 2.31 m; Engines 2 x Avco Lycoming T55-712 turboshafts.

The Chinook is a tandem-rotored, twin-engined medium-lift helicopter and the first aircraft entered service with the RAF in 1982. It has a crew of four (pilot, navigator and 2 x crewmen) and is capable of carrying 54 fully equipped troops or a variety of heavy loads up to approximately 10 tons. The triple hook system allows greater flexibility in load carrying and enables some loads to be carried faster and with greater stability. In the ferry configuration with internally mounted fuel tanks, the Chinook's range is over 1,600 km (1,000 miles). In the medical evacuation role the aircraft can carry 24 stretchers.

RAF Chinook aircraft were upgraded to the HC2 standard between 1993-1996 for some £145m. The HC2 upgrade modified the RAF Chinooks to the US CH-47D standard. New equipment included infra-red jammers, missile approach warning indicators, chaff and flare dispensers, a long-range fuel system, and machine gun mountings. In 1995, the UK MoD purchased a further 14 x Chinooks (6 x HC2 and 8 x HC3) for £240 million.

During 2003 the Chinook Night Enhancement Package (NEP) was installed in the HC2 fleet. The NEP was based upon experience gained during operations in Afghanistan in 2001 and allows Chinook aircraft to operate at night and in very low-light conditions, often at the limit of their capabilities.

HC2 aircraft are due to be phased out during 2010 and HC2A aircraft in 2015.

We await confirmation of the formal entry into service of the eight Chinook Mk3 helicopters configured for special operations. Current indications are that the first HC3 aircraft may enter service in 2007/2008 provided that additional funding can be found.

The total number of operational hours (monthly average per aircraft) flown by RAF Chinooks during the period July to December 2005 is as follows:

	Chinook
July 2005	3.58
August 2005	27.42
September 2005	76.20
October 2005	20.49
November 2005	93.06
December 2005	33.10
	253.85

PUMA
In service with:

33 Squadron	15 x Puma HC1	Benson
230 Squadron	18 x Puma HC1	Aldergrove

All the above aircraft are under the control of the Joint Helicopter Command (JHC).

Crew 2 or 3; Capacity up to 20 troops or 7,055 lb underslung; Fuselage Length 14.06 m rotors turning 18.15 m; Width 3.50 m; Height 4.38 m; Weight (empty) 3,615 kg; Maximum Take Off Weight 7,400 kg; Max Speed 163 mph/261 kph; Service Ceiling 4,800 m; Range 550 kms; 2 x Turbomeca Turmo 111C4 turbines.

Following the retirement of the last Wessex in 2003, the Puma is now the oldest helicopter in RAF service. The 'package deal' between the UK and France on helicopter collaboration dates back to February 1967. The programme covered the development of three helicopter types – the Puma, Gazelle and Lynx. Production of the aircraft was shared between the two countries, the UK making about 20% by value of the airframe, slightly less for the engine, as well as assembling the aircraft procured for the RAF. Deliveries of the RAF Pumas started in 1971. Capable of many operational roles, Puma can carry 16 fully equipped troops, or 20 at light scales. In the casualty evacuation role (CASEVAC), 6 x stretchers and 6 x sitting cases can be carried. Underslung loads of up to 3,200 kg can be transported over short distances and an infantry battalion can be moved using 34 Puma lifts. 41 x RAF Puma helicopters received an avionics upgrade between 1994-1998.

RAF Pumas are due to be phased out of service in 2010.

The total number of operational hours (monthly average per aircraft) flown by RAF Pumas during the period July to December 2005 was as follows:

	Puma
July 2005	27.09
August 2005	31.24
September 2005	27.38
October 2005	25.36
November 2005	28.40
December 2005	23.50
	162.97

EH101 MERLIN MK3

In service with:

28 Squadron	22 x Merlin Mk 3	Benson

All the above aircraft are under the control of the Joint Helicopter Command (JHC).

Crew 4; Capacity up to 24 combat-equipped troops, or 16 stretchers and a medical team, or 4 tonnes of cargo (2.5 tonnes as an underslung load). Length 22.81 m; Rotor Diameter 18.59 m; Max Speed 309 k/ph (192 mph); Engine 3 x Rolls Royce/Turbomeca RTM 322 turboshafts.

The EH101 Merlin Mk 3 is the newest RAF helicopter, the RAF having ordered 22 EH101 (Merlin) support helicopters for £755m in March 1995. Merlin is a direct replacement for the Westland Wessex, and it operates alongside the Puma and Chinook in the medium-lift role. Its ability to carry troops, artillery pieces, light vehicles and bulk loads, means that the aircraft is ideal for use with the UK Army's 16 Air Assault Brigade. Deliveries took place between 2000-2002.

The aircraft can carry a load of 24-28 troops with support weapons. The maximum payload is 4,000 kg and Merlin has a maximum range of 1,000 km, which can be extended by external tanks or by air-to-air refuelling. The Merlin Mk 3 has sophisticated defensive aids, and the aircraft is designed to operate in extreme conditions with corrosion-proofing for maritime operations. All weather, day/night precision delivery is possible because of GPS navigation, a forward-looking infra-red sensor and night vision goggle compatibility. In the longer term, the aircraft could be fitted with a nose turret fitted mounting a .50 calibre machine gun.

RAF Merlin Mk3 are due to be phased out of service in 2030.

The total number of operational hours (monthly average per aircraft) flown by RAF Merlins during the period July to December 2005 is as follows:

	Merlin
July 2005	59.38
August 2005	54.30
September 2005	67.16
October 2005	115.12
November 2005	68.51
December 2005	38.25
	402.72

SEA KING HAR3/3A

In service with:

22 Squadron	Headquarters	RMB Chivenor
A Flight	3 x Sea King HAR3/3A	RMB Chivenor
B Flight	3 x Sea King HAR3/3A	Wattisham
C Flight	2 x Sea King HAR3/3A	Valley
202 Squadron	Headquarters	Boulmer

A Flight	3 x Sea King HAR3/3A	Boulmer
D Flight	3 x Sea King HAR 3/3A	Lossiemouth
E Flight	2 x Sea King HAR 3/3A	Leconfield
203 (Reserve) Squadron	3 x Sea King HAR3/3A	St Mawgan
78 Squadron	2 x Sea King HAR3/3A	Mount Pleasant

Note. Both 22 and 202 Squadrons have 8 x Sea King HAR3/3A. Numbers of aircraft have been allocated to flights for rounding purposes.

Crew 4; Length 17.01m; Height 4.72 m; Rotor Diameter 18.9 m; Weight (empty) 6,201kg; Cruising Speed 129 mph/208 kph; Range 1,230 kms; Engine 2 x Rolls Royce Gnome H1400-1 turboshafts.

The Westland Sea King HAR3 Search and Rescue helicopter entered RAF service in 1978. The aircraft is fitted with advanced all-weather search and navigation equipment, as well as autopilot and onboard computer to assist positioning and hovering at night or in bad weather. In addition to four crew members, the HAR3 can carry up to six stretchers, or 18 survivors. Under normal conditions, expect the HAR3 to have an operational radius of approximately 448 km (280 miles). The Sea King HAR3A replaced the Wessex HC2 in the SAR role in 1996. An early 1990s MoD report concluded that a total of 25 Sea Kings was required to ensure that SAR duties were carried out effectively and an announcement was made in 1992 of an order for six more HAR3, to bring the total up to the required 25. Of these 25 aircraft, 16 are allocated for SAR duties in the UK, two in the Falkland Islands, three for conversion training and the remaining three form an engineering and operational pool.

RAF Sea King HAR3/3A are due to be phased out of service in 2017.

RAF WEAPONS

AIR TO AIR MISSILES

Sidewinder AIM-9L

Diameter 0.13 m; Span 0.63 m; Length 2.85 m; Total Weight 85.3 kg; Warhead Weight 9.5 kg; Propulsion Solid fuel rocket; Speed Mach 2.5; Range 10-18 km; Guidance Solid-state, infra-red homing system.

The Sidewinder missile, which is carried by all the RAF combat aircraft as well as the Hawk and Nimrod MR2, is an infra-red weapon which homes onto the heat emitted by a hostile aircraft's engines. Sidewinder can operate independently of the aircraft's radar, and provides the air defence aircraft with an alternative method of attacking targets at shorter ranges. Sidewinder has an excellent dogfight capability.

AMRAAM

Length 3.66 metres; Diameter 0.18 m; Span 0.48 m; Weight 161.4 kg/336 lbs; Cruising speed Mach 4; Range approx 30 miles; Guidance System Active radar terminal/inertial midcourse

AMRAAM (Advanced medium-range air-to-air missile) is a US air fighting weapon that matches the fire-and-forget capability of the ASRAAM, but with greater range. There is increased immunity over electronic countermeasures and a low-smoke, high-impulse rocket motor to reduce the probability of an enemy sighting the missile. This system is in use by Tornado F3, and will be used by the Typhoon. In addition, trials were underway during late 2000 with AMRAAM fitted to Jaguar GR1B. AMRAAM has been in service with the Fleet Air Arm since 1995, and the initial purchase was believed to be some 210 missiles worth some £50m. For Typhoon, the current cost for AMRAAM procurement is £214m with deliveries planned about to start.

ASRAAM

Length 2.9 m; Diameter 0.17 m; Weight 88 kg; Cruising speed Mach 3.5+; Range over 10 miles; Guidance Imaging IR 128x128 element focal plane array.

ASRAAM is a fast, highly agile, fire-and-forget IR missile for short-range air-to-air combat, able to counter intermittent target obscurity in cloud and severe infra-red countermeasures. It is carried on Tornado F3, Harrier GR7/9 and the Typhoon. It will replace Sidewinder AIM-9L albeit that this will remain in service in parallel for a period. The programme cost is some £857m. There were considerable technical problems and delays before service entry in 2002.

Meteor (BVRAAM)

The Beyond Visual Range Air-to-Air Missile (BVRAAM) (also known as *Meteor*) should provide Typhoon with the capability to combat projected air-to-air threats and sustain air superiority throughout the life of the aircraft. The weapon is required to operate in all weather conditions and will complement the Typhoon Advanced Short Range Air-to-Air Missile (ASRAAM). Until Meteor enters service, Typhoon will be armed with the Advanced Medium-Range Air-to-Air Missile (AMRAAM). Meteor is a collaborative programme with five partner nations; Germany, Spain and Italy (for Typhoon), Sweden (for JAS 39 Gripen) and France (for Rafale). The in-service date has slipped to 2012 and the projected overall cost is some £1.4bn.

AIR-LAUNCHED AIR-TO-GROUND CRUISEMISSILE

Storm Shadow

Length 5.1 m; Diameter 0.48 m; Span 2.84 m; Weight 1,300 kg; Range Estimate 350 km; Propulsion TRI 60-30 Turbofan; Guidance Navigation using TERrain PROfile Matching) system as well as GPS, Terminal guidance using imaging infra-red sensor, Autonomous target recognition algorithms, BROACH warhead.

Storm Shadow (also known as Conventionally-Armed Stand-Off Missile or CASOM) is a long-range, air-launched, stand-off attack missile that will allow the RAF to attack high-priority targets deep inside enemy territory without exposing the launch aircraft to high-intensity enemy air defences. The missile is the BAe version (with some UK enhancements) of the French Matra APACHE/SCALP missile and entered service in late 2002. It is fitted to Tornado GR4, Harrier GR7/GR9 and theTyphoon. The RAF is believed to have purchased an initial batch of 500 missiles. The programme cost is some £980m. Storm

Shadow was deployed operationally and fired with tremendous success during the 2003 Iraq War.

AIR-TO-GROUND ANTI-RADIATION MISSILE

ALARM
Length 4.3 m. Diameter 0.22 m. Span 0.72 m. Weight 265 kg. Propellant 1 x Royal Ordnance Nuthatch solid fuel two-stage rocket. Guidance Passive Radar Homing/Strap-down INS; Range 93 km.

ALARM stands for Air-Launched Anti-Radiation Missile and this type was introduced into RAF Service in the early 1990s. The missile is launched at low level near the suspected site of an enemy radar and, after launch, rapidly climbs to about 12,000 m. At this height, a small parachute opens and the missile descends earthwards while the on-board radar searches the broadband for emissions from enemy radar. Once a target has been identified, the motor is re-ignited and the missile makes a supersonic dive onto the target. The total RAF buy in the first manufacturing run was believed to be some 750 missiles. Since its original entry into service, radars have become increasingly more sophisticated in their ability to avoid detection and attack by anti-radiation weapons such as ALARM. As a result, the missile has received extensive upgrades.

Area Weapons

BL 755 Cluster Bomb
Length 2.45 m. Diameter 0.41 m. Weight 277 kg. Warhead 147 bomblets.

The BL 755 is a system that was designed to cope with some of the very large area targets that might have been encountered on the Soviet Central Front, especially large armoured formations of Regimental strength (90+ tanks) or more. The weapon can be carried by Tornado GR1, Harrier, Jaguar, Buccaneer and Phantom and consists of a large container which is divided into seven compartments. Each of these compartments contains 21 bomblets making a total of 147 bomblets in all. After the bomb has been released from the aircraft, the 147 bomblets are ejected and fall to the ground covering a wide area. As each individual bomblet hits a target, a HEAT charge is detonated which can fire a large slug of molten metal through up to 250 mm of armour. In addition, the casing of the bomblet disintegrates and hundreds of fragments of shrapnel are dispersed over a wide area, with resultant damage to personnel and soft- skinned vehicles. The BL 755 can be released at very low altitude and this is essential if pilots are to survive in high-density SAM conditions. Aircraft will only have the chance to make one pass over the target before the defences are alerted, and for a pilot to make a second pass to ensure accuracy would be suicidal.

It is intended that the Brimstone missile will replace the BL 755 in the anti-armour role.

Brimstone

Length 1.81m; Diameter 0.18 m; Weight 49 kg; Propulsion cast double-base propellant rocket motor; Guidance inertial guidance + seeker determination to target acquisition, then seeker control; Cruising speed boost to supersonic; Range 8 km.

The Advanced Air-launched Anti-Armour Weapon (AAAW), known as Brimstone, is an area weapon to attack enemy armoured forces as early and as far forward as possible. It replaces the BL755 cluster bomb in the anti-armour role, and will be carried by Tornado GR4/4a, Harrier GR7/9 and Eurofighter Typhoon. These fixed-wing aircraft will compliment the capability provided by the Apache AH64-D, which is armed with the Hellfire anti-armour weapon. Brimstone operates automatically after launch, which helps reduce the hazard to the attacking aircraft from enemy fire. Development and procurement of Brimstone has cost the RAF some £822m since 1996. The weapon entered RAF service in mid 2005.

AIR-TO-GROUND ANTI-ARMOUR MISSILES

Maverick

Length 2.6 m; Diameter 0.31 m. Span 0.71 m; Weight 286 kg; Range 27 km; IR Guidance (Laser and EO also available).

The Maverick missile, which is used by the Harrier GR7 as an anti-armour weapon, entered RAF service in early 2001 and is one of the latest additions to the RAF inventory. The missile has a number of seeker heads available for use in a variety of operational scenarios. The RAF bought the Maverick with an Imaging Infra-red (IIR) seeker head, which allows the missile to be employed both by day and by night and in poor atmospheric conditions. The Maverick missile will complement the Brimstone missile that is entering RAF service with a millimetric wave all-weather seeker head. The RAF version of the Maverick is a fire-and-forget weapon, which sends a picture from the IIR seeker head to the Multi-Purpose Colour Display (MPCD) in the cockpit. The pilot identifies the target, locks the missile onto it and fires the missile once the target is in range. The Maverick will then home onto the target while the delivery aircraft carries out escape manoeuvres, thus minimising its exposure to enemy air defence systems.

PRECISION GUIDED MUNITIONS

PAVEWAY II

Length 3.7 m; Weight 520 kg; Laser Guidance

Paveway II is the standard 1,000 lb (454 kg) general purpose bomb for used against moderately well-protected targets. Paveway II can be fitted with a laser guidance kit, and the bomb can be used in the freefall or retarded Mode. Used on the Tornado GR4, Harrier, Jaguar, and Eurofighter Typhoon.

PAVEWAY III

Length 4.4 m; Weight 1,130 kg; Laser Guidance

Paveway III is a 2,000 lb (908 kg) laser guided bomb (LGB) for use against well-protected targets. The bomb is guided to its target by a TIALD (Thermal Imaging and Laser

Designation) pod that is carried on the aircraft or by a ground based observer using a target designator. The weapon can be carried on the Tornado GR4, Jaguar, Harrier, and Typhoon. Unlike the Paveway II, this weapon uses proportional guidance – the control canards on the front of the bomb move only the exact amount necessary to guide the weapon. This conserves energy, improves accuracy capability and increases the range of the weapon, thus allowing delivery aircraft to engage their targets with greater stand-off. When the weapon is released, it flies a pre-programmed autopilot profile into the target area, using the energy given to it by the releasing aircraft. These autopilot profiles are designated to provide the best attack conditions for different types of target and also to use to maximum effectiveness the increased stand-off capability of the weapon.

Enhanced Paveway (EPW)
Length (EPW2)3.7 m; (EPW3) 4.4 m); Weight (EPW2) 545 kg (EPW3) 1,130 kg); GPS guidance.

Shortcomings in target acquisition during the 1999 Kosovo conflict resulted in a requirement for the RAF to obtain a weapon to satisfy all-weather 24-hour tasking. The Enhanced Paveway (EPW) family of weapons meets this requirement, and the EPWII entered service in 2001 and the larger EPWIII entered service in late 2002. Both EPWII and EPWIII are based on their laser-guided bomb variants, the Paveway II and Paveway III respectively, and utilise the same warheads and fin sections. However, the EPW weapons have a modified guidance section and wiring to accommodate a Global Positioning System Aided Inertial Navigation System (GAINS). EPW is carried by the Tornado GR4.

In Iraq, during Operation Telic in early 2003 the RAF used 360 x Enhanced Paveway PGMs, and 255 Paveway II/III LGBs. Enhanced Paveway was described by the RAF officers as "the weapon of choice".

Paveway IV
In late 2003 the UK MoD selected the Paveway IV PGM in preference to the Boeing Joint Direct Attack Munition (JDAM). Paveway IV has the ability to engage targets in all types of weather with laser guidance for high terminal accuracy.

The Paveway IV kit is equipped with a GPS/INS (Global Positioning System/Inertial Navigation System) and a SAL (Semi-Active Laser) terminal seeker. The total value of the contract is believed to be in the region of £100 million. Paveway IV is a is a joint development by the UK-based Raytheon Systems Ltd (RSL) and Raytheon Missile Systems (RMS) in the US.

Paveway IV kits, fitted to 227kg (500 lb) bombs, will enter service in late 2006 or early 2007.

Rockets

CVR-7
This is an air-to-air and air-to-surface rocket system. Each rocket pod, weighing 240 kg, carries 19 rockets. The HE warhead is designed for use against light armour, vehicles, small vessels and helicopters. Deployed on the Jaguar and Harrier.

Freefall bombs

Conventional 1,000 lb (454 kg) bombs are still in service, as are Mark 1 and Mark 2 bombs weighing 570 lb (260 kg). By adding the Hunting 118 retarding tail, the weight of the latter is increased to 670 lb (304 kg).

Anti-ship missile

Harpoon

Length 3.84m. Diameter 0.34m. Span 0.91m; Total Weight 526kg. Warhead Weight 225kg. Range 110km. Guidance Sea-skimming cruise monitored by radar altimeter, active radar terminal homing.

The US-designed Harpoon is an extremely powerful anti-ship missile that is carried in the bomb bay of the Nimrod MR2. The air to sea version of the missile has extremely sophisticated Electronic Counter Measures (ECM), and the ability to fly a sea-skimming course on a dog-leg path through three pre-programmed way-points. The warhead is extremely powerful and a hit from Harpoon is almost certain to result in the destruction or disablement of a major surface vessel.

Air-launched Torpedo – Sting Ray

Length 2.6 m; Diameter 0.34 m; Weight 267 kg; Warhead 45 kg of HE in a shaped charge; Speed 45 knots; Range 8-11 km; Depth 800 m; Propulsion magnesium/silver-chloride seawater battery (Pump-jet); Guidance active/passive sonar.

Sting Ray is a lightweight homing torpedo that is carried in the bomb bay of the Nimrod MR2. The torpedo is fully programmable, with a number of search options and has been designed to destroy submarines. The torpedo seeker can either home in on the sound of the submarine or detect and track the target using its own sonar. From 2003, Sting Ray was upgraded to Mod 1 standard. The upgrade includes new digital homing, guidance and control systems and the upgraded torpedo is planned to enter service in 2006.

Sting Ray first entered service with the Royal Navy and Royal Air Force in 1983, and there are plans to extend its life through regular upgrades thereby ensuring that the weapon remains in service until about 2020.

BALLISTIC MISSILE DEFENCE

In 2002, the unilateral withdrawal of the United States from the 1972 Anti-Ballistic Missile Treaty with the then Soviet Union opened the way for the deployment of limited national and theatre ballistic missile defence (BMD) systems. In early 2003, the UK government agreed to a US government request to upgrade BMEWS system at RAF Fylingdales for BMD applications. The UK MoD has been conducting studies on BMD – probably a Theatre High-Altitude Area Defence (THAAD) system – to defend the UK against incoming missiles.

In an early 2006 statement the Secretary of State for Defence said that "The UK Government have not yet decided whether or not to pursue missile defence for the United Kingdom, but continues to examine, with our NATO allies, the developing threat from ballistic missiles and the appropriate responses. We have agreed to the upgrading of the radar at RAF Fylingdales as part of the United States missile defence system, and we also have a programme of joint technical and research projects with the US exploring the relevant technologies."

We believe that the UK MOD appears to be interested in creating a layered anti-missile defence, capable of multiple attempts at hitting targets at ranges of over 100 miles at heights of over 100,000 feet, to shorter-range systems such as the US Patriot that could hit targets at much closer range. Recent fears of nuclear proliferation, and the problems of nuclear-capable delivery systems such as the former Soviet Scud missile and derivative missiles being used by nations who hitherto have not been able to mount a credible threat to the UK, have forced the MoD to look at the options offered by adopting a high-level missile defence.

Given the huge costs involved, it is likely that any UK programme in BMD would be collaborative,

RAF REGIMENT

The need to raise a dedicated specialist force to protect air installations became apparent during WWII when unprotected aircraft on the ground were vulnerable to enemy air and ground attack. Consequently, the RAF Regiment was raised on 1 February 1942 by a Royal Warrant of King George VI. At the end of WWII, there were over 85,000 personnel serving in the RAF Regiment manning 240 operational squadrons. As of 2006, the strength of the RAF Regiment is some around 3,000, including some 300 officers and 500 part-time reservists. The Regiment is generally formed into Squadrons of 100 to 150 personnel. Currently the RAF Regiment exists to provide defence for RAF installations, and to train all the RAF's combatant personnel to enable them to contribute to the defence of their units. RAF Regiment units are under the operational command of No 2 Group.

RAF Regiment restructuring

In July 2004 it was announced that the role of providing Ground Based Air Defence was to be transferred to the Army and the four Royal Air Force Regiment Rapier squadrons (15 Sqn; 16 Sqn; 26 Sqn and 37 Sqn) are to be disbanded.

The phased timings associated with this phased programme will allow the Army's Royal Regiment of Artillery to take over the overall UK Ground Based Air Defence (GBAD) in a progressive manner.

The UK MoD states that "As part of the changes, both 3 Squadron RAF Regiment, based at RAF Aldergrove, and the Queen's Colour Squadron, based at RAF Uxbridge, will be expanded by around 40 personnel each in order to enhance their operational capability to match that of the other four regular RAF Regiment Field Squadrons. This will improve the units' ability to deploy on operations and so enhance the operational flexibility of the RAF Regiment in its Force Protection role".

It is expected that about 340 RAF Regiment personnel posts will be affected by this restructuring. Other RAF Regiment elements will be affected by this restructuring as follows:

♦ 1 Squadron RAF Regiment will move from RAF St Mawgan to RAF Honington by March 2007

♦ 2625 (County of Cornwall) Squadron Royal Auxiliary Air Force Regiment, based alongside 1 Squadron at RAF St Mawgan, will be disbanded with effect from November 2006

In another restructuring announcement in March 2006 it was announced that "RAF Force Protection elements are being enhanced by integrating the RAF Regiment and the RAF Police to deliver a full range of capability from policing and security (including dogs) to close combat".

As of 1 April 2006, RAF Regiment units are as follows:

Field Squadrons

No 1 Squadron	St Mawgan	Field Squadron (Honnington March 2007)
No 2 Squadron	Honnington	Field /Parachute Sqn
No 3 Squadron	Aldergrove	Field Squadron
No 27 Squadron	Honnington	CBRN Defence (RAF element of Joint CBRN Regiment)
No 34 Squadron	Leeming	Field Squadron
No 51 Squadron	Lossiemouth	Field Squadron
No 63 (QCS)	Uxbridge	Ceremonial /Field Sqn

RAF Regiment Depot	Honnington
No 1 RAF STO HQ	Wittering
No 2 RAF STO HQ	Leeming
No 3 RAF STO HQ	Marham
No 4 RAF STO HQ	Honington (Survive to Operate Centre)

STO – Survive to Operate

Note: Joint CBRN Regiment: No 27 Squadron RAF Regiment provides some of the 244 personnel of the Joint CBRN Regiment alongside two squadrons of the Royal Tank Regiment all of whom are stationed at Honnington.

Air Defence

No 15 Squadron	Honnington	6 x Rapier (disbands by March 2008)
No 16 Squadron	Honnington	6 x Rapier (disbands by March 2007)
No 26 Squadron	Waddington	6 x Rapier (disbands by March 2008)
No 37 Squadron	Honnington	6 x Rapier (disbanded in March 2006)
Joint Rapier Training Unit	Honnington	2 x Rapier (disbanding)

Specialist RAF Regiment training for gunners is given at the RAF Regiment Depot at Honnington. On completion of training at the RAF College Cranwell officers also undergo further specialist training at RAF Honnington and, in some cases, the School of Infantry at Warminster in Wiltshire or the Royal School of Artillery at Larkhill. The RAF Regiment also mans the Queen's Colour Squadron (QCS) which undertakes all major ceremonial duties for the Royal Air Force. These duties involve mounting the Guard at Buckingham Palace on an occasional basis, and providing Guards of Honour for visiting Heads of State. The Queen's Colour Squadron also has a war role as a field squadron. The regiment is not alone in defending any RAF station. Every airman based at a station has a ground defence role and is trained to defend his place of work against ground attack and attack by NBC weapons. Training for this is given by RAF Regiment instructors who provide courses at station level for all personnel on various aspects of ground defence.

Royal Auxiliary Air Force Regiment (RAuxAF Regt)

Airfield defence is further enhanced by squadrons of the RAuxAF Regt who are recruited locally and whose role is the ground defence of the airfield and its associated outlying installations. An RAuxAF Regiment Squadron has an all-up strength of about 120 personnel and costs approximately £500,000 a year to keep in service. As a general rule, a squadron has a headquarters flight, two mobile flights mounted in Land Rovers and two flights for static guard duties. RAuxAF Regt squadrons are as follows:

2503 Sqn RAuxAF Regt	RAF Waddington	Ground Defence
2620 Sqn RAuxAF Regt	RAF Marham	Ground Defence
2622 Sqn RAuxAF Regt	RAF Lossiemouth	Ground Defence
2623 Sqn RauxAF Regt	RAF Honnington	Force Protection
2624 Sqn RauxAF Regt	RAF Brize Norton	Ground Defence

Note. 2625 Sqn RAuxAF Regiment (RAF St Mawgan) disbanded in November 2005.

Royal Auxiliary Air Force Regiment squadrons are generally based alongside regular units in order to maximise training opportunities and give the auxiliary personnel access to equipment held by the regular unit.

RAF Reserves

The reserve component of the Royal Air Force on 1 April 2005 was as follows:

RAuxAF & RAFVR Reserves	–	1,480 (290 x officers and 1,190 other ranks)
Royal Air Force Reserve	–	8,430 (590 x officers and 7,840 other ranks)
Individuals liable to recall*	–	26,720 (8,030 officers and 18,700 other ranks)
Total	–	36,630

*This number includes retired officers and airmen who have completed pensionable service.

The Controller Reserve Forces (RAF) is located at RAF PTC. He is responsible for all of the non-operational aspects of reserve forces policy and co-ordination, ranging from recruitment, through training, promotions and welfare to future planning. The following are the formed Reserve Units for which he is responsible.

Royal Auxiliary Air Force

3 Sqn	RAF Henlow	Tactical Provost Wing
501 Sqn	RAF Brize Norton	Operations Support Squadron
504 Sqn	RAF Cottesmore	Harrier Support Sqn
600 Sqn	RAF Northolt	HQ Augmentation Unit
603 Sqn	Edinburgh	Operations Support Squadron
606 Sqn	RAF Benson	Helicopter Support Squadron
609 Sqn	RAF Leeming	Operations Support Squadron
612 Sqn	RAF Leuchars	Airmobile Surgical Squadron
2503 Sqn	RAF Waddington	Operations Support Squadron
2620 Sqn	RAF Marham	Operations Support Squadron
2622 Sqn	RAF Lossiemouth	Operations Support Squadron
2624 Sqn	RAF Brize Norton	Operations Support Squadron
4624 Sqn	RAF Brize Norton	Operations Support Squadron
4626 Sqn	RAF Lyneham	Aeromedical Evacuation Unit

Royal Air Force Reserve Units

7006 Flight	RAF High Wycombe	Intelligence
7010 Flight	RAF High Wycombe	Photographic Interpretation
7630 Flight	DISC Chicksands	Intelligence
7644 Flight	RAF High Wycombe	Public Relations Squadron
Mobile Met Unit	RAF Benson	Meteorological Services
Marham Support Flight	RAF Marham	Ground Crew
1359 Flight	RAF Lyneham	Hercules Reserve Flight
TSS	RAF Shawbury	Training & Standardisation Sqn

Royal Auxiliary Air Force Defence Force Flights

RAuxAF Defence Force Flight	RAF Brampton
RAuxAF Defence Force Flight	RAF High Wycombe
RAuxAF Defence Force Flight	RAF Lyneham
RAuxAF Defence Force Flight	RAF St Athan

In war, these four flights would provide specialist assistance in public relations, foreign language interrogation, photographic interpretation and intelligence support.

Note. The RauxAF and the RAFVR were amalgamated on 5 April 1997.

CHAPTER 5 – MISCELLANEOUS

Joint Nuclear, Biological and Chemical Regiment (Jt NBC Regt)

The Joint NBC Regt was created following the Strategic Defence Review and is based at RAF Honington in Suffolk. The Regiment is composed of two squadrons from 1 RTR and 27 Sqn RAF Regiment plus supporting staff from other army units. The Jt NBC Regt fields specialist NBC defence equipment, specifically the Fuchs nuclear and chemical reconnaissance and survey vehicle, the Prototype Biological Detection System (PBDS) and the Multi-Purpose Decontamination System (MPDS). The PBDS is due to be replaced by greater numbers of a new and more capable Integrated Biological Detection System (IBDS) within the next few years. The Regiment will be an essential element of any joint force operation where there is an NBC threat, enhancing the integral NBC defence capabilities of the remainder of the force. Not only will the Regiment support Army formations but also other vital assets such as air bases, logistic areas and key lines of communication.

In peace the Army may be asked to provide Military Assistance to the Civil Authorities. In these circumstances, the Joint NBC Regiment may be called on to deal with radiological, biological or chemical hazards. The Joint NBC Regiment offers a new and challenging role to the Armoured Corps and the RAF Regiment, requiring new skills, innovative ideas and a significant intellectual challenge.

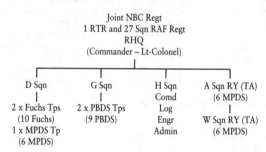

Defence Medical Services Department (DMSD)

The DMSD is the headquarters for the Defence Medical Services. The clinical director of the DMSD is the Surgeon General (SG) and he operates through four directorates as follows:

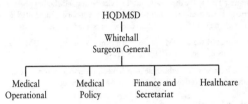

DMSD is a Joint Service organisation with personnel from all three services and MoD Civil Servants working together to ensure "Provision of strategic direction to the Defence Medical Services to ensure coherent delivery of all medical outputs".

The DCDS(H) (Deputy Chief of Defence Staff (Health)), is accountable to the VCDS (Vice-Chief of Defence Staff) for the overall performance of the Defence Medical Services.

Single Service Medical Care

The three armed forces maintain their own medical services who provide medical support worldwide in both peace and war.

Royal Naval Medical Service (RNMS)
Army Medical Services (AMS)
Royal Air Forces Medical Services (RAF MS)

Hospital Care

In the UK hospital care is provided at Ministry of Defence Hospital Units (MDHU).

The Defence Medical Services Department (DMSD) has contracts with the NHS for provision of care in MDHUs, which are run as military units embedded within selected NHS hospitals. There are MDHUs at Derriford (Plymouth), Frimley Park (Aldershot), Northallerton (near Catterick), Peterborough and Portsmouth.

In addition, the Defence Medical Services runs a number of other units which include the Royal Centre for Defence Medicine (Birmingham), Defence Services Medical Rehabilitation Centre (Headley Court) and the Duchess of Kent's Psychiatric Unit (Catterick). There are also two military hospitals, one in Cyprus and the other in Gibraltar.

In Iraq the 'Role 3' Field Hospital at Shaibah provides medical support that includes primary surgery, an intensive care unit, medium and low dependency nursing care beds and diagnostic support, as well as emergency medical care.

Service personnel serving in Germany who require hospital care are treated in one of the five German Provider Hospitals.

Royal Centre for Defence Medicine (RCDM)

The RCDM in Birmingham provides a centre for military personnel requiring specialised care, and incorporates a facility for the treatment of service personnel who have been evacuated from an overseas deployment area after becoming ill or wounded/injured. RCDM also acts as a centre for the training of Defence Medical Service personnel.

In operation since 2001 the RCDM operates on a contract between the DMSD and the University Hospitals Birmingham (UHB) NHS Trust.

The RCDM is a Joint Service establishment with medical personnel from all three of the armed services wearing their respective Naval, Army, or Air Force uniforms.

Service Health Professions

In March 2006 totals for health professionals in the Defence Medical Services were as follows:

Post	Number in post
Biomedical Scientist	60
Clinical Physiologist	7
Combat Medical Technician (Army)	1,620
Dental Hygienists	69
Dental Surgery Support	390
Dental Technicians	42
Environmental Health Officer	29
Environmental Health Technicians	100
Health Inspector	2
Medical Admin (RAF)	330
Medical Assistant (Royal Marine and Commando)	66
Medical Assistant (General Duties)	470
Medical Assistant (RAF)	370
Medical Assistant (Submarine)	86
Operating Department Practitioners	120
Pharmacist	10
Pharmacy Technician	43
Physiotherapist	83
Radiographer	33
Tri-Service Totals	3,930

Service Nursing Staff

Totals at 1 January 2006 were as follows:

Nursing Staff	In Post
QARNNS (Navy)	290
Officers	90
Other ranks	200
QARANC (Army)	840
Officers	270
Other ranks	570
PMRAFNS	420
Officers	120
Other ranks	300

Note:
QARNNS – Queen Alexandra's Royal Naval Nursing Service
QARANC – Queen Alexandra's Royal Army Nursing Corps
PMRAFNS – Princess Mary's Royal Air Force Nursing Service

Defence Dental Services (DDS)

The Defence Dental Services (DDS) is a tri-service area employing approximately 1,000 personnel from the three armed services and contracted civilians. In the majority of cases treatment is provided at Service Dental Centres worldwide.

The DDS is part of the Director General Healthcare area within the DMSD.

THE MOD'S CIVILIAN STAFF

The three uniformed services are supported by the civilian staff of the MoD. On the 1st January 2006 there were some 108,470 civilian personnel employed by the MoD (84,740 in the UK and 23,730 overseas-locally engaged). This figure has fallen from 316,700 civilian personnel in 1980.

In addition to the permanent UK based civilians, locally entered civilian personnel were distributed around the following locations:

Continental Europe	10,500 (1)
Gibraltar	360
Cyprus	2,790
Middle East	1,650 (2)
Far East/Asia	730 (3)
Africa	780 (4)
USA	200
Canada	20
Central/South America	50
Falkland Islands	50
Elsewhere/Unallocated	3390

Notes
(1) The overwhelming majority of this figure are 9,700 locally entered civilians supporting BFG (British Forces Germany) and 170 in the Balkans. (2) Includes Iraq, Egypt and Libya.(3) Includes Brunei and Nepal. (4) Includes 610 in Sierra Leone

In a recent statement the UK MoD stated that " The Department remains committed to a process of civilianisation. Increasingly, it makes no sense to employ expensively trained and highly professional military personnel in jobs which civilians could do equally well. Civilians are generally cheaper than their military counterparts and as they often remain longer in post, can provide greater continuity. For these reasons, it is our long-standing policy to civilianise posts and so release valuable military resources to the front line whenever it makes operational and economic sense to do so".

In general MoD Civil Servants work in a parallel stream with their respective uniformed counterparts. There are some 'stand alone' civilian agencies of which QinetiQ is probably the largest.

DEFENCE PROCUREMENT AGENCY (DPA)
From its headquarters at Abbey Wood in Bristol the DPA is responsible for the procurement of new equipment for the UK Armed Forces and for the provision of other procurement-related services. The DPA is an Executive Agency of the UK MoD and has been in existence since April 1999 when it replaced its predecessor the MoD Procurement Executive.

The DPA has approximately 4,500 staff of which 740 are service personnel (510 x officers and 230 soldiers) and approximately 3,760 are civilians. Of the civilian total some 1,800 are scientists or engineers. The annual DPA budget is in the region of £6 million with over 12,000 contracts in place during FY 2005 – 2006.

Inside its mission which is "to equip the UK Armed Forces" the DPA works to the following parameters:

♦ Buy weapons systems and platforms and manage major upgrades
♦ Deliver projects within defined performance, time and cost bands
♦ Provide certain procurement-related services, guidance and standards
♦ Participate in the UK's military nuclear programmes

DEFENCE LOGISTICS ORGANISATION (DLO)
Following the establishment of PJHQ at Northwood it became important to combine the separate logistics functions of the three Armed Forces. As a result, in 2000 the three distinct separate service logistic functions were fused into one and the DLO was formed.

With its mission "to sustain UK capability, current and future", the DLO spends approximately £8 billion a year to support front line operations. The DLO is responsible for keeping the services fully equipped and ready to act at any time, in war or peace.

The DLO employs approximately 20,700 people and is the single largest employer in the Ministry of Defence

Supply to the armed forces is maintained through the following departments:

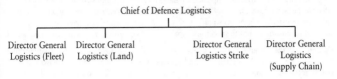

Chief of Defence Logistics

| Director General Logistics (Fleet) | Director General Logistics (Land) | Director General Logistics Strike | Director General Logistics (Supply Chain) |

Key customers for the DLO are the Front Line Commands and Permanent Joint Headquarters (PJHQ). There are also key relationships with the Defence Procurement Agency (DPA) and industry.

Supporting the front line means providing logistic support to UK Armed Forces involved in operations around the world, with the DLO currently supporting the following:

♦ Operation Banner – support to Northern Ireland in accordance with the Operational Commitments Plan.
♦ Operation Telic – support to coalition forces in Iraq.
♦ Operation Herrick – support to the International Stabilisation and Assistance Force (ISAF) in Afghanistan.
♦ Operation Oculus – support to all UK forces in the Balkans including the Kosovo Force and support to European Union forces in Bosnia (Operation Althea).
♦ Operation Tosca – the UK contribution to United Nations peacekeeping forces in Cyprus.

THE UNITED KINGDOM DEFENCE INDUSTRY

Despite uncertainties over future defence strategy and pressure on defence spending, the United Kingdom's Defence Industry has proved to be a remarkably resilient and successful element of our national manufacturing base.

Despite the rationalisation which is still taking place within the defence sector it is generally accepted that defence employment still provides a significant element of the broader UK economy via salaries paid throughout the supply chain.

Historically, the UK defence industry has possessed the capability and competence to provide a wide range of advanced systems and equipment to support our own Armed Forces. This capability, matched with their competitiveness, has enabled UK companies to command a sizeable share of those overseas markets for which export licence approvals are available. At home, UK industry has consistently provided some 75% by value of the equipment requirements of The Ministry of Defence. In simple terms, in recent years our industry has supplied £9 – £10 billion worth of goods and services for our Armed Forces annually while a further £3 -5 billion worth of business has accrued to the UK defence industry from sales to approved overseas customers.

The United Kingdom's defence companies are justifiably proud of their record in recent years in the face of fierce overseas competition. Reductions in the UK's Armed Forces and the heavy demands on our remaining Service personnel, who face an unpredictable international security environment, make it inevitable that considerable reliance will be placed upon the support and surge capacity offered by our comprehensive indigenous defence industrial base. Without this effective industrial base, the ability of the UK to exert independence of action or influence over collective security arrangements would be constrained. It is essential that government policies ensure that industry retains the necessary capabilities to support our forces in a changing world.

Up until now the United Kingdom's defence industry has been highly successful in supporting the United Kingdom's Armed Forces with high quality equipment and it has also made a significant contribution to our balance of payments. As a strategic resource it is vitally important that it should attract the appropriate levels of research and development funding to maintain the necessary technical excellence and production facilities to meet the needs of the future.

As importantly, the defence industry is not only a major employer but it is also the generator of high technology that is readily adaptable to civilian use in fields such as avionics and engine technology. The future of the UK's defence industry will almost certainly have to be properly planned if it is to remain an efficient and essential national support organisation in times of crisis. A look at MoD payments to contractors during FY 2004-2005 identifies some of the larger manufacturers.

MAJOR CONTRACTORS LISTING

Over £500 million
BAE Systems PLC

QinetiQ Group PLC

£250 to £500 million
Babcock International Group PLC
British Telecommunications PLC
EADS
Finmeccanica

General Dynamics Corps
Rolls Royce Group PLC
Serco Group PLC
Thales Defence PLC

£100 to £250 Million
BP International Ltd
EDS Defence Ltd
Fujitsu Services Holding PLC
Halliburton Corporation
Interserve PLC

Le Grand Annington Ltd
Lockheed Martin Corp
Raytheon Company
VT Group PLC

£50 to £250 Million
AMEC PLC
Aqumen Services Ltd
Atkins Facilities Management Ltd
The Boeing Corporation
Cobham PLC
International Business Machines UK Ltd
Lex Defence Management Ltd

Marshall Group PLC
Modus Services PLC
Sodexho Defence
Steria Ltd
Swan Hunter (Tyneside) Ltd
The Weir Group

QinetiQ
(Formerly known as the Defence Evaluation & Research Agency)

From 1 April 1995, the Defence Evaluation & Research Agency (DERA) assumed the responsibilities of its predecessor the Defence Research Agency (DRA). DERA changed its title to QinetiQ on 2 July 2001.

The name QinetiQ has been derived from the scientific term, kinetic (phonetic: ki'ne tik), which means 'relating to or caused by motion'. This in turn comes from the Greek, kinetikos based on 'kineo' which means 'to move'.

Following the 2001 restructuring, certain functions of DERA, encompassing the majority of the organisation's capabilities for defence and security and amounting to approximately three quarters of DERA, were formed into QinetiQ Limited, an entity which is a wholly-owned subsidiary of QinetiQ Group plc. In February 2006 QinetiQ was listed on the London Stock Exchange with a market capitalisation of £1.3 billion.

A quarter of QinetiQ has been retained within the MoD as the Defence Science and Technology Laboratory (DSTL) to manage the research programme and the International Research Collaboration, along with other sensitive areas such as CBD (Chemical & Biological Defence), Porton Down.

The total value of contracts awarded by the Ministry of Defence to QinetiQ from December 2002 to February 2006 (inclusive) was some £4,933 million. This includes the Long Term Partnering Agreement placed in February 2003, which was valued at £3,970 million at that time.

QinetiQ is organised into five major operational divisions:

Integrated Services (formerly Complex Managed Services)

♦ Test and evaluation
♦ Public sector strategic partnering, infrastructure rationalisation and operation
♦ Integrated acquisition support
♦ Asset management (e.g. logistics, calibration, technology upgrade, obsolescence management and disposal)

Sensors & Electronics

♦ Spectrum solutions
♦ Sensors, processing and integration
♦ Marine & acoustics
♦ Optronics

Knowledge and Information Systems

♦ Command & intelligence systems
♦ Information assurance

- Communications
- Technical consulting
- Human sciences
- Space

Future Systems and Technology

- Maritime
- Aerospace
- Vehicles, platforms and systems
- Weapons
- Energy
- Intelligence & control
- Materials
- Structures

North America

- Key focus on homeland security and defence markets.
- Major customers include US Department of Defence, Department of Homeland Security and DARPA (Defence Advanced Research Projects Agency).

THE DEFENCE ESTATE

The Ministry of Defence (MoD) is one of the largest landowners in the UK with a diverse estate of some 240,000 hectares (1% of the UK land mass) and is valued at some £15.3 billion. Typically, approximately £1.5bn per year is spent on maintenance and new construction. Some of these costs are offset against income from tenants and other land users.

Defence Estates (DE) is the MoD Agency responsible for the management of the defence estate and provides services to support all aspects of a very large and diverse estate.

The estate is made up of:

- Built Estate which occupies around 80,000 hectares and is made up of naval bases, barracks/camps, airfields, research and development installations, storage and supply depots, communications facilities, around 49,000 Service Families Accommodation and town centre careers offices.
- The Rural Estate occupies around 160,000 hectares which includes 21 major armed forces training areas, 39 minor training areas, small arms ranges, test and evaluation ranges and aerial bombing ranges.
- Significant overseas estate in Germany, Cyprus, the Falkland Islands and Gibraltar with major overseas training facilities in Canada, Norway, Poland and Kenya.
- There are 179 Sites of Special Scientific Interest (SSSIs) across the rural estate that is managed by the MoD, the largest number in Government ownership.
- There are currently around 650 listed buildings and 1057 scheduled monuments across both the built and rural estate. The defence estate includes the largest proportion of

statutorily protected buildings held by the government, 43% of all government heritage properties.

♦ The size, diversity and nature of the estate is dictated entirely by the Services requirements to fulfil the Defence Mission. The UK estate also includes facilities for US forces based in the UK.

THE SERVICES HIERARCHY

Officer Ranks

Army	Navy	Air Force
Field Marshal	Admiral of the Fleet	Marshal of the Royal Air Force
General	Admiral	Air Chief Marshal
Lieutenant General	Vice Admiral	Air Marshal
Major General	Rear Admiral	Air Vice Marshal
Brigadier	Commodore	Air Commodore
Colonel	Captain	Group Captain
Lieutenant-Colonel	Commander	Wing Commander
Major	Lieutenant Commander	Squadron Leader
Captain	Lieutenant	Flight Lieutenant
Lieutenant	Sub Lieutenant	Flying Officer
Second Lieutenant	Midshipman	Pilot Officer

Non Commissioned Ranks

Army	Navy	Air Force
Warrant Officer 1/2	Warrant Officer	Warant Officer
Staff/Colour Sergeant	Chief Petty Officer	Flight Sergeant
Sergeant	Petty Officer	Sergeant
Corporal	Leading Rate	Corporal
Lance Corporal	Able Rate	Senior Aircraftsman
Private	Ordinary Rate	Leading Aircraftsman/Aircraftsman

Note: In general terms the rank shown in each column equates to the other service ranks in the columns alongside.

PAY SCALES (FROM 1 APRIL 2006)

The following are a selection from the Army pay scales relevant from 1 April 2006. Approximate scales for the other two services can be identified by using the previous table of commissioned and non-commissioned ranks. Pay scales apply to both males and females.

Officers

Rank		Level	Daily	Annual
Brigadier	+4	Level 5	237.06	86,526
	+3	Level 4	234.62	85,636
	+2	Level 3	232.21	84,756
	+1	Level 2	229.79	83,873
	OA	Level 1	227.37	82,990
Colonel	+8	Level 9	209.51	76,471
	+7	Level 8	207.01	75,558
	+6	Level 7	204.51	74,646
	+5	Level 6	202.02	73,737
	+4	Level 5	199.53	72,828
	+3	Level 4	197.04	71,919
	+2	Level 3	194.55	71,010
	+1	Level 2	192.05	70,098
	OA	Level 1	189.56	69,189
Lt Colonel	+8	Level 9	180.95	66,046
	+7	Level 8	178.78	65,254
	+6	Level 7	176.61	64,462
	+5	Level 6	174.46	63,677
	+4	Level 5	172.31	62,893
	+3	Level 4	170.16	62,108
	+2	Level 3	168.01	61,323
	+1	Level 2	165.86	60,538
	OA	Level 1	163.69	59,746
Major	+8	Level 9	139.68	50,983
	+7	Level 8	136.79	49,928
	+6	Level 7	133.92	48,880
	+5	Level 6	131.04	47,829
	+4	Level 5	128.14	46,771
	+3	Level 4	125.27	45,723
	+2	Level 3	122.37	44,665
	+1	Level 2	119.51	43,621
	OA	Level 1	116.63	42,569
Captain	+8	Level 9	110.11	40,190
	+7	Level 8	108.86	39,733
	+6	Level 7	107.59	39,270
	+5	Level 6	105.10	38,361
	+4	Level 5	102.59	37,445

Rank		Level	Daily	Annual
	+3	Level 4	100.10	36,536
	+2	Level 3	97.58	35,616
	+1	Level 2	95.07	34,700
	OA	Level 1	92.59	33,795
Lieutenant/				
2nd Lieutenant	+4	Level 10	79.86	29,148
	+3	Level 9	77.95	28,451
	+2	Level 8	76.06	27,761
	+1	Level 7	74.16	27,068
	OA	Level 6	72.25	26,371
	2Lt	Level 5	60.11	21,940
Officer				
Cadet		Level 1	38.03	13,880
University				
Cadet Entrants	+3	Level 4	43.71	15,954
	+2	Level 3	40.04	14,614
	+1	Level 2	35.66	13,015
	OA	Level 1	31.06	11,336

Warrant Officers, Non-Commissioned Officers and Soldiers

Rank	Range 5	Higher Range		Lower Range	
		Daily	Annual	Daily	Annual
Warrant Officer 1	Level 7	114.17	41,672	107.74	39,325
	Level 6	112.45	44,044	104.78	38,244
	Level 5	110.48	40,325	101.92	37,200
	Level 4	108.54	39,617	99.97	36,489
	Level 3	106.58	38,901	98.03	35,780
	Level 2	104.78	38,244	96.09	35,072
	Level 1	102.76	37,507	94.26	34,404
	Range 4				
	Warrant Officer 2 Levels 5-9 only				
Staff Sergeant					
Levels 1-7 only	Level 9	105.62	38,551	96.77	35,321
	Level 8	104.13	38,007	94.63	34,539
	Level 7	102.16	37,288	93.42	34,098
	Level 6	101.21	36,941	92.01	33,583
	Level 5	99.02	36,142	88.03	32,130
	Level 4	96.82	35,339	86.85	31,700
	Level 3	94.63	34,539	84.86	30,973
	Level 2	92.42	33,733	82.19	29,999
	Level 1	90.24	32,937	81.13	29,612
	Range 3				

Rank	Range 5	Higher Range		Lower Range	
		Daily	Annual	Daily	Annual
Sergeant	Level 7	90.18	32,915	83.30	30,404
	Level 6	88.52	32,309	82.67	30,174
	Level 5	86.86	31,703	79.91	29,167
	Level 4	85.20	31,098	77.88	28,426
	Level 3	84.14	30,711	77.10	28,141
	Level 2	82.06	29,951	75.21	27,451
	Level 1	79.99	29,196	73.29	26,750
	Range 2				
Corporal	Level 7	81.03	29,575	72.87	26,697
	Level 6	79.30	28,944	72.34	26,404
	Level 5	77.69	28,356	71.77	26,196
	Level 4	75.86	27,688	71.21	25,991
	Level 3	74.13	27,057	70.67	25,794
	Level 2	70.67	25,794	67.38	24,593
	Level 1	67.38	24,593	64.48	23,535
	Range 1				

Lance Corporal Levels 5-9 only

Private					
Levels 1-7 only	Level 9	70.67	25,794	59.17	21,597
	Level 8	67.38	24,593	57.10	20,841
	Level 7	64.48	23,535	54.60	19,929
	Level 6	61.65	22,502	52.36	19,111
	Level 5	58.79	21,458	50.26	18,344
	Level 4	53.17	19,407	47.69	17,406
	Level 3	49.45	18,049	43.85	16,005
	Level 2	44.79	16,348	41.55	15,165
	Level 1	39.24	14,322	39.24	14,322

All New Entrants Rate   33.32 per day   12,161 Annually

Notes:
(1) Pay scales apply to both males and females. (2) These rates only show the most common basic pay rates. (3) From 1991 all recruits have been enlisted on an Open Engagement. The Open Engagement is for a period of 22 years service from the age of 18 or the date of enlistment whichever is the later. Subject to giving 12 months notice, and any time bar that may be in force, all soldiers have the right to leave on the completion of three years reckonable service from the age of 18.

CODEWORDS AND NICKNAMES

A Codeword is a single word used to provide security cover for reference to a particular classified matter, eg 'Corporate' was the Codeword for the recovery of the Falklands in 1982. In 1997 'Bolton' was used to refer to operations during the reinforcement of Kuwait and 'Op

Grapple' was used for operations in support of the UN in the former Yugoslavia. 'Telic' is the current Codeword for operations in Iraq. A Nickname consists of two words and may be used for reference to an unclassified matter, eg 'Lean Look' referred to an investigation into various military organisations in order to identify savings in manpower.

DATES AND TIMINGS

When referring to timings the Armed Forces use the 24 hour clock. This means that 2015 hours, pronounced twenty fifteen hours, is in fact 8.15pm. Soldiers usually avoid midnight and refer to 2359 or 0001 hours. Time zones present plenty of scope for confusion! Exercise and Operational times are expressed in Greenwich Mean Time (GMT) which may differ from the local time. The suffix Z (Zulu) denotes GMT and A (Alpha) GMT + 1 hour. B (Bravo) means GMT + 2 hours and so on.

The Date Time Group or DTG can be seen on military documents and is a point of further confusion for many. Using the military DTG 1030 GMT on 20th April 2006 is written as 201030Z APR 06. When the Armed Forces relate days and hours to operations a simple system is used:

a. D Day is the day an operation begins.

b. H Hour is the hour a specific operation begins.

c. Days and hours can be represented by numbers plus or minus of D Day

Therefore if D Day is 20 Mar 06, D2 is the 18 Mar 06 and D + 2 is the 22 Mar 06. If H Hour is 0600hrs then H+2 is 0800 hours.

PHONETIC ALPHABET

To ensure minimum confusion during radio or telephone conversations difficult words or names are spelt out letter by letter using the following NATO standard phonetic alphabet.

ALPHA BRAVO CHARLIE DELTA ECHO FOXTROT GOLF HOTEL INDIA
JULIET KILO LIMA MIKE NOVEMBER OSCAR PAPA QUEBEC ROMEO
SIERRA TANGO UNIFORM VICTOR WHISKEY X RAY YANKEE ZULU.

USEFUL QUOTATIONS

There are two groups – Military and General.

Military Quotations

Young officers and NCOs may find some of these quotations useful on briefings etc: There are two groups – Military and General.

Military

"It is foolish to hunt the tiger when there are plenty of sheep around."
Al Qaeda Training Manual 2002

"Information is something that you do something with. Data is something that just makes officers feel good! I keep telling them but nobody listens to me."
US Army Intelligence specialist – CENTCOM Qatar 2003

"If you torture data sufficiently it will confess to almost anything".
Fred Menger – Chemistry Professor (1937-)

"If you tell someone what needs doing, as opposed to how to do it, they will surprise you with their ingenuity"
General Patton

"An appeaser is one who feeds a crocodile in the hope it will eat him last"
Winston Churchill

"Amateurs talk tactics, professionals talk logistics."
Anon

"More delusion as a solution"
US State Department Official – Baghdad March 2005

"If you claim to understand what is happening in Iraq you haven't been properly briefed".
British Staff Officer at Coalition HQ 2004

"If you can keep your head when all about you are losing theirs and blaming it on you – you'll be a man my son".
Rudyard Kipling

"If you can keep your head when all about you are losing theirs – you may have missed something very important".
Royal Marine – Bagram Airfield 2002

Admiral King commanded the US Navy during the Second World War. His daughter wrote – "He was the most even tempered man I ever met – he was always in a rage. In addition, he believed that civilians should be told nothing about a war until it was over and then only who won. Nothing more!"

Mrs Saatchi explained her 12 month silence after her husband started living with Nigela Lawson by quoting Napoleon's dictum
"Never disturb your enemy while he is making a mistake"

"We trained very hard, but it seemed that every time we were beginning to form up in teams, we would be reorganised. I was to learn in later life that we tend to meet any new situation by reorganising, and a wonderful method it can be for creating an illusion of progress, while producing confusion, inefficiency and demoralisation".
Caius Petronius 66 AD

"Having lost sight of our objectives we need to redouble our efforts".
Anon

During the Second World War Air Marshal Sir Arthur (Bomber) Harris was well known for his glorious capacity for rudeness, particulary to bureaucrats. "What are you doing to retard the war effort today" was his standard greeting to senior civil servants.

"The military value of a partisan's work is not measured by the amount of property destroyed, or the number of men killed or captured, but the number he keeps watching."
John Singleton Mosby 18331916 – Confederate Cavalry Leader

"A few honest men are better than numbers."
Oliver Cromwell

"The beatings will continue until morale improves."
Attributed to the Commander of the Japanese Submarine Force.

"When other Generals make mistakes their armies are beaten; when I get into a hole, my men pull me out of it".
The Duke of Wellington after Waterloo

"Take short views, hope for the best and trust in God. "
Sir Sydney Smith

"There is no beating these troops in spite of their generals. I always thought them bad soldiers, now I am sure of it. I turned their right, pierced their centre, broke them everywhere; the day was mine, and yet they did not know it and would not run".
Marshal Soult (French Army) – Commenting on the British Infantry at Albuhera in 1811

"Confusion in battle is what pain is in childbirth the natural order of things".
General Maurice Tugwell

"This is the right way to waste money"
PJ O'Rourke – Rolling Stone Magazine (Watching missiles firing during an exercise)

" This is just something to be got round like a bit of flak on the way to the target".
Group Captain Leonard Cheshire VC Speaking of his incurable illness in the week before he died.

"Pale Ebenezer thought it wrong to fight,
But roaring Bill, who killed him, thought it right".
Hillare Belloc

"Everyone wants peace – and they will fight the most terrible war to get it".
Miles Kington – BBC Radio 4th February 1995

"The purpose of war is not to die for your country. The purpose of war is to ensure that the other guy dies for his country".
General Patton.

"War is a competition of incompetence – the least incompetent usually win".
General Tiger (Pakistan) -after losing Bangladesh.

"In war the outcome corresponds to expectations less than in any other activity".
Titus Livy 59 BC – 17AD

"Nothing is so good for the morale of the troops as occasionally to see a dead general".
Field Marshal Slim 1891-1970

"It makes no difference which side the general is on".
Unknown British Soldier

At the end of the day it is the individual fighting soldier who carries the battle to the enemy; Sir Andrew Agnew commanding Campbell's Regiment (Royal Scots Fusiliers), giving orders to his infantrymen before the Battle of Dettingen in 1743 shouted; "Do you see yon loons on yon grey hill? Well, if ye dinna kill them, they'll kill you! "

"The only time in his life that he ever put up a fight was when we asked for his resignation."
A comment from one of his staff officers following French General Joffre's resignation in 1916.

General Quotes
Homer Simpson's advice to his son Bart:
Homer to Bart: "These three little sentences will get you through life":
Number 1: "Oh, good idea boss".
Number 2: (whispers) "Cover for me".
Number 3: "It was like that when I got here".

"Don't worry about people stealing an idea. If it's original you will have to ram it down their throats."
Howard Aiken 1900-1973 (Howard Aiken completed the Harvard Mark II, a completely electronic computer, in 1947).

"It's like the old hooker said. It's not the work – it's the stairs that are getting me down"
Elaine Stritch – Actress 2003

"The primary function of management is to create the chaos that only management can sort out. A secondary function is the expensive redecoration and refurnishing of offices, especially in times of the utmost financial stringency".
Theodore Dalrymple 'The Spectator' 6 November 1993.

"Success is generally 90% persistence".
Anon

"It is only worthless men who seek to excuse the deterioration of their character by pleading neglect in their early years".
Plutarch Life of Coriolanus Approx AD 80

"They say hard work never hurt anybody, but I figured why take the chance".
Ronald Regan

"To applaud as loudly as that for so stupid a proposal means that you are just trying to fill that gap between your ears".
David Starkey – BBC (4 Feb 95)

"Ah, these diplomats! What chatterboxes! There's only one way to shut them up – cut them down with machine guns. Bulganin, go and get me one!"
Joseph Stalin – As reported by De Gaulle during a long meeting.

"Whenever I hear about a wave of public indignation I am filled with a massive calm".
Matthew Parris – The Times 24th October 1994

"It is a general popular error to imagine that the loudest complainers for the public to be the most anxious for its welfare."
Edmund Burke

"The men who really believe in themselves are all in lunatic asylums."
GK Chesterton

"What all the wise men promised has not happened and what all the dammed fools said would happen has come to pass".
Lord Melbourne

Extracts from Officer's Annual Confidential Reports

"Works well when under constant supervision and cornered like a rat in a trap."

"He has the wisdom of youth, and the energy of old age."

"This Officer should go far – and the sooner he starts, the better."

"This officer is depriving a village somewhere of its idiot."

"Only occasionally wets himself under pressure."

"When she opens her mouth, it seems that this is only to change whichever foot was previously in there."

"He has carried out each and every one of his duties to his entire satisfaction."

"He would be out of his depth in a car park puddle."

"This young man has delusions of adequacy."

"When he joined my ship, this Officer was something of a granny; since then he has aged considerably. "

"This Medical Officer has used my ship to carry his genitals from port to port, and my officers to carry him from bar to bar."

"Since my last report he has reached rock bottom, and has started to dig."

"She sets low personal standards and then consistently fails to achieve them."

"His men would follow him anywhere, but only out of curiosity."

"This officer has the astonishing ability to provoke something close to a mutiny every time he opens his mouth".

Finally

Drill instructor to an embarrassed cadet who appears to be completely incapable of identifying left from right – "Tell me Sir, as an outsider, what is your opinion of the human race? *Overheard at the RMA Sandhurst*

EXTRACTS FROM THE DEVILS DICTIONARY 1911

Accuracy: A certain uninteresting quality generally excluded from human statements.

Armour: The kind of clothing worn by a man whose tailor is a blacksmith.

Colonel: The most gorgeously apparelled man in a regiment.

Education: That which discloses to the wise and disguised from the foolish their lack of understanding.

Enemy: A designing scoundrel who has done you some service which it is inconvenient to repay.

Foe: A person instigated by his wicked nature to deny one's merits or exhibit superior merits of his own.

Foreigner: A villain regarded with various degrees of toleration, according to his conformity to the eternal standard of our conceit and the shifting ones of our interest.

Freedom: A political condition that every nation supposes itself to enjoy in virtual monopoly.

Friendless: Having no favour to bestow. Destitute of fortune. Addicted to utterance of truth and common sense.

Man: An animal so lost in rapturous contemplation of what he thinks he is as to overlook what he ought to be. His chief occupation is the extermination of other animals and his own species,

Overwork: A dangerous disorder affecting high public functionaries who want to go fishing.

Peace: In international affairs a period of cheating between two periods of fighting.

Plunder: To wrest the wealth of A from B and leave C lamenting a vanished opportunity.

Republic: A form of government in which equal justice is available to all who can afford to pay for it.

Resign: A good thing to do when you are going to be kicked out.

Revelation: Discovering late in life that you are a fool.

Robber: Vulgar name for one who is successful in obtaining the property of others.

Zeal: A certain nervous disorder affecting the young and inexperienced.

The following is a selection from the list of standard military abbreviations and should assist users of this handbook.

AAC	Army Air Corps
AAR	Air to Air Refuelling
AAAW	Advanced Anti-Armour Weapon
AAW	Anti-Air Warfare
AB	Airborne
ABLE	Automotive Bridge Launching Equipment
ac	Aircraft
accn	Accommodation
ACE	Allied Command Europe
ACLANT	Allied Command North Atlantic
ACOS	Assistant Chief of Staff
ACV	Armoured Command Vehicle
AD	Air Defence/Air Dispatch/Army Department
ADA	Air Defended Area
ADA	Air Defence Alerting Device
Adjt	Adjutant
admin	Administration
admin O	Administrative Order
ADP	Automatic Data Processing
ADR	Airfield Damage Repair
AEW	Airborne Early Warning
AFCENT	Allied Forces Central European Theatre
AFNORTHWEST	Allied Forces Northwestern Europe
AFSOUTH	Allied Forces Southern Europe
AFV	Armoured Fighting Vehicle
AGC	Adjutant General's Corps
AGLS	Autonomous Navigation And Gun Laying System
AHQ	Air Headquarters
AIFV	Armoured Infantry Fighting Vehicle
AIRCENT	Allied Air Forces Central Europe
Airmob	Airmobile
ALARM	Air Launched Anti Radiation Missile
AMF(L)	Allied Mobile Force (Land Element)
AMRAAM	Advanced Medium Range Air-to-Air Missile
AOC	Air Officer Commanding
AP	Armour Piercing/Ammunition Point/Air Publication
APC	Armoured Personnel Carrier
APDS	Armour Piercing Discarding Sabot
APO	Army Post Office
ARBS	Angle Rate Bombing System
armd	Armoured

armr	Armour
ARRC	Allied Rapid Reaction Corps
ARRF	Allied Rapid Reaction Forces
arty	Artillery
ARV	Armoured Recover Vehicle
ASRAAM	Advanced Short-Range Air-to-Air Missile
ASTOVL	Advanced Short Take Off and Vertical Landing
ASW	Anti Submarine Warning
ATAF	Allied Tactical Air Force
ATGW	Anti-Tank Guided Weapon
att	Attached
ATWM	Army Transition to War Measure
AVLB	Armoured Vehicle Launched Bridge
AWC	Air Warfare Centre
AWOL	Absent without leave
BALTAP	Baltic Approaches
BAOR	British Army of the Rhine
BC	Battery Commander
Bde	Brigade
BE	Belgium (Belgian)
BFG	British Forces Germany
BFPO	British Forces Post Office
BG	Battle Group
BGHQ	Battlegroup Headquarters
BK	Battery Captain
BMA	Battery Manoeuvre Area
BMEWS	Ballistic Missile Early Warning System
BMH	British Military Hospital
Bn	Battalion
Bty	Battery
c sups	Combat Supplies
C3I	Command, Control, Communications & Intelligence
CAD	Central Ammunition Depot
cam	Camouflaged
CAP	Combat Air Patrol
cas	Casualty
CASEVAC	Casualty Evacuation
CASOM	Conventional Attack Stand-Off Missile
CASTOR	Corps Airborne Stand Off-Radar
cat	Catering
CATO	Civilian Air Traffic Operation
CCM	Counter Counter Measure
CCP	Casualty Collecting Point

CCS	Casualty Clearing Station
Cdo	Commando
CDS	Chief of the Defence Staff
CEP	Circular Error Probable/Central Engineer Park
CEPS	Central European Pipeline System
CET	Combat Engineer Tractor
CGRM	Commander General Royal Marines
CGS	Chief of the General Staff
CinC	Commander in Chief
CINCENT	Commander in Chief Central European Theatre
CINCUKAIR	Commander in Chief UK Air
civ	Civilian
CJO	Chief of Joint Operations
CJRDFO	Chief of the Joint Rapid Deployment Force Operations
Cmdt	Commandant
CO	Commanding Officer
COBRA	Counter Battery Radar
Col GS	Colonel General Staff
comd	Command/Commander
comp rat	Composite Ration (Compo)
COMRFA	Commander Royal Fleet Auxiliary
COMSEN	Communications Centre
coord	Co-ordinate
COS	Chief of Staff
coy	Company
CP	Close Protection/Command Post
CPO	Command Pay Office/Chief Petty Officer
CQMS	Company Quartermaster Sergeant
CRC	Control Reporting Centre
CRP	Control Reporting Point
CTOL	Conventional Take off and Landing
CTTO	Central Trials and Tactics Organisation
CUP	Capability Upgrade Period
CV	Combat Vehicle
CVD	Central Vehicle Depot
CVR(T)	Combat Vehicle Reconnaissance Tracked
CVR (W)	Combat Vehicle Reconnaissance Wheeled
CW	Chemical warfare
DAA	Divisional Administrative Area
DAG	Divisional Artillery Group
DASS	Defensive Aids Sub-System
DAW	Department of Air Warfare
def	Defence
DERA	Defence Evaluation & Research Agency

det	Detached/Detachment
DF	Defensive Fire
DHFS	Defence Helicopter Flying School
DISTAFF	Directing Staff (DS)
Div	Division
DK	Denmark
DMA	Divisional Maintenance Area
dml	Demolition
DMR	Daily Messing Rate
DRA	Defence Research Agency
DROPS	Demountable Rack Off Loading & Pick Up System
DS	Direct Support/Dressing Station
DTG	Date Time Group
ech	Echelon
ECM	Electronic Counter Measure
EDP	Emergency Defence Plan
emb	Embarkation
EME	Electrical and Mechanical Engineers
EMP	Electro Magnetic Pulse
en	Enemy
engr	Engineer
EOD	Explosive Ordnance Disposal
eqpt	Equipment
ETA	Estimated Time of Arrival
EW	Early warning/Electronic Warfare
EWOSE	Electronic Warfare Operational Support Establishment
ex	Exercise
FAC	Forward Air Controller
Fd Amb	Field Ambulance
Fd	Field
FEBA	Forward Edge of the Battle Area
FFR	Fitted for Radio
FGA	Fighter Ground Attack
FLA	Future Large Aircraft
FLET	Forward Location Enemy Troops
FLIR	Forward Looking Infra Red
FLOT	Forward Location Own Troops
fmn	Formation
FOC	First of Class
FONA	Flag Officer Naval Aviation
FOO	Forward Observation Officer
FOSF	Flag Officer Surface Fleet
FOSM	Flag Officer Submarines

FOST	Flag Officer Sea Training
FR	France (French)
FRG	Federal Republic of Germany/Forward Repair Group
FRT	Forward Repair Team
FTS	Flying Training School
FUP	Forming Up Place/Forming Up Point
FWAM	Full Width Attack Mine
Fy	Financial Year
GDP	General Defence Plan/Gross Domestic Product
GE	German (Germany)
GOC	General Officer Commanding
GPMG	General Purpose Machine Gun
GPWS	Ground Proximity Warning System
GR	Greece (Greek)
GRSC	Ground Radio Servicing Centre
HAS	Hardened Aircraft Shelter
HE	High Explosive
HEAT	High Explosive Anti-Tank
hel	Helicopter
Hesh	High Explosive Squash Head
HOTAS	Hands on Throttle and Stick
HV	Hyper Velocity
HVM	Hyper Velocity Missile
Hy	Heavy
ICCS	Integrated Command & Control System
IFF	Indentification Friend or Foe
IFOR	Implementation Force
II	Image Intensifier
illum	Illuminating
Inf	Infantry
INTSUM	Intelligence Summary
IO	Intelligence Officer
IRF	Immediate Reaction Forces
IRG	Immediate Replenishment Group
IS	Internal Security
ISD	In Service Data
IT	Italy (Italian)
ITS	Inshore Training Squadron
IUR	Immediate Use Reserve
IW	Individual Weapon
JFHQ	Joint Force Headquarters

JHQ	Joint Headquarters
JRC	Joint Regional Command
JRDF	Joint Rapid Deployment Force
JSRC	Joint Sub-Regional Command
JSSU	Joint Services Signals Unit
KFOR	Kosovo Force
L of C	Lines of Communication
LAD	Light Aid Detachment (REME)
LANDCENT	Commander Allied Land Forces Central Europe
LGB	Laser Guided Bomb
LLAD	Low-Level Air Defence
LML	Lightweight Multiple Launcher
LO	Liaison Officer
Loc	Locating
Log	Logistic
LPH	Landing Platform Helicopter
LRATGW	Long-Range Anti-Tank Guided Weapons
LSL	Landing Ships Logistic
LSW	Light Support Weapon
LTW	Lyneham Training Wing
maint	Maintain
MAMBA	Mobile Artillery Monitoring Battlefield Radar
MAMS	Mobile Air Movement Squadron
MAOT	Mobile Air Operations Team
MATO	Military Air Traffic Operations
mat	Material
MBT	Main Battle Tank
MCM	Mine Countermeasures
MCMV	Mine Countermeasures Vessels
mech	Mechanised
med	Medical
MFC	Mortar Fire Controller
MG	Machine Gun
MIRV	Multiple Independently Targeted Re-entry Vehicle
MLRS	Multi-Launched Rocket System
MLU	Mid-life update
MNAD	Multi-National Airmobile Division
MND	Multi-National Division
MO	Medical Officer
mob	Mobilisation
MoD	Ministry of Defence
MoU	Memorandum of Understanding

MP	Military Police
MRG	Medium Repair Group
MRV	Multiple Re-entry Vehicle
msl	missile
MU	Maintenance Unit
NAAFI	Navy, Army and Air Force Institutes
NADGE	NATO Air Defence Ground Environment
NAEW-F	NATO Airborne Early Warning Forces
NATO	North Atlantic Treaty Organisation
NATS	National Air Traffic Services
NBC	Nuclear, Biological and Chemical Warfare
NCO	Non-Commissioned Officer
nec	Necessary
NGFSO	Naval Gunfire Support Officer
ni	Night
NL	Netherlands
NO	Norway (Norwegian)
NOK	Next of Kin
NORTHAG	Northern Army Group
NTR	Nothing to Report
NYK	Not Yet Known
OC	Officer Commanding
OCU	Operational Conversion Unit (RAF)
OEU	Operational Evaluation Unit
OIC	Officer in Charge
OOTW	Operations other than war
OP	Observation Post
opO	Operation Order
ORB	Omni-Radio Beacon
ORBAT	Order of Battle
P info	Public Information
pax	Passengers
PJHQ	Permanent Joint Headquarters
Pl	Platoon
PO	Portugal (Portuguese)
POL	Petrol, Oil and Lubrication
Pro	Provost
PTC	Personnel and Training Command
QCS	Queen's Colour Squadron
QM	Quartermaster

R & D	Research and Development
RA	Royal Artillery
RAC	Royal Armoured Corps
RAFASUPU	RAF Armament Support Unit
RAMC	Royal Army Medical Corps
RAP	Rocket-Assisted Projectile/Regiment Aid Post
RCMDS	Remote-Control Mine Disposal System
RCZ	Rear Control Zone
RE	Royal Engineers
rebro	Rebroadcast
rec	Recovery
recce	reconnaissance
Regt	Regiment
REME	Royal Electrical and Mechanical Engineers
RFA	Royal Fleet Auxiliary
rft	Reinforcement
RGJ	Royal Green Jackets
RHA	Royal Horse Artillery
RHQ	Regimental Headquarters
RLC	Royal Logistic Corps
RM	Royal Marines
RMA	Rear Maintenance Area/Royal Military Academy
RMAS	Royal Military Academy Sandhurst
RMAS	Royal Military Academy Sandhurst
RMP	Royal Military Police
RN	Royal Navy
RNMC	Royal Netherlands Marine Corps
RO	Retired Officer
Ro-Ro	Roll On-Roll Off
RP	Reporting Point
RPV	Remotely Piloted Vehicle
RRF	Royal Regiment of Fusiliers/Rapid Reaction Forces
RSA	Royal School of Artillery
RSME	Royal School of Mechanical Engineering
RSS	Royal School of Signals
RTM	Ready to Move
RTU	Return to Unit
SACLOS	Semi Automatic to Command Line of Sight
SACEUR	Supreme Allied Commander Europe
SAM	Surface-to-Air Missile
SAR	Search and Rescue
SAS	Special Air Service
SBS	Special Boar Service
SDR	Strategic Defence Review

Sect	Section
SH	Support Helicopters
SHAPE	Supreme Headquarters Allied Powers Europe
SIB	Special Investigation Branch
Sig	Signals
sit	Situation
SITREP	Situation Report
SLBM	Submarine-Launched Ballistic Missiles
SMG	Sub-Machine Gun
smk	Smoke
SNCO	Senior Non-Commissioned Officer
SOC	Sector Operations Centre
SP	Self Propelled/Start Point
SPS	Staff and Personnel Support
Sqn	Squadron
SSBN	Nuclear Powered Ballistic Missile Submarine
SSK	Single shot to kill
SSM	Surface-to-Surface Missile
SSN	Nuclear-Powered Attack Submarine
SSVC	Services Sound and Cinema Corporation
STC	Strike Command
STOBAR	Short Take-Off and Arrested Recovery
STOL	Short Take-Off and Landing
STOVL	Short Take-Off and Vertical Landing
TA	Territorial Army
tac	Tactical
TBT	Tank Bridge Transporter
TCC	Turret Control Computer
TCP	Traffic Control Post
TCV	Troop Carrying Vehicle
tgt	Target
THAAD	Theatre High-Altitude Area Defence
TIALD	Thermal Imaging Airborne Laser Designator
tk	Tank
TLAM	Tactical Land Attack Missile
TLAM-C	Tactical Land Attack Missile – Conventional
TLB	Top Level Budget
TMA	Troop Manoeuvre Area
TOT	Time on Target
tp	Troop
tpt	Transport
TTTE	Tri-National Tornado Training Establishment
TU	Turkish (Turkey)
TUL	Truck Utility Light

TUM	Truck Utility Medium
UAV	Unmanned Aerial Vehicle
U/S	Unserviceable
UK	United Kingdom
UKADGE	United Kingdom Air Defence Ground Environment
UKADR	United Kingdom Air Defence Region
UKMF	United Kingdom Mobile Force
UKSC (G)	United Kingdom Support Command (Germany)
UN	United Nations
UNFICYP	United Nations Forces in Cyprus
UNCLASS	Unclassified
US	United States
UXB	Unexploded Bomb
veh	Vehicle
VOR	Vehicle off the Road
WE	War Establishment
wh	Wheeled
WIMP	Whingeing Incompetent Malingering Person
wksp	Workshop
WMR	War Maintenance Reserve
WO	Warrant Officer
X	Crossing (as in roads or rivers)

This publication was produced by R&F (Defence) Publications
Editorial Office Tel 01743-247038 Fax 01743-241962

Website: www.armedforces.co.uk
E Mail:Editorial@armedforces.co.uk

Editor: Charles Heyman

Other publications in this series are:
The Royal Air Force Pocket Guide 1994-95
The Armed Forces of the United Kingdom 2006-2007
The Territorial Army 1999

Further copies can be obtained from:
Pen & Sword Books Ltd
47 Church Street
Barnsley S70 2AS

Telephone: 01226 734222   Fax: 01226 734438

5th Edition July 2006

HMSO Core Licence Number CO2W0004896
PSI Licence Number C2006009533
Parliamentary Licence P2006000197

Printed and bound in Great Britain
by Biddles Ltd, King's Lynn, Norfolk